Adventures in the Digital Playroom

This book transforms Minecraft from casual screen time into a meaningful therapeutic tool. It demonstrates how clinicians of all skill levels can harness the game's popularity to support children's mental health within an intentional, therapeutic setting.

Drawing on established play therapy modalities and contemporary neuroscience, the book presents a practical, seven-part approach. Through vibrant case vignettes, it details ways to help children work through big emotions, negative self-talk, trauma, and grief – all within the world of Minecraft. The book's seven-part framework also provides strategies for working with parents to navigate screen time and strengthen family bonds. Essential clinical considerations are also discussed, including treatment planning, documentation, privacy, and tips for engaging ADHD and neurodivergent clients.

Adventures in the Digital Playroom provides essential guidance for clinicians, from play therapists to school counselors, linking Minecraft's cultural influence with established clinical theory. It is also an invaluable resource for parents and families seeking to transform conflicts over gaming into opportunities for connection and growth.

Brian W. Keating, MA, LPC, is a synergetic play therapist who specializes in online play therapy and the therapeutic use of Minecraft.

Adventures in the Digital Playroom

The Seven Guiding Principles for Using Minecraft in Play Therapy

Brian W. Keating

Routledge
Taylor & Francis Group
NEW YORK AND LONDON

Designed cover image: Getty Images

First published 2027
by Routledge
605 Third Avenue, New York, NY 10158

and by Routledge
4 Park Square, Milton Park, Abingdon, Oxon, OX14 4RN

Routledge is an imprint of the Taylor & Francis Group, an informa business

ISBN: 978-1-041-01449-2 (hbk)
ISBN: 978-1-041-01448-5 (pbk)
ISBN: 978-1-003-61478-4 (ebk)

DOI: 10.4324/9781003614784

Typeset in Sabon
by KnowledgeWorks Global Ltd.

Access the Instructor Resources: www.routledge.com/9781041014485

Contents

SECTION VI
Appendices 253

Acknowledgments

I thank my wife, Stacey, for her unwavering support and for being my first reader. She now knows more about Minecraft and play therapy than she ever imagined. Thanks also to editor Anna Moore for her support over the past year, Bill Belanger for his encouragement as a first peer reader, and to my mentors Jeffrey M. Price, Gaea Logan, and Michelle M. May.

I am also profoundly grateful to the team of content experts who generously reviewed individual chapters. Their sharp insights, challenging questions, and specialist knowledge significantly improved the manuscript. Any errors that remain are, of course, my own. My particular thanks and gratitude to Lisa Dion, LPC, RPT-S, for her expertise on Chapters 5, 6, and 10; Gaela Mintz, MSW/RSW, for her feedback on Chapter 8; Micki Burns, PHd, for her input on Chapter 12; Stephanie Heitkemper, Phd, LPC, RPT-S, FT, for her comments on Chapter 13; Robert Jason Grant, EdD, LPC, NCC, RPT-S, for his knowledge on Chapter 14; and Zachary J. Thieneman, PsyD, HSP, CGP for his review of Chapter 15.

Thanks are also extended to the clinicians mentioned in Chapter 20, who graciously contributed their own descriptions of using this modality in groundbreaking ways. The field is much greater for their work and creativity.

Last, I would like to extend my gratitude to Ellie Finch for contributing the foreword and offering encouragement and support throughout the process.

Foreword

By Ellie Finch

It is 2020 and I am in the midst of a therapy session with a 13-year-old boy, we are in Minecraft and we are lost. Totally lost. We have lost the safe place he has made, a house he spent several sessions making just right. He is panicking and flying around his world looking everywhere for it, I am beginning to panic too and I am feeling like a failure: "Why didn't I make a note of the coordinates?" I think to myself, "I'm so stupid!" And then I pause and think oh wait is this how he feels about himself? We land on a mountain top together; the sun is setting. I say, "OK this is not where we wanted to be, we wanted to be at your safe place, but we are here. What can you see?" He looks around, "I see the sun going down and I see the sea." "What do you think our characters can smell?" I ask. He looks down at the grass around us, "The flowers," and then laughing a little, "And ... that smelly sheep over there." I laugh and agree the sheep is probably quite smelly.

As practitioners I imagine we might all end up with a story of how it first dawned on us that video games could be used therapeutically. For some of you it might be coming across this wonderful book. For me, it began in 2012, a year after Minecraft was launched. I was regularly playing the game online with my nieces and nephews and, at the time, I was training to be a social worker. I was a complete "noob," and I remember falling down holes, accidentally breaking their builds, and wandering around with the front door to their house in my hand for ages without realizing it.

At this time, I was writing my MA dissertation on engaging children and young people in online mental health services. I started to see how powerful Minecraft could be as a creative therapeutic tool. Still, it was not until 2020, when the pandemic pushed my practice online, that I began entering the game with clients as part of their therapy sessions. I soon discovered what I had suspected all along: Minecraft is an incredibly powerful therapeutic tool. I only wish I had not waited so long to use it.

I think this is what motivates me to share my work through my writings, videos, and trainings. And I imagine it is what motivates Brian Keating to share his work too: to encourage others to venture into this new way of working in the digital world and not take so much time about it as I did! Technology can feel intimidating for many of us practitioners. If you are not a gamer, or even if you are, inviting clients to join you in a digital space can feel overwhelming: *what if I cannot keep them safe? What if I look like I do not know what I am doing? What if I break something they made?*

This is why Brian's first of the seven principles written about in this book is so important as practitioners; we do not have to be an amazing player to use Minecraft in therapy. As Winnicott (1973) said, we just need to be "good enough." I am a strong advocate for practitioners seeing Minecraft as a tool, just as you would a sandtray or paints, through which you can incorporate your own therapeutic approach, training, and experience (Beckett & Finch, 2024). In this book, Brian, who is a Synergetic Play Therapist, illustrates this via Principle 4, where he describes how he uses the game to model regulation, build interoception, and increase the child's Window of Tolerance.

Minecraft is such an adaptable and flexible tool that practitioners I have trained across the world, from many different backgrounds (play therapy, support work, bereavement counseling), have each found their own creative ways to incorporate it into their services. In my trainings, I emphasize that we may feel deskilled when taking up the challenge of learning the controls of a new game for example, but we do not lose our professional skills and expertise; those remain with us. We do not need to be experts in Minecraft. Of course, we must know how to keep ourselves and our clients safe in digital spaces, but we do not need to match our clients' gaming expertise. In fact, that is nearly impossible. Have you ever tried to keep up with a 10-year-old who has been playing every day since they were five? By using creative digital tools like Minecraft, we are meeting clients in their comfort zone. We are going to them, instead of expecting them to come to us.

As a child and family counselor I regularly bring families together in Minecraft for their sessions. I am always struck by how often simple moments of shared enjoyment in the game, held with therapeutic intention, can foster as much connection and change as any formal intervention I might bring into their sessions (Finch & Rivett, 2026). In Principle 6, Brian describes how family sessions can provide a fantastic opportunity for the children to be the experts and guides for their parents within their Minecraft world, gently opening up new perspectives for parents on video games.

Brian's work is part of a much wider movement. Many practitioners have been using video games therapeutically for years, carefully integrating them into their services and sharing what they notice with colleagues. These everyday acts gradually change attitudes toward video games one conversation at a time. We need to share not just our successes, but (as

Brian does so bravely in this book) our mistakes too, so we can all learn to harness these tools. Whatever form our sharing takes, it matters. It changes children's lives.

I was at the very start of my journey using Minecraft therapeutically when I was on the mountain top with that 13-year-old boy searching for his safe place (an amalgamated and anonymized example). Since then, I have shared with colleagues the value of noting coordinates and creating containing spaces for therapy in Minecraft from island worlds to the Sandtray Therapy Minecraft World I later co-created (Finch, 2022; Finch, 2024). But that day, being lost led to something important: an opportunity to pause, to notice the beauty of the blocky world around us, to take in the plants and animals, and to realize we are in a safe place.

Ellie Finch – Founder and Director of PlayMode Academy

References

Beckett, M., & Finch, E. (2024). *Bridging the ChASM: Creating accessible services using minecraft—A guide* [Video recording]. University of Cambridge. https://www.educ.cam.ac.uk/research/programmes/chasm/

Finch, E. (2022). Using Minecraft as a sandtray. In J. Stone (Ed.), *Digital play therapy: A clinician's guide to comfort and competence* (pp. 190–192). Routledge.

Finch, E. (2024). Visit our sandtray world. PlayMode Academy. https://playmodeacademy.org/visit-our-sandtray-world

Finch, E., & Rivett, M. (2026). Systemic therapy through a pixelated lens: Using Minecraft in therapy with families that include autistic children and children with ADHD. *Journal of Family Therapy*. e70020. https://doi.org/10.1111/1467-6427.70020

Winnicott, D. W. (1973). *The child, the family, and the outside world*. Penguin.

Author's Preface

Using Minecraft in play therapy differs from a child playing the game with a fun family member or friend. When applied with clinical intention and combined with therapeutic theories and methods already used by clinicians working with children, Minecraft can become a powerful play-based intervention. This book explores how to utilize the game in play therapy with children and adolescents who may already be familiar with it or are discovering it for the first time. The upcoming sections and chapters offer a framework inspired by the questions and challenges discussed by clinicians worldwide who recognize the significant impact the game has on the children they see in their clinical practice and personal lives.

This book is written for anyone who works with, plays with, or supports children interested in Minecraft. It may be especially useful for clinical professionals working with children, such as play therapists, school counselors, social workers, and students in advanced programs. Parents might also find the clinical information helpful for understanding what they can expect from their child's Minecraft play therapy or for complementing their current work with a counselor, family therapist, or parent coach. Readers do not need to actively play Minecraft during a session to benefit from the topics discussed; a general understanding of Minecraft culture and gameplay dynamics can still encourage any adult to gain a deeper understanding of the children in their lives.

Throughout the book, clinical vignettes and case examples are included, often to introduce the topics of each chapter and illustrate key concepts. These snapshots are not about specific clients but are composite stories based on many children I have seen over the years. All identifiable information about real people has been removed or altered; however, the process, exploration, and growth depicted are true to what I have observed. My responses accurately reflect how I might react in real situations, and I have deliberately included my mistakes, as they also mirror my experiences. At the end of each chapter, a review of "helpful tips" will be provided, along with open-ended self-reflection questions to help readers integrate the material.

This book is built on the work of those who came before me. Many of them influenced me directly and will be recognized and introduced in the upcoming chapters. This includes play therapists, academics, and mental health clinicians who constantly push the boundaries of what we know about the brain, body, and interpersonal connections, offering insights into how Minecraft-based play therapy can be incredibly therapeutic.

Readers will also be introduced to clinicians around the world who utilize Minecraft in creative and innovative ways that surpass what I could have imagined or what I have implemented in my own practice. Many other play therapists and educators in the global community work tirelessly every day to advance our field and this modality, yet they are unseen and unknown. I know they are out there because I know there are so many children and adolescents playing Minecraft who are also suffering and are finding help through this modality.

While writing this book, I was amazed by the enthusiasm and support from colleagues, non-clinician friends, and acquaintances who encouraged me to make it a go-to resource, not just as a clinical reference, but also as a therapeutic validation for all Minecraft fans who had intrinsically known the benefits of playing. I was also surprised by stories from parents describing their children's excitement over the book's creation. It never occurred to me that a child would hear about this book and say, "I want to read that!" This is further proof that children continue to surprise me.

The importance of recognizing the children in our world cannot be overstated. As adults, we all have a role in supporting children, no matter our profession, vocation, or beliefs. This book is not just for play professionals or youth advocates; it's for anyone interested in tapping into their playfulness and creativity to see those same lively qualities in a child who matters to them. There might even be a child inside you, the reader, who is unexpectedly connecting with this material. To that child, I offer this welcome and invitation: "I am so glad you're here. Would you like to play Minecraft with me?"

About the Author

Brian W. Keating, MA, LPC, (he/him), is a Certified Synergetic Play Therapist and Certified Group Psychotherapist based in Colorado, USA, specializing in grief, childhood bereavement, and adverse childhood experiences. He has developed a niche in tele-play therapy and digital game-based interventions, with a focus on using platforms like Minecraft. His professional writing and speaking address these innovative clinical topics. Outside of his clinical work, Brian is a professional bass player in a Motown tribute band.

Section I

Introduction

Chapter 1

Introduction to the Use of Minecraft in a Clinical Setting

I answer the phone and begin speaking with a parent who is interested in play therapy for their child. We discuss details related to general administrative matters, including scheduling, insurance coverage, out-of-network costs, and in-person or online work. The parent inquires about my approach and background, so I describe my training, licensure, years in practice, and provide a brief overview of my clinical orientation and approach to client conceptualization.

"Oh, and if your child is interested in playing Minecraft, I can use that as a powerful play-based intervention. It is quite amazing, actually."

Although silent, I can hear the hesitation and apprehension in the pause on the other end of the call.

"Really? My child does like to play Minecraft. What does that actually look like?"

Mental health professionals, youth wellness advocates, and anyone working with children are likely familiar with the video game *Minecraft*. The brand's visual presence is evident in movies, music, and clothing, in all the ways one would expect from a pop culture phenomenon. Initially played in individual or family gaming spaces, the game can now be found in classrooms worldwide and even in therapeutic settings where clinicians meet with children. A natural fit for the evolution of mobile technology, children and adolescents can be seen playing Minecraft while in transit, passing time in public, or in the waiting room of a play therapy practice.

It is not unusual to greet a child before their play therapy appointment and see them playing Minecraft on a handheld gaming device, such as a Nintendo Switch, tablet, or phone. In many circumstances, the play therapist might express curiosity about the game and then reassure the child that they could return to it when they were done with the appointment. Parents, caregivers, and clinical supervisors would nod in agreement, and the device and game would be left behind.

DOI: 10.4324/9781003614784-2

This book asks, "What happens when we bring the game into the session with us?"

Following the release of Minecraft in 2011, play therapists worldwide began incorporating Minecraft into their play therapy sessions. The application of the game as a play-based intervention validated the importance of the child's interest in the game. Rather than leaving the game behind, the invitation to bring the game in created another therapeutic opportunity for the child to bring their whole world into the session. Using the game as a tool for expression and creativity, play therapists can utilize Minecraft as another resource in their play therapy toolbox to see what the child sees and to feel what the child feels. What was previously turned off could now be left on as a possible bridge for connection; another means of expression for the child to show us what was important to them, while allowing play therapists to say, "all of you can be here."

Playing Minecraft is a viable solution for meeting children's play-based needs, whether the game is provided by the play therapist, the child, or used as a topic of conversation to foster connection and build rapport. It is almost as though the game was designed to provide the atmosphere and exploration of a play therapy room. Minecraft's flexibility offers children opportunities to experience many of the benefits of a physical playroom in the digital world of the game. The following chapters address specific play-based dynamics, such as how play therapists can help their clients explore their identity through the design of their character, engage in collaborative or competitive play, participate in directive and non-directive interventions, discover creative play opportunities that can mimic *LEGO*, sand play, expressive arts projects, and initiate dynamic storytelling in the unrestricted nature of the game.

However, incorporating Minecraft into play therapy is not as straightforward as introducing a new toy into the playroom. As a video game, the idea of playing Minecraft in a therapy session can evoke hesitation, reluctance, and perhaps even explicit and implicit judgments about whether it can be beneficial for the child. Despite this work being done, there has been very little offered as a specific theoretical roadmap or understanding of what exactly makes playing the game a beneficial intervention for child clients in one's clinical practice. Consequently, play therapists who use Minecraft have faced the challenge of finding their own way and forging their own path.

Hannah Young (2025), a Certified Play Therapist based in the UK, selected Minecraft to demonstrate how a video game can initiate, facilitate, and strengthen play therapy interventions by correlating UNICEF's 11 digital play drivers with the therapeutic powers of play. This served as a crucial proof of concept, demonstrating that such a theoretical map could be drawn. This book moves beyond that initial step to present the Seven Guiding Principles as the first comprehensive theoretical framework, providing the detailed, practical field guide clinicians require.

Minecraft first became integrated into my work as a play therapist through my most significant and most influential teacher: the children themselves. As described in Chapter 3, my experience of using the game in play therapy for the first time included moments of frustration as I learned the game and considered how to apply the child's interest in playing to what was relevant to their therapy goals. Once learning how to play and feeling confident to host the experience in a comfortable way, I began to witness the new depths of discovery and growth that children had been telling me about all along; however, now I was empowered to listen in a new way, and I could help them go even further in their growth. Minecraft became more utilized in my sessions, and more time was devoted to exploring ways to use all aspects of the game with therapeutic intention.

The Benefits and Challenges of Traditional Toys in the Play Therapy Space

When a child enters a play therapy space, they are typically exposed to a variety of toys that encourage exploration and interaction. Garry Landreth (2012), founder and director of the University of North Texas's Center for Play Therapy, emphasizes that effective play therapy spaces should include toys that: (1) facilitate real-life and nurturing play experiences, (2) provide outlets for expressing aggression or fear, and (3) encourage creative expression and emotional release. The thoughtful arrangement and accessibility of toys, such as dolls and figurines, musical instruments, collaborative and competitive games, stuffed animals, *LEGO*, art supplies and materials, a sand tray or sandbox with various tools, and many other items can have a profound impact on a child's therapeutic experience.

The delight a child can express when they enter a new space for the first time and see something immediately familiar can be a decisive moment of creating safety. A child who might appear uncertain and guarded upon entering a play therapy space can suddenly appear relaxed and open as they see a toy or item and exclaim, "I know what that is! I have that at home!" This familiar experience with toys can build confidence and rapport with the adult by bridging the gap between their world at home and the new meeting space. Children may also choose to skip the toys altogether and move toward physically relational play by engaging in games such as hide-and-seek, dressing up in costumes, or initiating a sword fight with the play therapist.

Settings that are not explicitly designated as play therapy rooms may settle for a minimal number of toys available due to space, budget restrictions, and limited access. Counseling rooms at schools, playrooms in hospitals, rooms for children in churches and places of worship, and general community spaces may be limited in the toys and expressive items available. Art supplies and board games can be a valuable and accessible option in these instances, as they can be easily stored and have a less expensive initial cost than what would be commonly associated with a fully stocked playroom.

Some children who come into our practice are less fortunate and have limited access to toys or any play items at all. In those cases, being offered the invitation to enter into a space that exceeds their imagination for play can increase the willingness to engage in a therapeutic process, as they intrinsically know that there is something to be explored with these new toys. Play therapists may also have restricted access to toys for various reasons. Budget cuts for mental health support have limited the resources available to agencies, nonprofits, schools, and community centers. The costs and upkeep associated with a play therapy space can be stressed by the lower reimbursement rates provided by insurance agencies. Clinicians in different parts of the world may also encounter limited access to toys due to general accessibility issues and similar restricted budgets. An unfortunate reality is that not all play therapy spaces are outfitted the same, and not all children will have the same access to the same quality, quantity, and condition of items in a given space.

Play therapists, who first curate a play space, are confronted with initial purchase costs as well as the ongoing time investment required to clean and reset after each session. *LEGO* pieces that are scattered need to be collected and reorganized. Figurines and miniatures used need to be cleaned and returned to their designated shelf. Sand that has escaped from a tray needs to be carefully collected and returned to its container. Paint supplies also need to be cleaned, restocked, and reset for the next child to express themselves as freely as the previous one.

For a child telling a story in their play sessions, they depend on the same items being available week after week. Allowing children repeated access to the same toys may further support emotional processing and security as repeated themes can be played out in new ways (Axline, 1947; Schaefer & Drewes, 2014). The routine and consistency of available toys help create the safe boundary of expectation needed for growth and healing. Traditional toys in the playroom are also susceptible to wear and tear. It is not uncommon for play therapists to have experienced being in a playroom or play environment where a guitar sits in a corner with broken strings, cans of play-dough are dried up and crumble when touched, dolls are missing accessories or clothing items, and action figures are stuck in one position or are missing a limb or other critical pieces. Research suggests that broken toys can hold therapeutic value in play therapy settings, as they provide an opportunity for children to explore unconscious aspects of themselves that may feel broken or unhealed (Dion, 2022; Schaefer & Drewes, 2014). However, this can put an additional strain on play therapists if popular toys exceed functional wear and tear and need to be replaced frequently or throughout the course of a child's therapy.

Clinicians in certain circumstances may also face the challenge of disruption to their work environment when meeting rooms are changed due to limited space and other restrictions. A school counselor may meet with a child in a specific room one week and then meet with them in a different room the following week due to scheduling needs and conflicts. In those situations, one does the best they can, grabbing toys, items, and games that might be meaningful to the child or that they may have a history with from previous sessions. It is workable but not ideal for both the play therapist's efficiency and the expectations required for the child to be comfortable in their sessions.

The Significance of Minecraft in the Play Therapy Space

The upcoming chapters will explore the importance for mental health clinicians and anyone working with children to consider the impact Minecraft has had on the lives of their clients, while understanding the immense therapeutic benefits the game can offer when played in an intentional therapeutic setting. Through the discovery of game design, mechanics, and gameplay, play therapists will learn how to connect the game's possibilities to the theories, modalities, and skills they already use.

The dynamic, expressive world of Minecraft offers children the opportunity to explore creative, nurturing, caring, and engaging themes in real-life scenarios. This includes dynamic situations such as growing crops and tending to animals, managing energy and food to stay nourished, considering if items could be traded with a friendly villager, creating and finding safety in a distressing environment, and the opportunity to work with emotions related to consequences in the game. The Survival mode of gameplay further serves as a conduit for children to explore aggressive instincts and navigate potentially scary environments as they encounter a zombie apocalypse, running the risk of being defeated. Opportunities for creative expression and emotional release are endless, and the element of fantasy and wonder is always present as the child encounters magical beasts and can experiment with enchantments and potions.

The therapeutic value of these opportunities is underscored by research. Studying the play preferences of children aged 3–10, Ray et al. (2013) observed that sandbox and sand tray play were favored more frequently over other toys. This finding builds upon Landreth's (2012) categories and highlights the importance of pretend and fantasy play. The open-world, sandbox-style nature of Minecraft directly taps into this preferred mode of unlimited exploration. In fact, Minecraft can be seen as a fusion of sand play and *LEGO*, as a child can browse, choose, and select from a variety of blocks, dream up a creation, and begin to stack them together. This can happen individually or collaboratively with peers, caregivers, or a therapist. The crucial difference, however, is that all of this happens digitally, where there are no little pieces to clean up, no frustration over lost items, and nothing sharp to step on later in the day.

The world of Minecraft takes place in the child's digital device of choice: PC, Mac, tablet, phone, or gaming console. It can be played at home, in school, at a hospital, or in transit. The opportunity to play can be initiated by the child or the therapist, requiring a minimal amount of hardware to engage in play. Rather than the pressure to intentionally curate a play space or carry around toys in a backpack, everything needed for play can be easily accessible, depending on the chosen platform. This portability ensures that the Minecraft world serves as a container for therapeutic work, remaining consistent and accessible, thereby supporting consistent engagement wherever the session takes place.

In an article published in the *Journal of Infant and Adolescent Psychiatry*, Aronson (2017) explored the history of toys in play therapy, from the initial experiences of Anna Freud and Melanie Klein to his own experience of encountering Minecraft in the playroom. As he explored the allure of Minecraft in relation to the toys children and play therapists have used over the past many decades, he concluded that the relationship between the child and the play therapist is the most significant factor, regardless of which toy becomes the conduit for the relationship. The clinical intention presented in this book is not focused solely on playing Minecraft; it is about what happens between the play therapist and the child while playing the game.

Lisa Dion, creator of Synergetic Play Therapy and founder of the Synergetic Play Therapy Institute, has further emphasized the importance of the child's relationship with the play therapist in the playroom, regardless of the toys used. A core tenet of Synergetic Play Therapy emphasizes that "the therapist is the most important toy in the playroom" (2018). The powerful dynamic that can occur in the relationship between the child and play therapist, whether or not a toy is being used for play, helps to reframe the use of Minecraft in play therapy. Rather than Minecraft simply being a video game, it becomes another way for children to be in a healing relationship with their play therapist. Dion's work provides a strong foundation for the approach discussed throughout this book, including her concept of the "setup," sometimes also referred to as "the offering" which is referenced in Chapter 5 to describe how the experience of the child playing the game with the therapist can create powerful opportunities for healing as the child "offers" the therapist a look into their world.

A New Paradigm Bridging Minecraft Game Play with Clinical Theory

The mental health needs of youth have kept play therapists in high demand as the accessibility to online therapy and the normalization of asking for and receiving mental health support have undoubtedly increased. Youth seeking support are showing up in play therapy, reflecting a generational paradigm shift toward immersive interest and engagement with video games and the technology that accompanies them. What was once a hobby to pass the time has become an integral part of social, cultural, and generational identity. This shift has triggered a significant change in how clinicians in the clinical mental health field seek to understand how to implement the interest in games like Minecraft to support children in their practice.

Discussions surrounding the accessibility, attractiveness, and overall impact of games and technology have further entered play therapy spaces as parents seek to explore the implications of their child's gaming experiences at home. Mental health professionals interested in incorporating Minecraft into therapy also need to prepare for questions and challenges that may arise about how using screens in this line of work can be helpful and therapeutic. Questions related to screen use, gaming addiction, and violence in Minecraft are addressed further in Chapter 9. Acknowledging the intersecting impact and presence of the Minecraft phenomenon, it can be a startling shift to return to the concept that, at its core, Minecraft is a game that can be enjoyed as a toy for play.

The Seven Guiding Principles: A Therapeutic Framework for Using Minecraft in Play Therapy

The responsibility of a clinician using Minecraft in a therapy session is to understand how playing in a clinical setting differs from a client playing with a neighbor, friend, or family member. These Seven Guiding Principles serve as a framework for play therapists to implement Minecraft in their sessions with a clear clinical and therapeutic purpose. The principles will be referenced throughout the book to help readers see how interventions using Minecraft align with core theoretical ideas in play therapy. Through clinical vignettes, these principles will be translated into practice, demonstrating how to transform gameplay into meaningful therapeutic moments. Ultimately, this framework is not a rigid protocol but a flexible guide, empowering clinicians to personalize the Minecraft experience to meet the unique needs of each client and the individual style of each therapist (see Appendix A and Table 1.1).

Principle 1: The Play Therapist Does Not Need to Be a Skilled Player to Utilize Minecraft in Play Therapy

Grounded in the non-directive tradition of following the child's lead (Axline, 1947; Landreth, 2012), this principle asserts that the play therapist does not need to be a skilled player to utilize Minecraft in play therapy. An obstacle for clinicians new to using Minecraft in play therapy can be questions about their own skill with the game; however, one does not have to

Table 1.1 The Seven Guiding Principles for using Minecraft in Play Therapy

Guiding principles	*Core therapeutic function*	*Theoretical and clinical influences*	*Foundational references*
Principle 1: Gaming Experience Not Necessary	Acknowledging strengths, building confidence, modeling adaptive behaviors	Non-Directive Play Therapy	Axline (1947); Finch (2021); Young (2024)
Principle 2: Starting at the Beginning	Validation of client interests and creation of early therapeutic moments	Child-Centered Play Therapy	Axline (1947); Landreth (2012)
Principle 3: Being in the Game with the Child	Maintaining therapeutic intention and focus, observational assessment of internal states	Synergetic Play Therapy, Interpersonal Neurobiology	Dion (2018); Siegel (1999)
Principle 4: Coregulation and Working with Stimulation	Modeling regulation, building interoception, increasing child's Window of Tolerance	Polyvagal Theory, Interpersonal Neurobiology, Synergetic Play Therapy	Porges (2011); Siegel (1999); Dion (2018)
Principle 5: Practicing Positive Endings	Acknowledging and working with transitions and endings	Play Therapy Rituals, Limit-Setting	Landreth (2012)
Principle 6: Playing Together at Home	Strengthening family bonds, reinforcing positive attachment, and increasing communication	Attachment-Based Family Therapy for Depressed Adolescents	Diamond et al. (2014)
Principle 7: Bridging Online Play to Offline Play	Translating problem-solving skills and applying game strategies to real life	Therapeutic Metaphor	Mills and Crowley (2014)

be an experienced gamer to bring this modality into their practice (Finch, 2022; Young, 2024, 2025). In fact, many practitioners began this journey learning the game themselves along the way (Finch, 2021; Hembree, 2025). A clinician's novice status can, therefore, be leveraged as a therapeutic tool.

This approach enables the clinician to model essential skills, such as asking for help, tolerating the distress of feeling stuck, and persisting through challenges. Furthermore, it offers the child an opportunity to step into a teaching role, which can be a powerful way to acknowledge their strengths and build confidence. By being authentically themselves, clinicians build rapport and demonstrate that the benefits of the work come not from mastery of the game, but from the quality of the therapeutic connection. This principle also extends to parents and caregivers who play with their child as described in Chapter 8.

Principle 2: The Therapy Starts Even before the Game is Played

Offering Minecraft as a therapeutic option immediately shows the child that their interests matter and that the clinician is committed to understanding their world. This validating approach is important from the very first contact, including during the consultation, initial intake, and treatment planning. It also creates a neurodiverse-affirming method for children who may feel more comfortable expressing themselves through digital play. Even initial logistical tasks such as character design, starting a new world, and learning to navigate the technology for playing together become opportunities with therapeutic potential. These activities provide entry points for various therapeutic topics such as exploring identity and establishing routines, as explained in Chapter 4.

Principle 3: The Play Therapist Is Not Playing Minecraft for Their Own Enjoyment; They Are Playing to Be in the Experience of the Game with the Child

While playing Minecraft with clients can be enjoyable, our primary focus is on maintaining an attuned and observant presence within the game. This principle is grounded in the Synergetic Play Therapy concept of the "setup" and the interdisciplinary framework of interpersonal neurobiology (Dion, 2018; Siegel, 1999). The clinician's role is to maintain therapeutic intention, observing how gameplay stimulates the child's brain, body, and nervous system, and how our own thoughts, feelings, and nervous systems respond in tandem. This direct engagement with the child's internal world naturally leads to the co-regulatory work of Principle 4. Clinical vignettes in Chapter 5 illustrate the concept of being in the game with the child and how this differs from casual Minecraft play.

Principle 4: The Play Therapist Can Model How to Work with the Stimulation in the Game to Help the Child Learn More about Themselves While Playing

Drawing on Polyvagal Theory (Porges, 2011), interpersonal neurobiology (Siegel, 1999), and contemporary play therapy modalities (see Dion, 2018), play therapists can use their own experiences of being in the game to help model regulation, develop interoception, and expand the child's Window of Tolerance. By leveraging the benefits of coregulation, play therapists can help children regulate themselves in real-time as they navigate moments of distress during play. Additional clinical vignettes are provided in Chapter 6 to expand on the previous three principles and illustrate the concept of helping children better understand themselves.

Principle 5: How the Game Ends in a Session Is Practice for Endings and Transitions Outside of the Play Therapy Space

Inspired by the therapeutic use of rituals and limit-setting in play therapy (Landreth, 2012), this principle suggests that how the game ends in a session is practice for working with endings outside of the appointment. The intentional endings of the game provide a structured, relational container for the child to experience transitions, building a template for tolerating the distress of stopping a preferred activity and moving toward what comes next. As a natural segue into the final principles, Chapter 7 presents clinical vignettes that demonstrate how to practice positive and intentional endings.

Principle 6: Parents and Helping Adults Can Support Their Child in Having a Therapeutic Experience with Minecraft at Home by Being Curious and Learning about the Game Together

Rooted in the principles of Attachment-Based Family Therapy for Depressed Adolescents (Diamond et al., 2014), this approach guides parents to use Minecraft play as a purposeful play activity to strengthen family bonds and promote secure attachment. Following a split, family-systems model of exploring the caregiver's relationship to the game first, adults can be coached to engage with the child's interest through curiosity rather than direction. This helps create a conduit for improved communication, allowing the child to safely express their inner world through the metaphor of the game. This activity turns a shared experience into therapeutic opportunities for connection at home.

Principle 7: The Benefits of Playing the Game Reach far Beyond the Play Therapy Space and the Digital World of Minecraft

This principle harnesses the power of therapeutic metaphor (Mills & Crowley, 2014) to facilitate the transfer of in-game problem-solving skills and strategies to a child's real-world challenges. By intentionally focusing on the client's experience in Minecraft, the clinician can help build awareness of how competencies developed in the game, such as overcoming obstacles, managing frustration, and planning solutions, can be applied to external situations. Directive interventions are used to explicitly bridge this process from the session to experiences at home and beyond, ensuring the benefits of play extend far beyond the digital world.

Looking Ahead

The Seven Guiding Principles introduced in this book provide a clinical framework for using Minecraft to help children build vital skills in emotional regulation, distress tolerance, interoceptive awareness, and coping. The chapters ahead offer an in-depth exploration of this process, with focused applications for presenting issues including identity exploration, emotional distress, negative self-talk, trauma, bereavement, and neurodivergence. This work also thoughtfully addresses the essential balance of screen time, parent collaboration, and key clinical considerations from treatment planning and note-writing to assessing therapeutic fit.

This framework synthesizes a wide range of play therapy techniques and is grounded in the science of developing brain and nervous system. Readers will learn to assess a child's emotional development through their Minecraft play, understand how their brain and body perceive threat and safety within the game, and translate these insights into clear clinical conceptualization, documentation, and parent collaboration.

The interventions presented are based on my direct clinical experience, drawing from both the successes and challenges of implementing Minecraft in play therapy. While this book cannot encompass the entirety of play therapy literature, it is grounded in current research and inspired by a global community of pioneers who creatively use Minecraft in their work.

This book is designed to be a flexible resource. You may read it sequentially to build your understanding from the ground up, or dive directly into the sections most relevant to your practice. I encourage supervisors and colleagues to share specific chapters as needed. While you may find it helpful to keep this book nearby during a session, remember that the most powerful tool, as emphasized in Chapters 5 and 6, will always be your own authentic presence and curiosity within the game with the child.

The world of Minecraft and its therapeutic impact have expanded beyond just being a video game. While understanding gameplay mechanics can be helpful, this book is not intended as a build tutorial or gameplay guide for experienced players; nor does it cover mechanics such as redstone, coding, or modifying game elements. Although in-game features, mechanics, build ideas, and suggestions are referenced and discussed throughout, this is not a manual for designing or constructing. The goal of this book is to provide a clinical foundation for understanding how and why these approaches and focus areas are beneficial, useful, and therapeutic. It serves as a guide to developing a clinical and theoretical approach to using Minecraft as a play-based modality. As I tell the clients I work with, "You are the expert on what you can do in the game; I am here to help you understand yourself as you do it."

A Note on Terminology and Practice

To ensure clarity: the term "clinician" inclusively refers to all mental health professionals and helpers, while "caregiver" encompasses any supportive adult in a child's life. In clinical examples, "client" is used, though "child" or "adolescent" may appear in broader discussions. Italicized text represents dialogue to illustrate key interactions. My clinical experience referenced throughout primarily involves youth aged 7–18, with considerations for developmental readiness and technological support outlined in Chapter 9. While adults can also benefit from this modality, the focus here remains on the healing potential of play for children and adolescents.

Helpful Tips

- **Validate the child's interests** by bringing the game into the therapy session, creating a bridge for connection and expression rather than leaving the game behind.
- **The Seven Guiding Principles** are designed to translate gameplay into meaningful therapeutic moments, aligning Minecraft interventions with core theoretical concepts in play therapy.
- **Maintain therapeutic intention** by focusing on being attuned and observant while playing; the goal is to be in the experience *with* the child, rather than playing for personal enjoyment.
- **Use the game to model regulation and coregulation,** drawing on principles like Polyvagal Theory to help the child manage stimulation in real-time, develop interoception, and expand their Window of Tolerance.
- **Utilize the game's portability and consistency** as a therapeutic container; since Minecraft can be played on various devices, the world remains accessible and consistent, supporting engagement even when meeting rooms change.

Reflection Question

1 If I choose to bring the game into the session, how can I ensure that my engagement is driven by a clear "clinical and therapeutic purpose," thereby transforming the experience from casual gameplay into a

container for healing and growth as defined by the Seven Guiding Principles framework?

References

Aronson, S. (2017). We're not in Kansas anymore, or how I learned to embrace my inner Minecraft. *Journal of Infant, Child, and Adolescent Psychotherapy*, *16*(4), 261–264. https://doi.org/10.1080/15289168.2017.1360694

Axline, V. M. (1947). *Play therapy: The inner dynamics of childhood*. Houghton Mifflin.

Diamond, G. S., Diamond, G. M., & Levy, S. A. (2014). *Attachment-based family therapy for depressed adolescents*. American Psychological Association.

Dion, L. (2018). *Aggression in play therapy: A neurobiological approach for integrating intensity*. W.W. Norton & Company.

Dion, L. (2022). *The beauty of broken toys in the playroom*. YouTube; Synergetic Play Therapy Institute. https://www.youtube.com/watch?v=9RIwk8p7Dno

Finch, E. (2021). Therapeutic adventures in Minecraft. Playmode Academy; *BACP Children, Young People & Families*. https://playmodeacademy.org/resources-and-publications/featured-article-in-bacp-journal

Finch, E. (2022). *Thinking of using video games therapeutically?* Association for Counseling and Therapy Online. https://playmodeacademy.org/resources-and-publications/thinking-of-using-video-games-therapeutically

Hembree, D. (2025, September 10). *Minecraft therapy opens powerful world for children and teens*. MindSite News. https://mindsitenews.org/2025/09/10/minecraft-for-child-and-teen-therapy/

Landreth, G. L. (2012). *Play therapy: The art of the relationship* (4th ed.). Routledge.

Mills, J. C., & Crowley, R. J. (2014). *Therapeutic metaphors for children and the child within* (2nd ed.). Routledge.

Porges, S. W. (2011). *The polyvagal theory: Neurophysiological foundations of emotions, attachment, communication, and self-regulation*. W.W. Norton & Company.

Ray, D. C., Lee, K. R., Meany-Walen, K. K., Carlson, S. E., Carnes-Holt, K. L., & Ware, J. N. (2013). Use of toys in child-centered play therapy. *International Journal of Play Therapy*, *22*(1), 43–57. https://doi.org/10.1037/a0031430

Schaefer, C. E., & Drewes, A. A. (2014). *The therapeutic powers of play: 20 core agents of change* (2nd ed.). Wiley.

Siegel, D. J. (1999). *The developing mind: How relationships and the brain interact to shape who we are*. Guilford Press.

Young, H. (2024). Unlocking the potential of Minecraft as a therapeutic tool. *Play for Life—The Periodical for members of the International and UK Societies of Play and Creative Arts Therapies*, 11–16. https://static1.squarespace.com/static/65d620423bf68226c14ea353/t/66f57adeeb924e0860a2e261/1727363811541/Summer_PFL_2024.pdf

Young, H. (2025). Exploring the potential of Minecraft to embody the therapeutic powers of play, acting as a core agent for change in the play therapy process. *British Journal of Play Therapy*, *19*(1), 47–59.

Chapter 2

The History, Background, and Overview of Minecraft

A new world has been named; a new character created; the first day has started, and the game has begun. You spawn into a lush green biome, surrounded by rolling hills and rocky cliffs. Animals are scattered nearby, and gentle electronic music draws you further into the stimulation of this experience. You immediately start mining blocks to collect resources and craft items that will help you progress through the day. A shelter is built, and using a stone pickaxe, you make progress on mining materials for new items. Some basic food supplies are gathered, and even though there is so much more to do, the sun begins to set, and you can feel the creatures of the night gradually appearing. Mobs of zombies, oversized spiders, skeletons with bows and arrows, and creepers all lurk nearby. Cycles of day and night pass in the game, and hours at home go by in what feels like a few short breaths.

Minecraft is an open-world, sandbox-style video game that offers a 3D-like environment for players. Instead of following a strict storyline or set course of action, the open-world nature allows players to explore wherever their curiosity takes them. The sandbox gameplay encourages creative exploration by providing endless opportunities to shape and design the world in which the game takes place, without following specific objectives. Open-world, sandbox-style digital games are common in the gaming industry and may be familiar to veteran gamers. Titles such as *Animal Crossing: New Horizons* and *The Legend of Zelda: Breath of the Wild* are well-known examples of open-world, sandbox-style games, suitable for both children and adults. The online gaming platform *Roblox* also features many open-world sandbox games, like *Brookhaven RP* and *Welcome to Farmtown.* Minecraft stands out from others in the genre due to its dynamic, flexible, and creative gameplay, which can be fully experienced within a single game and gaming session.

Players in Minecraft find themselves in a world entirely made up of 3D digital blocks. These blocks are initially generated by the game across

DOI: 10.4324/9781003614784-3

different environments, or biomes. They can be generated randomly or specifically chosen by requesting a seed when creating a new world. The vast, endless feel of the environment is achieved as blocks continue to generate as the player explores. Blocks can be destroyed by the player and also built, placed, and rearranged in endless ways. The simple design of the block graphics creates a charming, familiar look, as everything the player sees is part of the block-shaped world's core design.

In Minecraft, players can select from various gameplay options and modes. For use in play therapy, this book focuses primarily on the game modes Creative and Survival. Creative mode provides players with endless choices, offering immediate access to an inventory of items that function like a well-stocked *LEGO* shelf or a drawer full of expressive art supplies. Survival mode presents a more specific challenge, requiring players to manage their health while navigating threats in the world and finding ways to stay safe through interaction, avoidance, or confrontation with mobs. The term "mobs" is short for "mobiles" and refers to characters that can be either threatening or harmless.

In Survival mode, the primary goal is to survive a zombie apocalypse that mainly happens when the game world turns to night. Players accomplish this by gathering materials through mining or breaking blocks, and then crafting or forming new blocks that serve as useful resources, such as wood for building structures and minerals like iron and diamonds for making weapons and other items. Players start in Survival mode with ten heart icons representing their health and a hunger bar made up of ten meat-style drumstick icons. Both the health and hunger bars can decrease during gameplay, making it important for players to protect their health and manage their hunger levels. A player is defeated if they are killed by a hostile mob or if their health bar runs out due to real-world factors like hunger, falling from a high place, or other causes of death. Heart health bars can regenerate if low, and if a player is defeated, they can respawn in various ways to continue the game.

As an optional goal, players can also explore traveling to other dimensions, such as the Nether and the End. In the End, players encounter the final mob known as the Ender Dragon, which, after being defeated, creates a portal to return to the Overworld and displays the credits of the game design team. Because the Ender Dragon is the final boss, this objective is considered the ultimate challenge in the game and serves as a key point for players seeking a sense of achievement.

Gameplay in Minecraft primarily takes place in the Overworld, which features familiar Earth-like landscapes, including green meadows, hills, mountains, cliffs, water, sand, and caves filled with lava. Other features resembling those on Earth include weather patterns such as rain and snowfall, along with elements like thunderstorms with lightning and fires. These features are fully customizable and can be modified for players, offering a therapeutic and clinical accommodation for clients who might be sensitive to these changes. The only things missing in the Minecraft world are the physical sensations of touch, taste, and smell, which will be discussed later in the book as therapeutic tools to introduce mindfulness skills with clients and help bridge the gap between playing the game on the screen and returning to the real world.

Another highly customizable feature of the Overworld is the day-and-night cycle, with a full day in Minecraft lasting 20 minutes (10 minutes for day and 10 minutes for night). This feature, along with the levels of difficulty and consequences of defeat, can also be tailored to suit the desired challenge and activation level of players. Sections 2 and 3 provide more detailed information about the clinical and therapeutic importance of these customizable features for a child's nervous system and Window of Tolerance (WOT), as well as their relationship to the Seven Guiding Principles.

There is much more to Minecraft and what the game offers. The upcoming chapters will help readers understand how the open-world, sandbox-style gameplay unique to Minecraft can be therapeutic for clients, including clinical vignettes to demonstrate the benefits of non-directive interventions when playing the game in session, as well as directive interventions for specific clinical populations. Strategies for using game concepts and dynamics outside of gameplay, such as reframing the players' health and hunger bars to increase a child's awareness of needs and coping strategies, will also be covered. Last, the Appendices and Handouts in Section 6 provide quick reference guides for therapists to integrate this framework into their sessions.

History of the Game

Officially launched to the public in November 2011, Minecraft has sold over 300 million units worldwide, making it the best-selling video game of all time (Curry, 2025). To compare with current pop culture phenomena, Taylor Swift has sold approximately 200 million albums (and digital unit equivalents) since her debut in 2006 (Wares, 2025). Alpha and beta versions of the game were first released for PC in 2009 by game developer Markus "Notch" Persson (Cadet, 2024; Curry, 2025). For the two years prior to its official launch, Mojang Studios refined the game under the creative leadership of Jens Bergensten, who still oversees the Bedrock Edition (Cadet, 2024; Curry, 2025). Minecraft is now owned by Microsoft, which acquired the game in 2014. Following the acquisition, Minecraft: Education Edition was introduced in 2016 with tailored controls, features, and content to help teachers incorporate Minecraft into their classrooms. Mobile versions for iOS and Android were also released in September and

October 2017 (Cadet, 2024). The game's popularity continued to grow with the release of expanded franchise titles, such as Minecraft Dungeons in 2020 and Minecraft Legends in 2023.

Current data show the global popularity and accessibility of the main Minecraft game, with 186 million registered players worldwide. The player demographics are as follows: 20.59% of players are under 15 years old, and 43% are between 15 and 21 years old (Cadet, 2024). About 21% of active players are based in the US, followed by 6.2% from Brazil, 5.6% from Russia, 5.1% from Germany, 4.6% from the UK, and the remaining 57.5% from other countries (Cadet, 2024). Given the global interest and participation in Minecraft, it is encouraging for clinicians that children are attracted to the game as a way to express and process their inner worlds.

The data also show that 80% of children play multiplayer Minecraft, including friends, family members, and players from the global online community (Cadet, 2024). The ability to connect and play with others reflects the increasing demand for mobile sales of the game, which account for 41% of total sales, allowing players to access the game from anywhere (Cadet, 2024). During the COVID-19 pandemic, interest in playing Minecraft for entertainment and social connection led to record-breaking sales, an increase in active users, and overall heightened engagement. Data from 2020 indicate a 25% increase in players and a 40% rise in sales, with an average monthly user base of 131 million, compared to 62 million in 2024 (Cadet, 2024).

In the current mental health landscape, social isolation is contributing to increased symptoms of anxiety and depression in children and adolescents (Almeida et al., 2021). The growing interest in Minecraft as a form of social play, combined with the increasing number of children initiating online interactions globally, offers an accessible way to help reduce the mental health impacts of loneliness. Considering Minecraft's tremendous popularity and its long-standing availability to children and teens, it is crucial for helping adults working with youth to consider how to leverage their training and background to intentionally enhance the therapeutic benefits of playing the game.

Minecraft in Pop Culture

Minecraft has become a staple in modern pop culture, with licensing extending to nearly every market outside the original game: music, books, movies, clothing, toys, and accessories, all feature items related to the Minecraft universe. The 2011 soundtrack of the original game, "Minecraft: Volume Alpha" by Daniel Rosenfield, has been inducted into the National Recording Registry by the Library of Congress for being "culturally, historically, and/or aesthetically significant" (Ulaby, 2025). The Minecraft movie, released in 2025, made a significant impact in the United States and worldwide, grossing as much as $162.8 million and $313 million, respectively, making it Warner Bros' third-highest-grossing opening weekend film. The brand's visibility, especially during April 2025 when the film was released, took on the qualities of a pop culture phenomenon, with media appearing in grocery store checkout lanes, on clothing racks at department stores, and in social media posts and memes across the internet.

Minecraft as an ESport

Minecraft has also secured a spot in the competitive esports scene. Similar to athletic events, esports provide competitive opportunities for players and entertainment for spectators. The history of video game competition began in 1972 at Stanford University's Artificial Intelligence Laboratory. It naturally expanded during the 1980s and 1990s with the rise of arcade gaming and the development of multiplayer gaming consoles. The following decades saw the growth of high-speed internet and a wider selection of multiplayer games with online features, which continued to increase interest and create opportunities for players worldwide to compete. Online streaming platforms have also enabled spectators to participate more actively, boosting the entertainment value of competitive gaming. Minecraft has become part of the esports industry as another way for players to connect their passion for the game with other aspects of their lives.

Although Minecraft was not originally a competitive game, its popularity and the evolving uses of modifications encouraged players to set creative benchmarks for competition. The combination of widespread popularity, rising skill levels, and a constant stream of new content has made Minecraft a rapidly growing force in esports. Organized groups and leagues for Minecraft esports players can be found in schools and universities, as well as in privately organized after-school programs, summer programs, and intensive camp-like experiences.

Minecraft Education

Before the official public release in 2011, educators who played the initial version of the game immediately noticed the creative and inventive benefits of integrating the game into the classroom (Duncan, 2011). Duncan's (2011) article, "*Minecraft: Beyond Creative and Survival,*" seems to be one of the first journal articles documenting the game's immediate appeal as an instructional platform in educational settings, referencing its niche use in 2009 and 2010. Educator and gamer Joel Levin, known as "The Minecraft Teacher," is recognized explicitly for early efforts to implement Minecraft in classrooms, primarily to foster creativity and critical thinking in young students through puzzles in pre-made worlds (Duncan, 2011; Levin, 2011; Webster, 2011).

Launched in 2016, Minecraft: Education Edition is a modified version of the Bedrock Edition that supports up to 30 student players simultaneously (Cadet, 2024). More than 35 million teachers and students are licensed to use the game, with over 100,000 educators officially trained, reaching classrooms across 115 countries (Cadet, 2024). Before the Education Edition was released, educators had already explored ways to adapt the game for classroom use (Dikkers, 2015; Gallagher, 2014; Nebel et al., 2016; Whale & O'Hanlon, 2014). The move toward a classroom-friendly version of the game was a natural step for educators seeking to boost student interest, motivation, and engagement. Studies conducted in 2022 and 2023 showed that the game encourages students to collaborate and taps into their creativity through an immersive learning environment (Andersen & Rustad, 2022; Slattery et al., 2023). According to Slattery et al. (2023), researchers also observed that using the game in classrooms continued to improve students' digital literacy and tech skills. These learning experiences also benefit teachers, as they can build their technology skills while observing how students understand and engage with new learning methods (Singh & Sun, 2025).

Classroom research has also examined the advantages of using Minecraft in STEM/STEAM (science, technology, education, arts, and math) programs, with a special emphasis on math-specific learning. Educators observed that students' familiarity with and interest in the game were significant motivators for learning about math-related principles, concepts, and ideas (Dezuani & Macri, 2020). As this book discusses in later chapters, involving parents and caregivers in a child's therapy promotes full family engagement, and the same is true for connecting classroom educational content to the home (Ellison et al., 2016).

Using Minecraft Education in the classroom also creates more opportunities to explore how the game can be used therapeutically. The collaborative and social aspects that often emerge when integrating the game into class activities can lead to further observations and questions about how students interact with one another and the effects of those interactions. A 2024 study on college students' social-emotional development used the game in both collaborative and competitive settings to assess communication, problem-solving, understanding, and empathy (Lee et al., 2024). Using the game this way introduces similarities with individual therapeutic goals, group work, and the benefits of ongoing research, regardless of the specific game edition or content.

The gameplay, environment, and features closely resemble the standard Minecraft edition; however, the Education Edition provides teachers with greater control and flexibility in classroom management and social restrictions. The Education Edition supports multiplayer interaction within a secure learning environment dedicated to the game licenses and classroom server. This prevents players from connecting outside the classroom, thereby reducing the game's casual social aspect. It creates a clear boundary that effectively communicates the specific learning goals for each session. Other educational features include comprehensive tutorials, pre-designed lesson plans, and extensive coding resources that support STEM-focused classroom objectives. These options offer helpful choices for play therapists when selecting which operating systems and game editions to use with their clients, especially if the option to use pre-built worlds is an incentive.

Minecraft in Play Therapy

As educators have found the game helpful in motivating and engaging their students, it became clear that the game could appeal to children and adolescents who might be curious or resistant to play therapy. Gaining the child's buy-in at the start of therapy helps establish the safety and comfort necessary for building a positive relationship between the child and the play therapist (Blackwood, 2025). Caregivers, clinicians, and mental health advocates can use the child's interest in Minecraft as a powerful starting point to improve the chances of a successful beginning to play therapy and related topics.

Research and peer-reviewed studies on the therapeutic benefits of Minecraft are limited, as the game's use as a clinical intervention is still in its early stages. Despite these limitations a growing body of research is emerging with studies on the efficacy of the game in working with neurodivergent and autistic youth (Blackwood, 2025) and the acknowledgment of global practitioners finding creative ways to support their clients (Stuart, 2025; Hembree, 2025) – a topic that will be explored in greater detail in Chapter 20. However, it's clear that Minecraft began to make an impact outside the classroom shortly after its release. In a literature review on the benefits of playing video games, Granic et al. (2014) recognized the potential of Minecraft as a therapeutic tool because of its popularity and flexible gameplay; however, they provided no specific details due to the game's early adoption.

Bridging the gap between the collaborative benefits of using Minecraft in the classroom, a study by Rachael Cilauro (2015) explored the growing interest and creative methods of using the game to connect intergenerational communities in Australia. The survey involved librarians partnering with young library patrons to organize a Minecraft Gaming Day, promoting socialization, identity, and community building across generations. The study demonstrated how both groups could collaborate, not only in the online world of Minecraft but also as community members responsible for organizing the event. This work introduced the potential future use of Minecraft in therapeutic groups and highlighted how in-game skills could be applied to real-world interactions.

Because many play therapy methods adopt a family-systems approach, understanding how parents perceive their children's Minecraft play is crucial when using the game in clinical settings. Research by Mavoa et al. (2017), involving parents aged 36–45 of children aged 3–12, found that 91.4% recognized Minecraft's benefits, including increased creativity, problem-solving skills, resource management, and improved social interaction with peers, siblings, and online collaborators. Parents also noted that the game promoted enjoyment, self-esteem, and a sense of achievement in their children. However, 46.8% expressed concerns about excessive screen time reducing physical activity or homework, as well as cyber safety risks such as exposure to inappropriate content or interactions with strangers. Other concerns included physical issues like poor posture or eyesight, addictive behaviors, and occasional aggression when ending gameplay or during conflicts within the game. Nonetheless, parents emphasized these issues were occasional and situational (Mavoa et al., 2017). This book will further explore these concerns in Chapters 7, 9, and 19.

Looking Ahead

Minecraft is not merely a fleeting digital trend, but a pervasive cultural force that has profoundly reshaped the landscape of childhood expression and engagement. With over 300 million units sold, making it the best-selling video game of all time (Curry, 2025), and an ecosystem that encompasses educational curricula, competitive esports, and a massive impact on pop culture, Minecraft has established itself as a global phenomenon that demands serious attention from helping professionals. For the play therapist, ignoring this pervasive environment where 186 million registered players worldwide (Cadet, 2024), predominantly youth, spend countless hours, is to overlook the language and context through which many children express and process their inner worlds.

This immense popularity and accessibility of the game serve as a powerful starting point to secure the child's buy-in, creating the essential foundation of safety and comfort required for any therapeutic journey to begin successfully. Furthermore, given that social isolation is a contributing factor to heightened symptoms of anxiety and depression (Almeida et al., 2021), the fact that 80% of children utilize Minecraft for social, multiplayer interaction (Cadet, 2024) positions it as a platform worthy of further inquiry for mitigating the mental health impacts of loneliness.

The mandate to take this game seriously, however, extends beyond its cultural reach; it rests in its therapeutic viability. The game's open-world, sandbox design uniquely offers the dynamic, flexible, and creative environment necessary for play therapy, mirroring the unlimited potential of a traditional playroom. Whether a client needs the immediate resources of Creative mode or the challenge of survival and resource management in the face of threats presented by Survival mode, the game mechanics provide a tailored canvas for intervention.

Moving forward, the clinical framework of the Seven Guiding Principles will reveal how these customizable features, from adjusting the day-and-night cycle to managing health and hunger bars, can be intentionally adapted to support a child's nervous system, enhance their awareness of needs, and expand their WOT. The question is no longer whether Minecraft belongs in therapy, but how clinicians can use this culturally meaningful game to foster profound growth.

Helpful Tips

- **Sandbox Gameplay:** Minecraft is a sandbox-style video game that features an open-world environment, allowing players to explore creatively by placing and rearranging digital blocks within a 3D space.
- **Key Therapeutic Modes:** Two primary game modes are emphasized: Creative mode, which provides instant access to countless items like a fully stocked *LEGO* shelf, and Survival mode, which involves managing health and hunger while defending against threats (mobs).
- **Customizable Features:** The game is highly flexible, offering customizable features such as the day-and-night cycle, difficulty, and weather patterns that can be tailored for players to support a child's nervous system or expand their WOT.
- **Global Phenomenon:** Minecraft is the best-selling video game of all time, with over 300 million units sold. Its widespread popularity and cultural significance among youth help therapists gain a child's buy-in at the start of therapy.
- **Social/Therapeutic Viability:** The game's open-world, dynamic design offers a flexible environment suitable for play therapy. Since 80% of children use Minecraft for social, multiplayer interaction, it can help alleviate the mental health effects of social isolation and loneliness.

Reflection Question

1 Given Minecraft's widespread cultural significance and therapeutic potential, what is one aspect of your current play therapy practice that you would need to adapt or learn more about to confidently use the game with your clients?

References

Almeida, I. L. L., Rego, J. F., Teixeira, A. C. G., & Moreira, M. R. (2021). Social isolation and its impact on child and adolescent development: A systematic review. *Revista Paulista De Pediatria*, *40*(40). https://doi.org/10.1590/1984-0462/2022/40/2020385

Andersen, R., & Rustad, M. (2022). Using minecraft as an educational tool for supporting collaboration as a 21st century skill. *Computers and Education Open*, *3*, 100094. https://doi.org/10.1016/j.caeo.2022.100094

Blackwood, L. (2025). Legend land: An evaluation of a telehealth videogame for the emotional regulation of autistic children. *Good Autism Practice*, *26*(1), 35–44. https://www.ingentaconnect.com/contentone/bild/gap/2025/00000026/00000001/art00007 https://www.ingentaconnect.com/contentone/bild/gap/2025/00000026/00000001/art00007

Cadet, L. (2024). *36 mind-blowing Minecraft statistics*. HostingAdvice.com. https://www.hostingadvice.com/how-to/minecraft-statistics/

Cilauro, R. (2015). Community building through a public library Minecraft Gaming Day. *The Australian Library Journal*, *64*(2), 87–93. https://doi.org/10.1080/00049670.2015.1015209

Curry, D. (2025). *Minecraft Revenue and Usage Statistics* (2020). Business of Apps. https://www.businessofapps.com/data/minecraft-statistics/

Dezuani, M., & Macri, J. (2020). *Minecraft: Education edition for educational impact*. https://research.qut.edu.au/dmrc/wp-content/uploads/sites/5/2019/10/MEE-Research.pdf

Dikkers, S. (2015). *Teachercraft: How teachers learn to use Minecraft in their classrooms*. Etc Press.

Duncan, S. C. (2011). Minecraft, beyond construction and survival. *Well Played: A Journal on Video Games, Value, and Meaning*, *1*(1), 1–22. https://stacks.stanford.edu/file/druid:qq694ht6771/WellPlayed-v1n1-11.pdf

Ellison, T., Evans, J., & Pike, J. (2016). Minecraft, teachers, parents, and learning: What they need to know and understand. *School Community Journal*, *26*(2). https://files.eric.ed.gov/fulltext/EJ1123979.pdf

Gallagher, C. (2014). *An educator's guide to using Minecraft® in the classroom*. Peachpit Press.

Granic, I., Lobel, A., & Engels, R. C. M. E. (2014). The benefits of playing video games. *American Psychologist*, *69*(1), 66–78. https://doi.org/10.1037/a0034857

Hembree, D. (2025, September 10). *Minecraft therapy opens powerful world for children and teens*. MindSite News. https://mindsitenews.org/2025/09/10/minecraft-for-child-and-teen-therapy/

Lee, S., Jang, W., & Rollins, M. (2024). *Using Minecraft Education Edition to enhance 21st century skills in the college classroom: A mixed methods study*. https://scholarspace.manoa.hawaii.edu/server/api/core/bitstreams/8679fb3f-ff72-4538-a579-d39e1915b7e6/content

Levin, J. (2011). *The Minecraft Teacher*. Tumblr. https://minecraftteacher.tumblr.com/

Mavoa, J., Carter, M., & Gibbs, M. (2017). *Beyond addiction: Positive and negative parent perceptions of Minecraft play*. Proceedings of the Annual Symposium on Computer-Human Interaction in Play. https://doi.org/10.1145/3116595.3116638

Nebel, S., Schneider, S., & Rey, G. D. (2016). Mining learning and crafting scientific experiments: A literature review on the use of *Minecraft* in education and research. *Educational Technology & Society*, *19*(2), 355–366.

Singh, M., & Sun, D. (2025). Evaluating Minecraft as a game-based metaverse platform: Exploring gaming experience, social presence, and STEM outcomes. *Interactive Learning Environments*, 1–23. https://doi.org/10.1080/10494820.2025.2459200

Slattery, E. J., Butler, D., O'Leary, M., & Marshall, K. (2023). Primary school students' experiences using Minecraft education during a national project-based initiative: An Irish study. *TechTrends*. https://doi.org/10.1007/s11528-023-00851-z

Stuart, K. (2025, July 14). The way a child plays is the way they live: How therapists are using video games to help vulnerable children. The Guardian. https://www.theguardian.com/games/2025/jul/14/the-way-a-child-plays-is-the-way-they-live-how-therapists-are-using-video-games-to-help-vulnerable-children

Ulaby, N. (2025). *National Recording Registry adds Tracy Chapman, Hamilton and the Minecraft game soundtrack*. NPR. https://www.npr.org/2025/04/09/nx-s1-5352774/national-recording-registry-tracy-chapman-elton-john-hamilton-minecraft

Wares, A. (2025). *Big story: The value of swiftnomics*. Platinum Media Group. Platinummediagroup.co.uk. https://www.platinummediagroup.co.uk/dynamic/2025/01/big-story-the-value-of-swiftnomics/

Webster, A. (2011). Educational building blocks: How Minecraft is used in classrooms. *Ars Technica*. https://arstechnica.com/gaming/2011/04/educational-building-blocks-how-minecraft-is-being-used-in-the-classroom/

Whale, D., & O'Hanlon, M. (2014). *Adventures in Minecraft*. John Wiley & Sons.

Section II

The Seven Guiding Principles

Chapter 3

The Modern Era of Video Games

The Author's Journey (Principle 1)

A child is describing to me how they like to "chill out" playing Minecraft. They find the music very relaxing and share that they might even turn on a YouTube video of the game's music to help them fall asleep. I asked if they played in Survival mode, and they replied that they did not; it was too stressful because of the pressure from threats that attack at night. Instead, they enjoy creating a peaceful space with things they want to look at, such as happy pigs, lots of flowers, parrots flying around, and axolotls swimming nearby.

They also described having a room with a large bookshelf because they enjoyed reading, and they wanted a reading nook in the game. I was immediately struck by the mindfulness and grounding skills this client had been developing through the intention of their gameplay and the detailed description of what sounded like a "Happy Place," an intervention I often used as a prompt in a sand tray build or during an expressive art activity.

"Actually, I could show it to you over the screen. Would you like to see it?"

"Yes!"

My journey as a play therapist began with working with bereaved children. In the playrooms where I met children and adolescents, I played games like *UNO* and *Battleship*, observed creations made with *LEGO*, and watched deeply vulnerable, personal stories unfold in the safe container of a sand tray. While watching children play, I often thought about video games and the nature of play associated with them.

During the COVID-19 pandemic, I adapted my playroom activities for online meetings. To build rapport and meet the goals of treatment plans in this new digital space, I adapted by playing *UNO* online, using a digital sand tray, and exploring a variety of other traditional board games used in play therapy that could be played online. Throughout this period, I had consistently heard about Minecraft but had dismissed it as a game without clinical relevance.

However, my perspective began to shift as I heard about the benefits clients described from playing video games. Engaging with clients through

DOI: 10.4324/9781003614784-5

their interests in games like *Fortnite* or others played on the *Roblox* platform started to show how self-awareness and coping skills could be recognized in a medium that felt authentic to them. These experiences, combined with increasing discussions in online communities of therapists using these methods creatively, led me to reconsider my clients' strong interest in Minecraft.

The sessions began to shift as I focused more on how children related to their interest in Minecraft. Many had played before logging into our session or planned to play afterward. I was amazed at how detailed clients were when describing their characters or the "skins" they intentionally chose to express themselves in the game. There were also many different play styles that felt unique to each client.

One might share how they built a village in Survival mode, farming food, raising animals, and expanding their homestead to survive a zombie apocalypse. Another might talk about watching building tutorials on YouTube and challenging themselves to replicate what they saw. Their game worlds could include a digital hobby room where they showcased everything they created over the month. I saw pride on their faces as they mentioned the increasing difficulty and time they dedicated to their recent builds. It was this consistent display of engagement, self-expression, and mastery that convinced me to move from observing their interest to formally integrating Minecraft as a core therapeutic intervention.

Connecting Traditional Play to Minecraft Play

My work in traditional playrooms taught me the core processes of child engagement. When I moved online, I discovered that Minecraft could digitally support these same processes. Where I once thought I was at a disadvantage online, lacking items such as sand trays, Minecraft could address that need. When children would benefit from creating a memory box, instead of needing art supplies at home to decorate and personalize it, they can craft something just as meaningful and memorable in Minecraft. Helping caregivers stay connected to their child's experience through these activities was accessible, since many of these caregivers knew their children played Minecraft and had even tried playing it themselves.

Working with bereaved children led me to pursue advanced trainings such as Eye Movement Desensitization and Reprocessing (EMDR) for trauma, and Attachment-Based Family Therapy for Depressed Adolescents (ABFT) to help caregivers repair relationships with their adolescents. Further training in Synergetic Play Therapy (SPT) taught me to consider the interpersonal and neurobiological dynamics in play therapy between the therapist and client. It was through this advanced lens that I began to see Minecraft not just as a playful diversion, but as a platform capable of supporting profound therapeutic processes such as trauma processing, attachment repair, and emotional regulation. While observing how Minecraft could benefit my online practice and how my advanced training could integrate with the expansive play experiences offered by Minecraft gameplay, I realized I needed to learn more about how to play the game and the technology behind it.

Learning Minecraft to Meet the Needs of Children During the COVID-19 Pandemic

After conceptualizing Minecraft's therapeutic potential, I faced my biggest practical challenge: mastering my own technological learning curve, which far exceeded the Nintendo systems I grew up with. My initial research revealed a confusing amount of information, and I wrestled with basic, logistical questions: do I need a different platform to match each child? What subscriptions are necessary for each device? What are the confidentiality and privacy concerns?

Next, I needed to understand the game itself as a clinical tool: what is the clinical significance of Creative mode versus Survival mode? How might player-versus-player (PVP) dynamics differ from cooperative play? What are the practical and clinical implications of using a Realm versus a world?

Finally, ethical and theoretical concerns arose: how could I confidently explain the therapeutic benefits to caregivers? How would I document in-game processes? Most importantly, was there a community of clinicians already doing this work from whom I could learn?

Faced with these complex questions, I actively sought out other professionals and realized I was not alone. During the COVID-19 pandemic, therapists frequently shared their experiences and resources on social media. Facebook groups such as Tele-PLAY Therapy Resources, Geek Therapy Community, Play Therapy Community, and Synergetic Play Therapy Learning Community became essential peer support networks. The Let's Play Therapy Institute offered training, and advocates and pioneers like Ellie Finch of PlayMode Academy in the UK provided visible validation for the clinical importance and impact of this work. To start my own Minecraft groups, I connected with Laura Morlock of Play Therapy Connections for direct advice on running online sessions for 2nd to 5th graders.

The Author's Initial Experience Using Minecraft in Play Therapy Sessions

As I learned more about the game and sought answers to my earlier questions, it became clear how my clinical background would inform the interventions I used with Minecraft. Just as I had previously worked with a variety of toys, sand trays, and other play accessories, Minecraft was simply another tool for play, both online and in person. The clinical decision-making I previously drew upon was equally relevant in adapting a child's interest in Minecraft to support their treatment plans and goals.

Challenges Faced

Making this transition was not always smooth. The challenges fell into three main categories: the technical learning curve, the investment in clinical preparation, and navigating my own personal engagement with the game.

Mechanics and Connectivity

The sheer complexity of Minecraft was my first hurdle. Unlike the simple, self-explanatory toys in my playroom or the minimal learning curve of traditional online games, Minecraft required dedicated practice. Since I had never played the game before, I had to understand what the items on the screen represented, how they differed between the two gameplay modes, and learn basic skills, like how to survive the first night. As many of the children I work with will tell you, I still need lots more practice.

Connectivity posed another significant barrier. Josh Vensor, a Licensed Clinical Social Worker (LCSW), and colleague who used Minecraft with grieving children, helped me practice connecting online and joining a shared virtual world. This was challenging at first and can still be an obstacle to work out with a client, while also having therapeutic value as explored in Chapter 10. Recognizing all the digital "moving parts" was essential for me to feel confident and present.

Clinical Preparation

The time investment required to become "therapy-ready" with Minecraft was unlike anything I had encountered with other play therapy tools. While I could quickly learn the rules of a new board game, learning Minecraft was a continuous process. I made time outside my play therapy sessions to familiarize myself with the game, reframing this not as a burden, but as a necessary and valuable form of clinical continuing education. Just as I might read journal articles or books on therapy, the time spent learning the basics of Minecraft was a direct investment in my clinical skills. This hands-on learning, while a labor of love, was crucial for competent practice.

Personal and Clinical Boundaries

Perhaps the most unexpected challenge was navigating my own enjoyment and its impact on clinical boundaries. Playing the game skillfully was harder than I expected, but I also faced the learning curve of not being prepared for how much fun I would have. As my clients made progress, I found it easier to get lost in the play. Instead of always following the guiding principle of being present with the child, there were times I was simply playing. Adjusting to this made me aware of a blind spot, where it was easy to lose track of time. There were moments when it felt incredibly difficult to honor my ethical and clinical promise not to enter the shared world without the client to finish a build. Even now, it remains challenging not to succumb to the tempting pull of plain fun.

Principle 1 in Practice: The Clinician as a "Good Enough" Player

Navigating my inexperience with the game and the challenges of the learning curve led directly to the first of the Seven Guiding Principles: the play therapist does not need to be a skilled player to utilize Minecraft in play therapy. A common obstacle for clinicians is anxiety about their own gaming skill, but research and practice indicate that one does not need to be an expert to effectively use this modality (Finch, 2022; Young, 2024, 2025). In fact, many practitioners begin by learning the game alongside their clients (Finch, 2021; Hembree, 2025). A clinician's novice status can be leveraged as a therapeutic tool embodying the concept of the "good enough" player (Finch, 2021). This posture enables the clinician to model essential socioemotional skills, such as asking for help, tolerating the frustration of being stuck, and persisting through challenges. Furthermore, it inverts the traditional dynamic, offering the child a valuable opportunity to step into the role of the competent teacher, which can powerfully build self-esteem and acknowledge their strengths (Finch, 2021). This aligns with the core of child-centered play therapy: effectiveness stems not from the therapist's mastery of the medium, but from the quality of the therapeutic relationship and the condition of being fully present with the child in their world (Landreth, 2012). This principle of the "good enough" player also benefits parents and caregivers who play with their child at home, a concept explored in Chapter 8.

Looking Ahead

The following sections and chapters provide a detailed overview of how I adapted my previous experience in play therapy and family systems to align seamlessly with what many children and adolescents already do in Minecraft. Referring to the Seven Guiding Principles, readers will be introduced to a theoretical and clinical framework that highlights the importance of the relationship between the child and play therapist as the most vital therapeutic element. Section 2: The Therapeutic Nature of Minecraft and Section 3: Clinical Applications and Special Focus Populations offer further insights into how to implement the game in work with various clinical presentations in play therapy, such as emotional distress and dysregulation, negative self-talk, building self-esteem, grief and bereavement, supporting trauma experiences, working with neurodivergent populations, and group therapy applications. Addressing the development of a healthy relationship with screen time and gameplay is also included as a key concern for many clinicians and families.

Section 4 discusses additional clinical practice considerations raised by mental health professionals during conversations and after presentations I have given at professional conferences. Section 5 emphasizes the significant presence Minecraft currently has within the mental health community and explores potential future developments as we prepare for advancements in technology and mental health advocacy. Finally, Section 6 provides appendices and handouts that offer quick reference answers to questions addressed throughout the book, helping readers begin to integrate this work into their practice immediately.

Helpful Tips

- **Client-Led Discovery:** Minecraft was formally integrated after consistently observing clients demonstrate engagement, self-expression, and mastery when discussing the game, revealing its therapeutic potential.
- **A Clinical Container:** Advanced training in modalities like EMDR and Synergetic Play Therapy informed the recognition of Minecraft as a valid platform for deep therapeutic work, including trauma processing and attachment repair.
- **Embrace the "Good Enough" Player (Principle 1):** Clinical effectiveness does not require gaming expertise. A novice stance can model vital socioemotional skills, such as asking for help, and empowering the child to become a competent guide.
- **The Relationship Is the Intervention:** View Minecraft as another tool in the playroom. The healing power flows from the therapeutic relationship and the clinician's attuned presence, not from technical mastery of the game.
- **Commit to Clinical Preparation:** Integrating Minecraft requires overcoming a technological learning curve and dedicating time to understanding the clinical implications of game modes (e.g., Creative vs. Survival) and mechanics.

Reflection Question

1 What is one aspect of Minecraft's mechanics (like game modes or player dynamics) that I would need to understand more deeply to feel confident using it for play therapy?

References

Finch, E. (2021). Therapeutic adventures in Minecraft. Playmode Academy; *BACP Children, Young People & Families*. https://playmodeacademy.org/resources-and-publications/featured-article-in-bacp-journal

Finch, E. (2022). *Thinking of using video games therapeutically?* Association for Counseling and Therapy Online. https://playmodeacademy.org/resources-and-publications/thinking-of-using-video-games-therapeutically

Hembree, D. (2025, Septeber 10). *Minecraft therapy opens powerful world for children and teens*. MindSite News. https://mindsitenews.org/2025/09/10/minecraft-for-child-and-teen-therapy/

Landreth, G. L. (2012). *Play therapy: The art of the relationship* (4th ed.). Routledge.

Young, H. (2024). Unlocking the potential of Minecraft as a therapeutic tool. *Play for Life—The Periodical for members of the International and UK Societies of Play and Creative Arts Therapies*, 11–16. https://static1.squarespace.com/static/65d620423bf68226c14ea353/t/66f57adeeb924e0860a2e261/1727363811541/Summer_PFL_2024.pdf

Young, H. (2025). Exploring the potential of Minecraft to embody the therapeutic powers of play, acting as a core agent for change in the play therapy process. *British Journal of Play Therapy*, *19*(1), 47–59.

Chapter 4

The Start

Identity Exploration and Expression (Principle 2)

Using the controls, I toggle to see myself onscreen from a third-person point of view. In real life, I have a beard, but in the game, my smooth face is looking back at me with joyful eyes. My brown hair has been replaced with a shade that falls between grey and white. I know my hair is changing color as I age, and I am embracing this change through my Minecraft character. A large, high-top pompadour is chosen for my hairstyle as a tribute to my love of 1950s music. The children I work with may not know this about me, but I smile inside, knowing that a part of my life, which I keep hidden, can be visible on the outside - even if only to me. My character is wearing what appears to be a soft grey sweatsuit. I imagine what it might feel like on my body, and I notice a sense of relaxation. On my feet are a pair of large boots that I chose because they remind me of Napoleon Dynamite. My clients are not familiar with this reference, but it is a small detail that I enjoy.

As an advocate and ally for the LGBTQIA+ community, my character has the added accessory of wearing a rainbow colored cape, designed like the Pride flag. My client logs into the game and notices my character. "It looks like you're wearing pajamas!" I smile, in real life on the video screen. "Oh, you have the Pride cape. I'm going to put that on too." On video, I see their attention focused on another screen. A moment later, their character is wearing the same cape. We are already in connection and in a relationship together.

The Second Guiding Principle of using Minecraft in play therapy is that the therapy starts even before the game is played. This chapter introduces one of the first therapeutic moments a child encounters: choosing their character. Before any gameplay takes place, Minecraft brilliantly and effortlessly tasks the child with a question of inner exploration: how do they want to express on the outside how they feel on the inside? Or, more simply, for the child playing the game: what do you want to look like?

This form of inner exploration is familiar to play therapists. Children are naturally drawn to costumes or toys in the playroom that express who they are and how they might like to be seen. A closet or chest full of

DOI: 10.4324/9781003614784-6

wardrobe items and accessories can act as a portal to magical lands where the child's imagination can express hidden powers. A child may discover a large purple wizard hat with gold stars and a silver tassel dangling from the top. They put it on, and suddenly they have magical powers that can turn a toy cash register into a mystical chest that provides tokens of invisibility. Disappearing in front of your eyes, they giggle when you ask where they have gone.

Play therapists who use sand trays typically have shelves or containers filled with figurines that represent a diverse range of body types, skin tones, occupations, and abilities. There are also specific figurines for magical and mystical creatures, as well as items that represent power, strength, or destruction. These options provide nonverbal explorations into how the child wishes to express themselves and represent others as well. As any well-stocked playroom has access to these items, Minecraft does as well, albeit in a digital format that is branded with recognizably familiar alternatives, offering even more flexibility and room for expression. Imagine the freedom of being able to change how you are viewed and how you express yourself multiple times within just a few short moments.

Some clients may appreciate and prefer the opportunity to choose an identity that is very different from how they present in real life. Clients who are exploring gender identity and expression may decide to try something new in the game first by representing themselves differently. If they are exploring the use of different pronouns and identifiers, the Minecraft space can be a safe and accepting environment for them. A client may even request that their in-game character be referenced by one set of pronouns and then transition to another set outside of the game. This can provide further safety for youth clients who are apprehensive about disclosing their current curiosity to their parents or caregivers. For clients transitioning from individual therapy to group therapy, there is an additional opportunity to try something new in a safe and confidential setting. What a gift it is for them to have a loving and accepting place to do that in the game with you.

The concept of players expressing themselves differently in a game has also been explored in pop culture. The Ernest Cline (2011) novel *Ready Player One* tells the story of teenagers playing a game in a digital dystopian future where they interact as avatars (or characters) of their real selves. Among other characters who changed their genders, one character in particular changed their avatar in the game to represent a White heterosexual male with an athletic build, only later to be revealed outside of the game as a Black queer female. The reveal of the character's identity outside the game sparks important discussion among readers as they reflect on the significance of representation, power, and privilege in a digital world.

A considerable drawback of many video games is that players often have no choice but to rely on an inaccurate and inauthentic portrayal of their identity, as alternative options are not available. Youth from marginalized backgrounds may feel underrepresented in current game offerings, and unintentional harm can occur when their identities do not match the pre-designed characters (Gray et al., 2025). Themes related to race, gender identity, sexuality, systemic oppression, and how culture and society influence identity are common concerns for children and adolescents we encounter in our practice. The ability to try out different "skins" and customize characters creates an inclusive and diverse experience for all players, especially those seeking more representation for their in-game avatars. The Minecraft Character Creator in the Bedrock Edition includes prosthetic arms and legs for players who want an accurate physical depiction; however, the game does not offer mobility aids as options. Despite some limitations and areas for improvement, the extensive flexibility and numerous customization options in Minecraft make it a valuable tool for clinicians seeking to support children and adolescents as they explore their identities.

Meeting Together in the Game

Playing the game with a child in session brings a new consideration for play therapists, as their digital in-game identity also becomes a point of interest and curiosity. The initial moment of seeing one another in the game is just as important and powerful as seeing one another over video or in real life. The child you are working with will naturally be curious about how you are represented in the game as they become more familiar with your presence. They may comment on how you have equipped your character, whether it resembles you or not, if you have new accessories, or if they are older.

When children see me in the game for the first time, they often comment on the difference in my appearance: "You don't have a beard!" "Your hair doesn't look like that!" I then ask if they would prefer my character look like I do in real life. If they say yes, I make the necessary changes. This can also lead to a playful exploration of giving the child power, as they might make other requests. I go along with these requests as much as I am comfortable. In my experience, this is similar to being in a playroom's costume corner and having a child hand me a fuzzy pink scarf, oversized sunglasses, and a wide-brimmed hat, saying, "Here, put this on." Not all play therapists have to accept requests that do not feel right to them, and it is up to the clinician to decide where they may need to set a boundary regarding what is comfortable.

It is also unhelpful to explain one's character choice and design to a child unless they ask. In many cases, I log in to the game, and the other player says, "I see you; I'm coming over." As with a play therapist who would not discuss themselves or their toy objects in a play session, the approach is the same here. If I take the time to discuss my skin and the approach to creating it, then I am making the session about me, and it is no longer focused on the child. There are, however, moments when discussing the clinician's choices can be a powerful therapeutic intervention.

Clinical Vignette

Referencing the scene described at the start of this chapter, when a child comments on my character and says, "It looks like you're wearing pajamas," I use the opportunity for an intentional therapeutic moment. When I first heard this, I laughed to myself, since I had not intentionally chosen an outfit for a pajama look. However, I recognized that I do enjoy wearing pajamas because they are soft, relaxing, and comfortable, and they remind me of the self-care choice of slowing down with something soothing. In this instance, I can use the child's comment as an opportunity not to correct or defend the choice I made, but instead to introduce an initial reflection on a felt sense, while also building interoception and introducing the idea of coping skills. With that in mind, I may reply by saying:

> *You see these as pajamas (acknowledging their observation). I can imagine how soft it might feel to wear pajamas (bringing awareness to a felt sense), my body can feel so relaxed inside when I'm wearing pajamas (prompting interoception) - sometimes wearing pajamas is a coping skill I use when I want to rest and relax (introduction of coping skills). I know the game can get intense sometimes, and remembering how I can relax is helpful for me (bridging game experience to real-world coping).*

Of course, not everyone will have this response, and that's okay. I can respond in this way because it is true for me; I love wearing soft, comfy things to destress! What is essential in our gameplay with our clients is that we be ourselves, show up, and respond in the ways that are most natural to us. A child's observations of our choices in the game (even in the first task of creating a character) can be used as therapeutic experiences, rather than addressing our needs and wants, which might be different if we were playing casually.

Another response could focus on acknowledging and reflecting the child's observation and curiosity. This is another way to bring the attention back to the child and what their inner experience may be like. An example of this type of response could be:

> *What else do you notice about what I'm wearing? (encouraging their curiosity about me) Do you have pajamas that look like these? (bringing curiosity back to the child) What do you imagine it would be like for you to wear pajamas in the game?*

This last question might be too abstract and confusing. Sometimes my questions do not come out clearly or are not the proper intervention in that moment, and that is okay. This clunky question reflects what might happen in a session, and sometimes we just might move on to playing the game.

The therapist's character expressions can also lead to observations and questions that plant the seeds for further exploration and expression of the child's personal identity. An example of this is the child's observation of my rainbow-colored Pride cape, which represents that I am a safe ally to the LGBTQIA+ community. Many children in my practice recognize and identify it right away. Along with being on display via my character, when a child comments on it, I use it as an opportunity to express my allyship to the LGBTQIA+ community. Similar to displaying allyship on a website, business card, and office door, this image, as part of my character, communicates safety and opens the door for further character expression.

While the child's skin may change multiple times in a game and over the course of working together, I keep my character the same every time we log in. Making this choice is intentional and therapeutic, as it helps create the familiarity that allows the child to feel safe and trust that I am a dependable and stable support. Just as we may play dress-up with our clients in the play therapy space, it is also okay to change our skin within a game if the client requests it. I always ask for the child's guidance along the way, so I adjust to their needs and wishes, rather than my own individual desire to play the game a certain way. This approach also reflects the need for clinicians to have separate Minecraft accounts for their personal and clinical play, so that the child is not surprised by a significant change one might have made while playing casually.

The Client's Character

Similarly, you may feel drawn to observe and acknowledge what you see in the child's character as well. It is essential for the child to feel seen by us. Voicing our observations of their character can be a powerful way for the child to feel seen and further integrate the choices they made in creating their character. Statements that observe and reflect can be powerful remarks when first entering the game together. *I see you have long hair, are wearing different colors, and I notice a cape on your back, too!* These observational statements let the child feel seen without feeling judged or criticized. Naturally, you may also be surprised if their online character does not match their in-person identity. You may be drawn to their choices, or you may have an aversion to choices you would not make for yourself. No different from a child we meet in real life, it is clinically and therapeutically important not to insert our opinions on their choices and expressions. We want to avoid remarks such as:

> *"Oh, that doesn't look like you-you don't have long hair,"* or *"Why did you choose that skin? I don't like all that color."*

The expressive character options extend beyond wardrobe choices, just as toys in the playroom can include various accessory choices that alter the tone and expression of a child's play. In the playroom, toy figurines may come with interchangeable tools and additional accessories that can be swapped out for specific functions and tasks. For example, a toy that holds a shield can have a very different feel and experience from a toy that holds a sword. The option to choose and express these different actions is essential because they communicate behaviors with deep emotional undercurrents, such as protecting or attacking.

Other items in the playroom can also inspire a child to use their imagination for personal expression. A pool noodle may represent a gun, sword, rocket cannon, or fire hose, while a pillow may be used as a shield, a surfboard, or just a pillow to take a rest. These personal and behavioral expressions are essential for helping the child show us more of their internal experience when words are not available. Thankfully, Minecraft has options for this as well.

The accessible and interchangeable items in Minecraft provide opportunities for children to express themselves and represent others in similar ways. A child might choose to equip themselves with powerful weapons, potions of invisibility or healing, and abilities to transport and magically flee a dangerous situation. Similar to being in a play therapy room, the child may also describe how they want the play therapist to be equipped. When a client is preparing to engage in battle with the play therapist, they may say that the clinician is only allowed wooden tools, which are weaker than the child's iron or diamond tools. Perhaps the child chooses to wear armor, but says that it is not permitted for the therapist's character to wear (Beckett & Finch, 2024).

As a child adds items to their inventory and equips themselves in a session, the play therapist might ask themselves: what is it the child wants to demonstrate? What are they feeling internally that they want to have communicated externally? Are there wishes about their character or identities that they want to express? Is there something that changes in between appointments that needs to be expressed differently from one week to the next? What is it that I am feeling when there is a big disconnect in our play? The following two chapters answer those questions and address the Third Guiding Principle: the play therapist is not playing Minecraft for their own enjoyment; they are playing to be fully immersed in the experience of the game with the child.

Directive Interventions: Checking In and Mindfulness Skills

There are as many different ways to begin playing the game as there are play therapists and children with big imaginations. How the game begins can also change over the course of a child's time in therapy. The focus here is on setting the frame for the first session with a child and ways an intentional beginning can evolve over the course of their work. Fred Rogers, the beloved host of Mister Rogers' Neighborhood, emphasized the importance of consistent, dependable routines for beginning and ending work with children, a principle he modeled on his television show (Fred Rogers Institute, n.d.).

Mr. Rogers greeted viewers at the start of the show as he picked out a sweater to wear and sat down to tie his shoes. The show ended with the routine of taking his shoes off and returning the sweater to the hanger. In applying intentional beginnings and endings in Minecraft, there are typically two interventions that, in my experience, have blended well with the use of Minecraft: a subjective units of distress scale (SUDS) and a beginning mindfulness exercise to help bring the awareness of a child's body and senses in real life into the experience of the game.

Checking In

Subjective units of distress scales (SUDSs) are often used in therapy as a cognitive, self-reflective intervention that invites the child to consider their level of activation or worry. In trauma-focused modalities like Eye Movement Desensitization and Reprocessing (EMDR), SUDS is a standardized measure within the treatment protocol (Shapiro, 2001). In trauma work,

SUDS assessments are specifically related to the overall discomfort or activation that is recognized when thinking of a specific target event or situation. As the Second Guiding Principle acknowledges that the therapy starts before the game is played, utilizing a SUDS assessment is an intentional way for the child to consider how they feel before playing the game. The scale can also be used at the end of the game to help build the child's capacity to reflect on what they gained from playing the game and their time with their play therapist, as discussed further in Chapter 7.

Depending on the child's interest and style of communication, the SUDS assessment may range from zero to ten, one to five, or some other creative option. Fun ways to check in and out of sessions could be using colors, emojis, weather reports, animals, or emotion charades, where the before and after feelings are acted out. Adolescents may come up with fun and expressive ways to communicate their feelings before and after, which could include sharing a meme, identifying a song or sound, or using pop culture characters from anime shows, movies, or books. When adapting the SUDS check-in to work with Minecraft, it's not essential how the child communicates their check-in – it is the process of intentionally considering how they are feeling before they start. What is most important about using this intervention is that it provides an opportunity for self-reflection at the beginning and end of the sessions, playing Minecraft in an intentional way.

Introducing Mindfulness to Bridge the Gap Between the Child and the Game

Play therapists can utilize various mindfulness skills as effective coping tools across different play therapy approaches (Wonders, 2025), including modalities like Acceptance and Commitment Therapy (ACT) or Dialectical Behavioral Therapy (DBT) (see Hayes et al., 2012; Linehan, 2015). In the context of Minecraft play therapy, mindfulness can be defined as a state in which the child is fully present and aware of their moment-to-moment experience within the game world. Introducing a mindfulness activity at the start of a session can help clients develop curiosity about their own mind-body connection while making the digital environment feel more tangible and real.

One powerful strategy is to guide the client through a brief, five-senses meditation as they enter the game. The clinician can prompt them to imagine being physically present in the Minecraft world by exploring:

Sight: What do they see directly in front of them? What details are visible in the distance?

Sound: What immediate sounds do they hear? What fainter sounds can they imagine in the background?

Touch: What might they feel under their feet? What is the sensation of the block in their hands? Is the air warm or cool on their skin?
Smell: What scents are carried on the air – the earthiness of grass, the smokiness of a torch?
Taste: What might the air taste like?

This exercise seamlessly bridges the gap between the physical and digital realms, centering the child in the therapeutic "here and now" of the game.

The role of developing these mindfulness skills is to make the Minecraft world as realistic as possible, while also planting seeds for the child to consider how their five senses can be accessed and utilized beyond the Minecraft world. This concept is explored further in Chapter 13.

Looking Ahead

This chapter establishes the critical importance of the Second Guiding Principle for utilizing Minecraft in play therapy, emphasizing that the therapeutic process begins before gameplay starts. This is most clearly shown through character selection, which acts as a powerful, nonverbal form of inner exploration and self-expression, similar to a child choosing costumes or figurines in a traditional playroom. The flexibility of customizing characters in Minecraft, from selecting different "skins" to accessories and equipment, creates an inclusive space for youth, especially those from marginalized identities, to explore race, sexuality, gender identity, and expression in a safe and confidential environment.

Beyond the child's character, the play therapist's digital identity is also a vital therapeutic tool; maintaining a consistent appearance ensures the therapist is perceived as a dependable and stable support, while intentional responses to a child's comments about the character can introduce powerful concepts such as felt sense, interoception, and coping skills, all which will be explored more in the upcoming chapters.

Furthermore, setting an intentional frame for the session is crucial, often accomplished through directive interventions like the SUDS for self-reflection before and after play, and mindfulness exercises (such as the five-senses meditation) to help ground the child and bridge the gap between their physical reality and the digital game world. Ultimately, recognizing the therapeutic potential in these initial choices and relational interactions prepares both the client and the clinician for the in-depth clinical work that follows, which aligns with the Third Guiding Principle of fully immersing oneself in the game experience with the child.

Helpful Tips

- **Therapy Starts Before Gameplay:** The Second Guiding Principle holds that therapy begins even before the game is played, as the initial task of choosing a character (or "skin") is a powerful, nonverbal opportunity for identity exploration and self-expression.
- **Identity Exploration for Safety:** The game's extensive flexibility and numerous customization options create an inclusive and safe environment for youth to explore concerns related to race, gender identity, sexuality, and expression.
- **Consistent Digital Presence:** The play therapist's digital character is a vital therapeutic tool; maintaining a consistent appearance every time you log in helps the child feel safe, viewing the therapist as a dependable and stable support.
- **Use Directive Check-Ins:** Setting an intentional frame is crucial, often accomplished through directive interventions like the SUDS to invite the child to self-reflect on their level of activation or worry before and after play.
- **Bridge Physical and Digital Realities:** Clinicians should use mindfulness exercises (such as a five-senses meditation) at the start of the session to help ground the child and intentionally bridge the gap between their physical reality and the digital game world, making the environment feel more tangible.

Reflection Question

1 Beyond character creation, what other seemingly "technical" aspects of starting a Minecraft session (like choosing a world name or game mode) could I view as intentional clinical interventions?

References

Beckett, M., & Finch, E. (2024). *Bridging the ChASM: Creating accessible services using minecraft—A guide* [Video recording]. University of Cambridge. https://www.educ.cam.ac.uk/research/programmes/chasm/

Cline, E. (2011). *Ready player one.* Turtleback Books. (Original work published 2011)

Fred Rogers Institute (n.d.). *Fundamentals of learning and growing inspired by Fred Rogers and educator practice.* Saint Vincent College. https://www.fredrogersinstitute.org/files/resources/97/sixfundementalsredesign_v5_compressed.pdf

Gray, K. L., McPherson, T., Russell, G., & Anderson, R. (2025). Video games and race. In D. A. Christakis & L. Hale (Eds.), *Handbook of children and screens: Digital media, development, and well-being from birth through*

adolescence (pp. 291–295). Springer Nature Switzerland AG. https://doi.org/10.1007/978-3-031-69362-5_40
Hayes, S. C., Strosahl, K. D., & Wilson, K. G. (2012). *Acceptance and commitment therapy: The process and practice of mindful change* (2nd ed.). Guilford Press.
Linehan, M. M. (2015). *DBT skills training manual* (2nd ed.). Guilford Publications.
Shapiro, F. (2001). *Eye movement desensitization and reprocessing (EMDR): Basic principles, protocols, and procedures* (3rd ed.). Guilford Press.
Wonders, L. L. (2025). *Mindfulness-based play therapy: A transtheoretical and neurobiological approach to psychotherapy with children and families*. Taylor & Francis.

Chapter 5

Being in the Game

What Is the Child Showing Us? (Principle 3)

It is the first session with a child who has experience playing Minecraft. I create a new world and randomly spawn in a snowy atmosphere. I ask how they would like to start, and they tell me I can do "whatever" I want. I tell them that I'll wait for them to log in, and we can meet each other by introducing our characters in the game.

There is no reply, and over the video screen, I can see that the child is focused.

An alert appears in the game, stating that the child has joined the world. I continue to wait in the silence, thinking that maybe there is a lag or delay with the online connection.

After a few moments that feel like forever, the child says, "You're never going to be able to find me."

"Would you like me to?"

"You can try, but you're never going to be able to."

In the game, I scroll my character's view around the landscape. It seems endless, and the other player could be anywhere. I look for clues, such as blocks that may have been broken or a gamer tag that might be hovering somewhere, yet I do not see anything.

"Have you started looking?"

"It feels overwhelming, and it would also be so exciting to find you!" I hear a giggle and see the child smile at themselves on the video screen.

We have just begun a game of hide and seek.

This chapter focuses on the third of the Seven Guiding Principles: the play therapist is not playing Minecraft for their own enjoyment; they are playing to be in the experience of the game with the child. This is achieved by observing how gameplay stimulates the child's brain, body, and nervous system. It is through this process that we gain insight into the child's inner world. Thus, this principle reframes the activity: children are not simply playing a video game in therapy; they are engaging in a deeply therapeutic process that can provide valuable insights for the helping adults who are playing with them.

DOI: 10.4324/9781003614784-7

The experience of play therapy provides children with an opportunity to use play as their primary means of communication (Grimmer, 2025; Renshaw, 2025). Just as adults debrief and process verbally, children express themselves through the exploration, discovery, and creation that is play. However, parents and caregivers may prefer a child to use words, wishing they could explain a bad mood or what they were thinking before an outburst. While children can describe events in simple terms, grasping the personal meaning and profound impact of an event often requires more than words can convey alone. For all humans, we often just need our hurt or distress to be seen and understood from our perspective.

Playing Minecraft together provides a powerful opportunity for the child to use the characters, mechanics, and experiences within the game to communicate their world in a way that words may not. In Minecraft, whether children play individually or with others, all aspects of the game become an integral part of their play. When a child is engaged and stimulated by the gameplay, the opportunity for expression and storytelling expands. The digital world offers control, flexibility, and dynamic elements that encourage the vast, expansive possibilities of a child's creative mind within a safe container. The possibilities are endless when we are committed to truly seeing and understanding this expression.

The shift from simply playing Minecraft to using it therapeutically stems from how we, as trained play therapists, can be in the game with the child. The therapist's role shifts from being a fun playmate to listening, observing, and feeling the play in a different way. This Third Guiding Principle sets the therapeutic foundation for the clinician to be fully engaged in the experience with the child. By directing our attention to how they are playing and what the play might be communicating, we increase the volume of what the child wants us to know.

Many play therapy models are built upon the core condition of being present with the child in their play. Following the child's lead is a central tenet of non-directive and child-led approaches, including Child-Centered Play Therapy (CCPT), Attachment-Based Play Therapy (ABPT), and Synergetic Play Therapy (SPT). This is particularly evident in SPT and its concept of the "setup," which posits that the child projects their internal experience onto the therapist and the environment (Dion, 2018). In Minecraft, the game becomes a microcosm of the client's world. The child's engagement and interactions with the digital world become the "setup," allowing us to experience what it feels like to be them through their experience with the game.

A wide variety of play therapy approaches agree that activities like sand play, board games, and expressive arts are therapeutic on their own. Minecraft provides the most accessible way to combine the benefits of these traditional methods with the unique aspects of a digital playroom. This chapter will explore this connected framework through a clinical vignette, examining how the SPT lens helps us decode developmental tasks and play styles within the game.

The "Setup" from Synergetic Play Therapy

My training in SPT changed the way I approached play and provided the foundation for understanding what was happening in a child's play within the Minecraft world. Lisa Dion (2018), creator of SPT and founder of the SPT Institute, introduced clinicians to the concept of the "setup," also referred to as "the offering." These terms describe the nonverbal, interpersonal communication that can occur during the play therapy process. Similar to a projective process, the setup allows the play therapist to form a hypothesis based on their own experience in response to what the child is showing in the game. The hypothesis may or may not be accurate; however, our primary goal as clinicians is to remain curious about how a child's perception of their world might be communicated to us through their play, leading to a deeper understanding of the child.

Inspired by the science of interpersonal neurobiology and the role of mirror neurons, play therapists encounter rich opportunities for the child to setup the clinician to feel what the child is working through while playing Minecraft. The experience a child has while playing the game can also influence the clinician's experience when they are with the child in a focused way. A groundbreaking 1996 study examining the premotor cortex of monkeys laid the groundwork for discovering mirror neurons by looking at how monkeys' brains executed and observed each other's actions (Gallese et al., 1996). Research by Kohler et al. (2002) showed that neurons in the premotor cortex of monkeys were linked to audiovisual actions that activated across subjects, whether the actions were performed, observed, or heard. Rizzolatti and Craighero (2004) further explored how actions between humans impact us, highlighting the importance of observation in imitation, learning, and understanding within a social setting. These studies not only reveal the discovery and role of mirror neurons but also open up new ways to understand how sound and behavior create neuronal resonance. This research suggests that a focused and tuned-in clinician can experience the child's internal state as if it were their own, which is the core of receiving the "setup."

This concept extends directly into the digital world. Specifically regarding video games, Karen Collins, an Associate Professor in the Department of Communication Arts at the University of Waterloo (2011, 2013), explored mirror neurons and introduced the theory of embodied cognition to explain the crucial role of sound in player immersion. Collins explained how players' engagement with sound in the game can act as a catalyst for deep immersion, blending the digital game environment with the physical, embodied experience of the player. Referencing Collins' concept of embodied cognition, Yvonne Stingel-Voigt (2020) examined the function of sound in video games, particularly focusing on how characters' voices contribute to the atmospheric and emotional depth of the gamer's experience. In Minecraft, this is strengthened through the application of the Third Guiding Principle, when what the child demonstrates can be better understood by how the play therapist vocally shares their experience of playing the game together.

The following clinical vignette illustrates how a "setup" can manifest in a Minecraft session. Analyzing it through the SPT lens reveals the underlying developmental tasks and play styles at work.

Clinical Vignette

It is the first session with a middle school-aged child, and they request that I join a world they had already created. This world is new to me, and I have no idea what to expect. Immediately, I become apprehensive and notice an attitude of hypervigilance. My senses feel heightened in real life, even though I am entering into the unknown circumstances of a digital Minecraft world.

Once I spawn on the screen, the child tells me to follow them. They lead the way to a dark cave. I am hesitant and can feel myself becoming alert. There is a part of me that wants to explore the cave differently. I have the thought that if I were playing by myself or with a friend, I might head off in another direction. Meanwhile, the child hangs torches along the way through the cave so we can see, yet I am still nervous and uncertain about where this is leading. We come to the edge of a large pit; standing closely near the ledge, I look down.

"I'm worried I'll fall down there and won't be able to get out." I am unsure of what to do next, and recognize there are very few options.

"It's okay, just jump down, it won't take all your hearts." We are in Survival mode, and the child is reassuring me that the impact and consequence of the fall would not lead to immediate defeat.

I take a big breath and jump down. A large number of hearts are sacrificed by the fall, but there are still a few left. I look up at the child in the game, and they begin flying away, using their commands to put us in two separate modes of gameplay. They have all the control, and I am stuck, unable to get out due to the depth of the fall. It feels like this world is an unpredictable and dangerous place.

"Oh no! Am I going to be down here all by myself?"

"You'll be fine ..."

Standing in the bottom of the pit, I feel scared, alone, hopeless, angry, and confused. I look up at my video screen and notice the child taking glances from their device to see my reaction.

In a situation like the one above, I strive to immerse myself in the experience of the world as much as possible, holding the consideration in mind that the child wants to show me something about how they might experience and perceive the real world.

What is it that you are noticing for yourself as you might have imagined being in this experience? Did you experience similar feelings of fear, anger, and confusion? Were there other feelings? If you were playing for fun, would you have navigated the situation differently from following along with the child?

Every child has unique and individual experiences, and as such, each child will play in a distinctly different way. Was this child working through experiences of being in unknown, scary situations? Trying to process being powerless and feeling scared? Is it possible that they were asking an emotionally developmental-oriented question of "Is the world okay?"

Developmental Tasks and Themes

This case vignette is an example of how the setup/offering can emerge through the experience of being in the game with the child's play. Following the child's lead, putting aside my own desires for how I would have liked to play, and voicing my experience along the way, my engagement with the game was a way of listening to what the child wanted me to know through the circumstances unfolding before us. This led me to consider: were they working through experiences of going into scary situations? Were there experiences of feeling alone and not knowing how to ask for help? It is possible that multiple dynamics were being worked through, such as feeling scared and also being told that they "will be fine."

To conceptualize this, I rely on the foundational concepts of the Developmental Tasks as identified in SPT training through the adaptation of

Duey Freeman's Developmental Model (L. Dion, personal communication, March 11, 2020). Developmental Tasks in play therapy serve as a framework for working with children who may exhibit themes of emotional developmental regression in their play. This is based on the understanding that while a child may be a specific chronological age, the theme and activity of their play might represent a much younger emotional age and emotional "task" that their psyche is working through.

This process of assessing emotional age is a key clinical focus. As Lindsay Stenzel (2025), a Licensed Clinical Social Worker and Synergetic Play Therapist, explains, during times of high stress, a chronologically older child may regress to the themes of an earlier developmental stage to work through the challenges associated with that task. The ages related to each task represent when the child would first encounter the emotional milestone, which is why the themes work with an expression of regressive behavior.

The case vignette at the start of this chapter, for instance, describes a first session with a child who is using the game to play a digital version of hide-and-seek. Typically, an older child between the ages of 8 and 11 may not initiate hide-and-seek play. When that emerges, I lean into the question of what theme the play might be communicating.

Initially, the model began with the task of "Is the world okay?", and was later modified by SPT parent coach and equine therapist Heather Gunther, who noticed a developmental theme emerging around the experience of "Do I exist?" This task is often played out in the physical playroom with children who use play tunnels, powers of invisibility, and the game of hide-and-seek.

In the first example, the theme of "Do I exist?" can serve as a key exploration of affirming worth, value, and a sense of being – especially during the first play therapy appointment when a child meets a new person. A child who has control over the outcome of a task (such as navigating a world as vast as Minecraft) can explore the eventual feeling of being found, discovered, and affirmed. As British Psychoanalyst Donald Winnicott (1963/2016) famously wrote, "It is a sophisticated game of hide-and-seek in which it is joy to be hidden but disaster not to be found" (p. 6).

In that specific example, the child was somewhat transparent about initiating the game; other times, it may not be that direct. A child can be nonverbal and disengaged, or express the desire to be alone and not approached in the game. For the play therapist, this could lead to the experience of wondering, "Do I matter?" or "Does it even make a difference that I am here?" The challenge that the play therapist may encounter relates to the child's experience of being seen in real life.

The experience of the play therapist and the conceptualization of the child's play may relate to one or more of the developmental tasks that manifest as different themes in the play. These developmental tasks, their corresponding ages, and potential presentations in Minecraft are outlined in the following list:

- **Do I (or Can I) Exist? (Conception–Birth):** Ignored play, feeling alone in the world, invisibility, hide-and-seek, and a thematic emergence of the client's character.
- **Is the World Okay? (Birth–18 months):** Bumping up against challenges in the world, hypervigilance and fear of external threats, not trusting the environment of the game, rules, and/or permissions changing without notice or explanation.
- **Am I Okay? (18–36 months):** Not feeling good enough, unsure if one is ready or prepared, negative self-statements or thoughts, and perfectionist tendencies.
- **How Much Can I Do? (3–6 years):** Quickly moving from one thing to the next, excessive builds that might be new to the client, keeping track of quantity in the game, and repeated play styles such as spawning and attacking the same mobs to reach an achievement or accomplishment-related goal.
- **How Well Can I Do It? (7–11 years):** Initiating building challenges, working out strategies related to game play, exploring confidence in comparison with others, seeking out and focusing on challenges in the game, interest in trophies or accomplishments, and speed runs.
- **Who Am I? (11+ years):** Focus on identity and character creation, meaning making, and what makes the game significant, playing the game while discussing external interests or challenges, and taking on leadership roles in a group.

Beyond the thematic content of the play, *how* the child engages relationally offers another crucial layer of clinical data. The familiar play themes and what the child is showing us in the game can provide more information about what the child might need help working through, tolerating, and making friends with inside themselves. Minecraft provides the outlet for the expression of aggression, fear, loss of control, being overpowered, feeling helpless, instances of bullying, peer pressure, discomfort/dislikes, expectations being worked through, over-/under-stimulation, working with the unknown, negative self-talk, and relational distress and ruptures. Empowering growth-oriented themes like working with confidence, being brave and taking on challenges, resilience, persistence, and not giving up can also be assessed through how the child is interacting with the clinician and the game through their style of play.

As the play therapist builds their working hypothesis of their experience being in the game with the child, it is essential to consider the child's history, goals for the session, and any other relevant information about the child's life. To fully grasp and conceptualize the above vignette, the play therapist would need to know more about how the session progressed and what themes continued to arise in future sessions. The following chapters in this book will continue to reference this concept and provide further detail on how play therapists can work with these moments, bringing more awareness to the child to integrate their inner world in ways that build awareness, tolerance, and helpful coping strategies for the circumstances they are working through.

Play Styles

Being in the game with the child provides the play therapist with valuable observations of how the child plays, which offers further insight into their emotional age and developmental stage. The style and engagement of the play can be conceptualized in terms of Developmental Tasks to assess the emotional age and developmental stage the child may be presenting.

To conceptualize this, we can integrate the six developmental play stages. Registered Clinical Counselor and SPT Supervisor Johanna Simmons (2020) draws on Mildred Parten's primary developmental play stages, which include: solitary play, onlooker play, parallel play, associative play, co-operative play, and games with rules (p. 243). Simmons (2020) further outlines the six levels of play related to chronological age, as defined by the York Region Preschool Speech and Language Program (2014, as cited in Simmons, 2020, p. 243):

- **Solitary play:** Birth to 2 years of age
- **Parallel play:** 2.5 to 3.5 years of age
- **Associative play:** 3 to 4.5 years of age
- **Co-operative play:** 4 to 4.5 years of age
- **Games with rules:** 6 years and on
- **Onlooker play:** At all ages

In Minecraft, these play styles manifest in distinct ways:

- **Solitary and isolated play** occurs when the play therapist and child are in the same world but are working and playing separately, with a distance that can seem as though both are alone. Oftentimes, this is enacted by a child when they say that they do not care what you do, or that you can do whatever.
- **Parallel play** can often emerge when isolated play moves closer in proximity, perhaps with an invitation from the child that you can play in a

part of the game where both players are visible. This fosters a relational dynamic of being together in solitude.
- **Collaborative, cooperative play** happens when the child asks for help, offers guidance and instructions, expresses interest in your play, and wants to demonstrate what they have been engaged with.
- **Competitive play, or games with rules,** can include activities like games, challenges, and even battles, where the play therapist may be invited to join in a duel with the child.

Play style themes can be apparent in a single session, and they can evolve and become more identifiable over multiple sessions. Reconsidering the chapter's vignettes, the play style offers another layer of interpretation.

In the first vignette at the start of the chapter, the challenge to find the player could be considered competitive play if the child continued to taunt, elude, or give clues along the way. If that were the case, I would consider how the theme relates to the closer chronological age represented by competitive play, suggesting the question of "How well can I do it?". However, if a child were hidden in the game and provided very little verbal interaction, it would lead me to consider it solitary play, which is more congruent with the younger theme of the developmental task.

This can be further expressed in Minecraft through clients that possess knowledge of commands within their world, which can enhance the invisibility of their character or provide methods to hide their in-game name, making them much harder to locate. For the play therapist, this experience of being ignored and seemingly alone could lead to the experience of wondering, "Do I exist?" "Do I matter?" or "Does it even make a difference that I am here?".

The second example presents similar challenges, as more information is required depending on how the rest of the play unfolds. The offer to follow the child into the cave could initially be viewed as collaborative, yet it quickly turns into the question of "Am I okay?" To learn more, one would have to observe how the play therapist and child continued to interact.

This observational play assessment can serve as an additional reference point for how play therapists conceptualize their client sessions when integrated with other theories and modalities in their toolboxes. Understanding these concepts provides the play therapist with awareness and an invitation to relate to the child's Minecraft play on a deeper level, one that goes beyond simply playing a video game. Parents who are not trained professionals can still benefit from a general understanding of these concepts, as it further validates the benefit and need for a child to use Minecraft as a medium for emotionally expressive play, even if the adult does not know the clinical theory underlying the themes. On the surface, it may appear that the child is blowing up creepers and enchanting swords, but clinicians understand it as much more.

Looking Ahead

Being in the game with the child requires a conceptual shift, as play therapists must also be aware of their own impulses. Given this relational focus, the clinician's experience profoundly affects the child. The next chapter will explore this in detail, introducing the Fourth Guiding Principle: the play therapist can model how to work with the stimulation in the game to help the child learn more about themselves while playing. These concepts of the setup, developmental tasks, and play styles will be referenced and expanded upon throughout the following chapters, and a practical framework for specific clinical presentations is provided in Section 3. Support for parents will be provided in Chapter 8. For clinicians interested in deeper training on the SPT concepts discussed here, I encourage exploring the SPT Institute.

Helpful Tips

- **The Third Guiding Principle Reframes the Activity:** The play therapist is not playing for enjoyment, but to be fully immersed in the experience of the game with the child, shifting the role from playmate to an observer who listens, observes, and feels the play.
- **Nonverbal Communication:** Minecraft offers a powerful opportunity for children to utilize the characters, mechanics, and experiences within the game to communicate their world in a way that words may not convey alone.
- **The Clinical "Setup":** Drawing from concepts in SPT, the child's play becomes a "setup" (or "offering") where the therapist is invited to feel what the child is working through in their internal world, treating the game as a reflection of the client's reality.
- **Decoding Emotional Age:** Clinicians conceptualize play by integrating Developmental Tasks (such as "Is the world okay?" or "Do I exist?") to assess the emotional age and underlying themes a child may be attempting to process, often through regressive behavior.
- **Observing Play Style:** The therapist gathers essential clinical information by observing the child's play style (e.g., solitary, parallel, or competitive play), which offers another reference point for understanding the child's developmental stage and relational needs.

Reflection Questions

1 Reflecting on a current or past client, how might viewing their Minecraft play through the lens of "emotional age" rather than chronological age change my understanding of their needs and my therapeutic approach?

References

Collins, K. (2011). *Making gamers cry: Mirror neurons and embodied interaction with game sound*. In Proceedings of the 6th Audio Mostly Conference: A Conference on Interaction with Sound (AM '11). Association for Computing Machinery, New York, NY, USA, 39–46. https://doi.org/10.1145/2095667.2095673

Collins, K. (2013). *Playing with sound: A theory of interacting with sound and music in video games*. The MIT Press.

Dion, L. (2018). *Aggression in play therapy: A neurobiological approach for integrating intensity*. W.W. Norton & Company.

Gallese, V., Fadiga, L., Fogassi, L., & Rizzolatti, G. (1996). Action recognition in the premotor cortex. *Brain*, *119*(2), 593–609. https://doi.org/10.1093/brain/119.2.593

Grimmer, T. (2025). Challenging play. In A. Bradbury (Ed.), *Play matters* (pp. 92–97). Early Years Reviews.

Kohler, E., Keysers, C., Alessandra Umiltà, M., Fogassi, L., Gallese, V., & Rizolatti, G. (2002). Hearing sounds, understanding actions: Action representation in mirror neurons. *Science*, *297*(5582), 846–848. https://doi.org/10.1126/science.1070311

Renshaw, K. (2025). Play therapy. In A. Bradbury (Ed.), *Play matters* (pp. 89–91). Early Years Reviews.

Rizzolatti, G., & Craighero, L. (2004). The mirror neuron system. *Annual Review of Neuroscience*, *27*(1), 169–192. https://doi.org/10.1146/annurev.neuro.27.070203.144230

Simmons, J. (2020). Moving toward regulation using synergetic play therapy. *Canadian Journal of Counselling and Psychotherapy*, *54*(3), 242–258.

Stenzel, L. [@lindsaystenzelcounseling]. (2025). Developmental tasks in the playroom [8 slides; Carousel post]. Instagram. https://www.instagram.com/p/DIgy201gbij/?img_index=1

Stingel-Voigt, Y. (2020). Functions and meanings of vocal sound in video games. *Journal of Sound and Music in Games*, *1*(2), 25–43. https://doi.org/10.1525/jsmg.2020.1.2.25

Winnicott, D. W. (2016). Communicating and not communicating, leading to the studies of certain opposites—BPAS (not final version), 15 May 1963. In R. Adès (Ed.), *The collected works of D. W. Winnicott: Volume 12, appendices and bibliographies* (p. 6). Oxford University Press. *(Original work written 1963)*

Chapter 6

The Experience of the Clinician

Coregulation, Building Interoception, and the Window of Tolerance (Principle 4)

I am hosting a play therapy group with five middle school-aged clients, who are playing Minecraft. Throughout the session, there were complaints and frustrations that the game was becoming "laggy." Initially, the reports from group members were sporadic and inquisitive.

"Is anyone having a hard time placing blocks?"

"Argghhhh, this is being SO SLOW! Is it just on my screen?"

As the game progressed, the frustrations increased, and possible reasons were being discussed.

"Maybe there are too many players?"

"Is someone lighting fires?" Both of these things might cause a game to lag.

Towards the end of the session, the game became almost frozen as mobs began spawning in drastic and dramatic numbers.

"There are hundreds of them!"

"What's going on?!"

"All I see on my screen are Iron Golems everywhere!" The energy in the group is increasing, and the members are becoming more upset and distracted.

My screen is also freezing in short bursts, and everything looks like utter chaos. I can feel the energy vibrating in my body as well, and I'm having a hard time concentrating in my role as the group facilitator. My brain feels fuzzy; I have been tense everywhere and have not realized it. My thoughts are scrambled, and quite frankly, I have no idea what is going on.

The clinician's experience of playing Minecraft with their clients represents a significant shift in understanding what it means to use the game therapeutically. When the play therapist is fully immersed in the child's experience of the game, anything that happens in the game can affect both of them, even if the child is not aware of it. Initially, this can include the play therapist noticing internal somatic activation, such as their stomach dropping when looking down or falling from tall heights, feeling tense during stressful parts of the game, and then experiencing relief when those moments pass. Being aware of what is happening in these moments provides

DOI: 10.4324/9781003614784-8

the play therapist with the opportunity to help their client become more curious and aware of what they might be feeling while playing the game. As one can imagine, this is a very different goal from playing Minecraft just for fun.

When a clinician begins to recognize their experience of being impacted by the game and communicates that to the child, the child's prefrontal cortex activates and begins to engage in self-reflection. Siegel (2012) describes this as a process of reflective dialogue that can help children integrate their own previously unknown experiences at the neural level. For example, if the play therapist notices tensing up in certain moments or feeling afraid or overwhelmed, they can identify this and name their experience. This could be saying, "My arms were so tense as we were fighting to get through that battle." Or "I'm scared that there are so many zombies around me, and I don't have any armor crafted." These statements offer the child opportunities to become curious and self-reflective about their experiences in those moments.

Relating to the experiences we have while playing the game helps the child turn inward and begin to question if they might be having those experiences as well. These moments help our clients learn more about their brains and bodies, enabling them to recognize stimulating moments for themselves, not only while playing the game but also while engaging in the many other activities children enjoy when not playing Minecraft. Imagine having a special flashlight in your play therapy space that you could use to help the child see what is happening in their body and mind, allowing them to learn to be more responsive rather than reactive. By becoming aware of and verbalizing our own sensations, thoughts, and experiences, we can offer the child that special tool of awareness.

A child who can recognize what is happening in their body can then identify what they might need in the moment to feel better or address a specific emotion connected to the feeling. This is the skill and power of interoception. Building interoceptive awareness can help children verbalize what needs may arise from different feelings, leading them to find ways to get those needs met (Mahler, 2016). For example, if a child is afraid of heights and looks down into a vast chasm, they might not realize their stomach is feeling woozy and perhaps even scared. When the play therapist helps the child recognize these moments through their own experience, it supports the child in learning to do so for themselves. Sometimes this may involve offering statements about internal thoughts or physical responses. At other times, it may involve more active coping strategies, such as shaking things out and taking slow, intentional breaths. This is the process that occurs during coregulation.

Play therapists who are attuned to how their bodies are activated by gameplay use their own personal sense of interoception to help the child become more aware of their potential internal experiences. This approach can be a significant shift for clinicians and represents a crucial distinction in how the Seven Guiding Principles provide a framework for play therapists to approach the game differently, with clinical intention. When we play Minecraft casually for fun, it can be easy to overlook how the game affects us. This is, of course, true for children as well. Clinicians who become focused on the game's activation can learn to regulate it, allowing them to stay present and engaged with the child. This process becomes workable and leads to teachable moments in the play therapist-child relationship, as both are stimulated by the game experience. The therapist's ability to recognize activation and regulate themselves leads to powerful moments of coregulation when the child is playing.

Coregulation between the play therapist and the child is crucial because it models and teaches a workable solution that the child can learn and internalize for self-regulation. For children to self-regulate, the fields of interpersonal neurobiology, contemporary play therapy, and emotionally attuned parenting have taught that children first need to experience coregulation through the connection with an attuned adult (Delahooke, 2022; Dion, 2018; Gobbel, 2023; Kennedy, 2022; Siegel & Bryson, 2021). When a child experiences this connection and attunement in a relationship, it helps them develop their own skills of awareness and recognition, leading to a better understanding of the impact of external triggers and moments of stimulation. It is through the experience of coregulation with the play therapist during distressing or activating parts of playing Minecraft that children begin to learn, understand, and *feel* the skills, strategies, and experiences necessary to develop their self-regulation abilities.

The Play Therapist as an Attuned Player

Reflecting on my personal experience playing video games, I recall memories of playing with a friend and being unaware of how my body was responding. One might imagine our bodies moving wildly; upper body jerking to the side, arms tense with focus on the controls, and our breath held before letting out big sighs. This example is likely familiar to players as their bodies respond to the game's intensity. Readers may even picture someone playing a driving game, waving the controllers back and forth as if they were the actual steering wheel of a car. Players become immersed in the game's stimulation and environment, and even though one knows it is not real, it feels real inside. Unless something unexpected happens, such as a cup of soda being knocked over or players accidentally colliding, it is possible to remain unaware of how the game is affecting their bodies.

Having an attuned adult play with us and recognize and name that the game was getting intense could have helped us develop skills of internal awareness and intentional coping, so that the energy did not manifest in unintentional ways.

Being with our clients while playing Minecraft through a clinical lens requires intentional focus and practice to recognize that the child is looking to follow our cues for how to regulate themselves when the game stimulates their brains and bodies. This orientation is uncommon for adults during casual gameplay or everyday interactions with the children in their lives. For many families who bring their children to our practices, experiences of coregulation can be rare. A deficit in experiences of coregulation could be impacted by a parent's experience of trauma as well as generational, cultural, and historical factors as families pass down what they simply observed from those that came before (Atlas, 2023; Perry & Szalavitz, 2008). Although phrases like "it's not a big deal, I don't know what you're crying about", or "suck it up and get over it" might all be well-meaning ways of not wanting a child to be stuck in a big emotion, they do not help the child learn what is happening inside themselves and what to do with those experiences. Our role as play therapists is to utilize the gameplay of Minecraft to provide various relational opportunities for the child, which we can also teach to parents and caregivers, as explored in Chapter 8.

The Fourth Guiding Principle describes this orientation: the play therapist can model how to work with the game's stimulation to help the child learn more about themselves while playing. This chapter explores why this process is so necessary and beneficial for the child, as well as how we, as play therapists and helping adults, can enhance the experience for the child by also understanding what is happening within our own bodies in the room, over a video call, and while playing in the game.

The Experience of the Play Therapist: Getting to Know Oneself

Mindfulness, Grounding, and Regulation

To be fully present in the game with their client, the play therapist must develop and utilize mindfulness, grounding, and regulation skills. Child and adolescent therapists may be familiar with mindfulness as a helpful coping tool in play therapy approaches (Wonders, 2025) and in specific interventions, such as Acceptance and Commitment Therapy (ACT) or Dialectical Behavior Therapy (DBT). Within the framework of the Seven Guiding Principles, Minecraft play is utilized to foster mindfulness as a state of awareness in which the play therapist is present to their moment-to-moment experience as they enter into the game-play relationship with the client. Setting the intention to be present and aware helps open the play therapist to the full range of stimulation that can be provided by playing the game.

A helpful strategy for this can include steps similar to Dan Siegel's (2018) "Wheel of Awareness" exercise, where one's attention is placed on the five senses before turning inward toward the sixth sense of internal sensations, noticing thoughts as the seventh sense, and last recognizing the interconnectedness of relationships as the eighth sense. This practice can be quick and even used as a routine starting point before each session. One way this could look involves bringing attention to one's breath and adding slow exhalations. With each breath out, one can become aware of what their body might feel like in their physical space, then notice what they see, hear, smell, and taste. Next is the invitation to turn inward and become curious about what one's emotional state is going into the session: perhaps there is energy left over from the previous appointment, maybe there is distraction from something that happened earlier in the day or week, or there could also be excitement about seeing this current client and what might be expected while playing together. All thoughts and mental activity are welcome and can also be observed. Last, one can open up to the connection of others in their lives – this could even be a reminder of one's mission and drive to do this powerful, healing work. Practicing mindfulness in this way involves simply observing and paying attention to whatever arises in the moment.

Mindfulness skills provide a window into the clinician's experience. In contrast, grounding skills can help the clinician regulate their internal activation, ensuring the session's experience does not exceed their ability to be an effective helper. Grounding skills are essential to help ease the distress that may have been experienced during the previous mindfulness check-in, as well as to assist the clinician in staying present and connected with the child in session. How the play therapist grounds themselves also sets up the strategies and practices they may use for coregulation.

Grounding activities can include intentional use of all five senses as a way to stay present. Some examples include:

- **Physical:** Tapping and moving one's toes and feet, rubbing hands on the thighs, using a fidget item, clenching and releasing big muscle groups, or simply being aware of the weight of one's body in their seat or on the ground.
- **Sight:** Locating objects of specific colors, naming items directly in front of one's view, looking at items that feel safe and soothing, like a particular picture or figurine.

- **Sound:** Listening to what is in the room or outside the room, focusing on the sound of one's breathing, intentionally humming, playing music, or listening to the music in the game.
- **Smell:** Noticing the smells in the room, keeping an object nearby with a soothing aroma, such as a scented stuffed animal, or using a lotion or essential oil roller for a light scent.
- **Taste:** Keeping a water bottle or beverage nearby, having a snack at the end of a session, or before the next session begins.

Developing mindfulness and grounding skills is essential for the play therapist to become an aware observer of the thoughts and feelings that arise during the play therapy session. Helping children develop mindfulness and grounding skills, specifically as a direct intervention, is addressed in Chapter 13.

The term "regulation" refers to how helping adults can modulate the activation occurring for them by utilizing the skills of mindfulness and grounding, either in a play therapy session (Dion, 2018) or when parenting (Gobbel, 2023), to stay present and aware with the children connected to them. This concept is essential when integrating Minecraft into a play therapy session, as it helps keep the clinician focused on the therapeutic intent of playing the video game.

The possibility of playing casually is often anecdotally cited as a primary concern by parents and cautious therapists when expressing uncertainty about how playing the game can be a helpful therapeutic intervention. In a play therapy session using Minecraft, intentional focus on regulation is an essential concept for the therapist, as the process of taking care of one's own thoughts and nervous system responses to be present and connected with the child's play is what moves the sessions away from playing casually toward what makes this approach so valuable.

Countertransference

The approach of relating to the game and the child from our own experience can be hard at times for many reasons. Along with the task of being able to recognize and regulate the reactions we have while playing, there are also the more personal experiences we have to work with, such as how we feel if the child is providing distractions that draw our attention in different places, and how we work with requests for help and specific tasks they want to complete. There are also times when the play therapist may have agenda items that parents want them to address, and then there are moments when the game play can be enticing and fun. These moments can present as personal struggles for clinicians, as they may be caught in moments of uncertainty and find themselves relating to the client in a way that differs from their typical style of intervention. When a play therapist experiences personal feelings and impulses during play therapy sessions, it is referred to as the clinical dynamic of countertransference.

Countertransference is a foundational concept in psychotherapy with roots dating back to Freud et al.'s (2001) initial theories of psychoanalysis in 1910, followed by Axline's (1947) exploration of the therapist's emotions in play therapy, through contemporary explorations by Landreth (2012) and many others. As the vast history of the study of countertransference demonstrates, this clinical dynamic is present in the therapist when working with both adults and children. When working with adults, the clinician's experience of countertransference may be activated more through the verbal and cognitive processing that one would expect with traditional talk therapy. In contrast, with children, it can be activated through the process of play. Similar to the previous description of the setup in Chapter 5, countertransference refers to the feelings and experiences that the play therapist experiences when in a relationship with the child in the room. It can manifest as emotions, conflicting thoughts, and even a general sense of being out of sync with one's typical feelings.

This dynamic becomes uniquely complex in the immersive world of Minecraft.

Here, the clinician must navigate two powerful, often overlapping, streams of experience: the child's "setup" (Dion, 2018) and their own internal reactions triggered by the game itself. The "setup" is the child's nonverbal invitation for the therapist to feel what they feel, a process facilitated by the shared digital environment. However, the game world can also directly activate the therapist's own personal material, such as their own history, fears, and desires. The clinical imperative, therefore, is to differentiate what is being communicated by the child from what is being activated within oneself.

This distinction is the cornerstone of effective practice with the Seven Guiding Principles. The clinician must learn to identify their own visceral reactions to the digital environment. This foundational skill of self-awareness is perfectly illustrated by Finch (2021), who identifies common triggers, such as claustrophobia in caves or vertigo on mountains, and frames the core question as discerning "what's my 'stuff' and what might be my clients' 'stuff'" (p. 11). Without this skill, a therapist risks misinterpreting their own triggered anxiety as part of the child's emotional offering. It is this very discernment that allows the "setup" to become a clear channel of communication rather than a muddied confluence of intersecting experiences.

It is vital to recognize that a therapist's "stuff" extends beyond visceral, in-the-moment reactions. It also includes pre-existing barriers, such as conscious or unconscious biases against video games, a lack of familiarity with the digital platform, or even economic constraints, which shape their perception and approach and can become a source of countertransference that impacts the therapeutic alliance (Young, 2025).

Subjective Countertransference

Geltner (2006), citing Spotnitz, used the term "*subjective countertransference*" to describe the feelings and reactions the therapist has toward the client that are motivated by and unique to their own personal history and needs. When playing Minecraft with a client, subjective countertransference may include a desire and pull to excel and be competitive, as well as the potential to become so engrossed in the game that time gets lost. Questions to ask oneself to consider if this dynamic is arising include: "Am I doing this for the client, or because of my own anxiety about what I want to do or think that I am supposed to be doing?" "What is happening for me that I want to play so hard and win at all costs?" "How did I lose track of time?" This is similar to what happened in my early sessions described at the end of Chapter 3.

Other reactions could include making suggestive game-play directives based on the play therapist's own interests or desires, such as building something intricate that they have just learned about or exploring a specific biome with which they have a personal affinity. Because subjective countertransference experiences are unique to each individual, the actual experiences are personal to the play therapist. They can change throughout the course of appointments, as well as from one session to the next. Ongoing supervision, peer consultation, and continuing education can all be helpful ways to stay curious about our subjective countertransference and how to work with it, as well as the unique ways it arises.

The mindfulness and grounding skills described above are also helpful in being aware of one's subjective countertransference, as what is happening in one's body and thoughts can help one become more empowered to stay present and engaged with the child. For example, if a play therapist is experiencing the desire to play well and try their hardest to outplay the client, becoming aware of that desire, recognizing it as subjective countertransference, and orienting back to the sights, sounds, smells, and physical sensations in the moment can help them consider what might be underneath those feelings. Being aware of our countertransference in the session allows the play therapist to become more mindful of their experiences with the child and the game, which can lead to rich opportunities for attunement and coregulation.

Coregulation, Interoception, and Window of Tolerance

Coregulation

As established, the "setup" from the previous chapter means the play therapist can experience what the child might be feeling through the game. Due to the interpersonal nonverbal communication process occurring through the mirror neuron system, the child can also experience cues from the play therapist. Not only is the child setting us up to feel their experience, we can also help them feel what it is like to soothe and work through symptoms of distress that arise in the game through the way our interconnected experiences resonate with one another. How the play therapist manages and regulates experiences of distress using their skills of mindfulness and grounding can become the prompt for the child to experience a similar feeling of soothing comfort. This is the process of coregulation.

Consider a moment where a child intentionally hides in the game world, as illustrated in the clinical vignette from Chapter 5. From one perspective, this is a powerful "setup" (Dion, 2018) – a nonverbal invitation for the therapist to feel the child's experience of isolation, anxiety, or perhaps a desire for pursuit. The therapist's initial feeling of panic or disorientation is crucial data. However, this is also the critical juncture where the therapist must differentiate this data. Is this feeling primarily the child's projected experience, or is it being amplified by the therapist's own "stuff" (Finch, 2021), such as a personal fear of losing control?

This moment of self-awareness is what unlocks coregulation. As Young (2025) observes, once the therapist has navigated this internal distinction, the scenario becomes a prime opportunity to model how to regulate their nervous system. By consciously choosing to remain grounded, present and connected to themselves despite the activation, the therapist embodies the essence of coregulation. They demonstrate that distress can be managed, transforming a potential reenactment of abandonment or chaos into a new experience of safety and connection.

The play therapist, by remaining present and regulated, offers a nervous system for the child to "borrow." This is equally true in other high-activation scenarios, such as when a child becomes frustrated and wants to quit the game entirely. Chapter 10 will explore these and other scenarios in detail, providing specific language and interventions to support them. The core principle remains: the therapist's regulated presence provides the co-regulatory resource that helps the child expand their own Window of Tolerance (WOT).

The discovery and research into the interpersonal process of mirror neuron activation have shown that the resonant experience of feeling another person can occur with both individuals in the dyad as described in Chapter 5. An example of this is when you feel rested and at peace, yet enter a busy public space or building. After a few short moments of interacting with the sudden shift of chaotic and restless energy in the new space, you may notice your sense of ease diminish as your heart rate and blood pressure rise. Parents may have similar experiences with their children. They may pick their child up from school feeling one way, and their experience could shift after hearing emotionally charged stories or general behaviors of distress. This process occurs when a large amount of activated energy unexpectedly connects with another body and nervous system. Coregulation occurs when the process happens in the opposite direction, where a sense of soothing and connection is shared with the body and nervous system that need it the most.

During moments of distress and emotional activation, the experience of a grounded connection to one's own body can be communicated and shared with another person. Parents can soothe and stay connected with their children when the activation is too big, and adults can coregulate one another when someone is asked to sit beside them or hold their hand. Coregulation occurs when someone's internal emotional battery is too low and needs to borrow energy from someone else whose emotional battery is higher and available.

The play therapist being available with their own charged emotional battery and being able to share that resource is part of the coregulation that happens during the play therapy process while playing Minecraft. A child may become increasingly distressed as the game becomes more difficult or frustrating. Then a big, unfortunate event occurs that might lead them to throw a controller or immediately turn off the game. This interaction provides an opportunity for coregulation, where the play therapist can utilize their mindful, grounded experience to help soothe the child's distress and be present with them to ride out the wave of energy and activation. Part of what makes coregulation useful and beneficial with the play therapist is that they have a higher WOT. What is upsetting for the child may not be as unsettling for the play therapist in the room. The play therapist's nervous system has more space to be helpful and available.

Interoception

Pediatric occupational therapist Kelly Mahler (2016) writes about interoception as an additional and often underappreciated sense of the original five senses that provide adults and children with information about their bodies from the inside out. In her book "*Interoception: The Eighth Sensory System*," Mahler (2016) provides research that draws the connections between what is felt in the body to a need that is being communicated and the relief that occurs when the need is met. It is the sense of interoception that interprets the signal of a full bladder as the feeling of needing to urinate. One's recognition of the discomfort associated with that need leads to using the bathroom to relieve the urge and meet the need to feel better.

Adults and children have different strengths of interoception, just as there are different strengths of the other primary senses. Children experience different levels of awareness and tolerance for cues in their bodies that indicate they are cold and need something warm, or that they are hungry and require a snack. Internal somatic cues can also serve as clues to emotions, providing helpful information for recognizing what might be happening internally before an external behavior arises. The connection between these internal emotional clues and what the emotion needs in that moment can be so difficult for children to recognize.

Play therapists using Minecraft to help children develop interoception can draw on their own experience of interoceptive awareness, which is activated when playing the game together. For example, statements such as "My heart is beating so fast when we're in this battle" or "My stomach just felt queasy when I died and lost all of my items" can build the internal reflective awareness for the child. The gameplay can also be used as an external prompt for interoceptive awareness.

For example, clinicians can bring curiosity to their character's experience of internal cues: "This iron sword must be so heavy to carry; my character must be really strong," or "My hunger bar is getting low; my character's stomach might be rumbling right now!" Questions related to interoceptive cues can be explored in how children play the game, as well as in their relationship to the game itself: what do their hands feel like after they have been playing for the entire session? Do they feel their body becoming tense when their character is hit with arrows from a skeleton?

The process of coregulation helps build a child's sense of interoception as the play therapist identifies and names internal sensations that they are experiencing in the play relationship and then models managing, tolerating, and staying in the big moments of the emotion by regulating. The focus of the play therapist is on taking the moments of activation and stimulation offered by the game and then bridging them to moments of staying present, connected, and aware together with the child. This is how a child's WOT is expanded.

Window of Tolerance

The term and concept of the WOT were popularized in Siegel's (1999) *The Developing Mind*. Related to the process of emotional regulation and the autonomic nervous system, the WOT concept describes the fluctuating capacities children and adults can accommodate before experiencing a state of sympathetic or parasympathetic nervous system activation (Porges, 2011). Awareness of one's WOT can be a powerful tool for managing distress, stimulation, and activation, allowing us to adjust and accommodate for our needs as best as possible. Understanding how one's WOT is experienced and managed is essential for the child and everyone in the child's life, as it enables helping adults to learn more about the child's experience. In helping the client in session, it is also vital for the play therapist to be aware of their own experiences and levels of activation before and after each session.

Play therapists who are aware of and attuned to their clients' WOT can help coregulate when they notice the child's window, or capacity for distress, reaching its limits. This process allows the child to understand their experiences internally, even if they do not know the cognitive, logical process behind what is happening. The gameplay in Minecraft naturally cycles through levels of activation based on the perceived intensity of the day and night cycle. In Survival mode, the night cycle triggers a zombie invasion aimed at destroying the player's character. As the sun rises in the morning, the threatening mobs disappear or burn from the sunlight.

Daylight can be experienced as a relief of the previous night's threats, resetting the player's WOT as they can once again feel safe and continue to work on preparing for the next night. Chapter 10 provides more detail about working with the client's WOT during the game. The concept is introduced here to emphasize the importance of the play therapist's awareness of this dynamic and how their attunement and relationship with the child can provide valuable insights. Using Minecraft in a play therapy session transforms from a casual video game into an intervention that helps the play therapist learn more about the child while the child learns more about themselves through the play therapist's presence.

Progress in coregulation, interoception, and expanding a child's WOT is evident when the play therapist observes the child beginning to practice these skills independently during sessions. This self-awareness then translates to their experiences at home, school, and with peers. These are also skills and ways of engagement that parents might be doing intuitively or can learn how to adapt with their current parenting skills, as discussed further in Chapter 8.

The following three clinical vignettes are provided to offer a more detailed description of how the therapist's understanding of themselves, utilizing the skills of mindfulness and grounding while playing the game, can coregulate with their clients and increase their skill of interoception, thereby expanding their WOT. The first vignette references the example at the start of the chapter of a Minecraft play therapy group, and how the group facilitator draws on their experience of the game play to bring awareness to interoception and coregulation with the group. The second vignette highlights the potential challenge of the therapist's countertransference reaction while also drawing attention to the child's experience when having a big reaction to the circumstances of the game. The final vignette illustrates the observation of the child's WOT and working together toward coregulation. These vignettes also set the stage for the specific clinical focus chapters in Section 3.

Clinical Vignette 1

This chapter begins with an example of a play therapy group using Minecraft, which starts to go awry when mobs begin to spawn, overwhelming the game and creating a frustrating experience for everyone in the group. The example illustrates that something uncertain was happening and started to create distress for the group members. Initially, subtle cues, expressions, and communications began to emerge within the group. The clients were picking up on it before I was. As the group moved forward and the message was not becoming clear, the intensity increased, and the volume of what needed to be communicated in the group grew louder. This is a typical dynamic that often occurs in the play therapy relationship. Additionally, in everyday interactions with the children in our lives, when the message is not being heard, the intensity of play and nonverbal communication can increase.

It was not until the character movement lagged, the blocks of the world failed to load, the screen froze, and the excessive spawning of mobs directly impacted me that I could recognize the potential message. Once I began to notice the emerging feelings of discomfort in my mind and body, I could then make the connection between my experience and how chaotic things appeared. If I were feeling it at that point, I could only assume that the children in the group were feeling the same way. Additionally, because I was feeling it so strongly, I needed to regulate that experience for myself so I could continue to be effective in my therapeutic role as the group facilitator and bring in the experience of coregulation for the others in the group. This is an example of how that process might occur.

> *"Wow! I'm noticing that my head is feeling really fuzzy right now, and I'm having a hard time concentrating on what's going on! There are so many things happening in this world, and I'm finding myself so distracted. I realize I've been really tense too, as I'm focusing so hard, even though I can't control all the things that keep changing. I'm going to step away from the screen for a minute and shake things out."*
>
> *"Yeah, me too!"*
>
> *"I have no clue about this right now."*
>
> *"I'm going to log out and refresh my world." When a group member suggests refreshing the world, I agree and use that as an opportunity to bring in the idea of resetting as a coping skill.*

"Yes, great idea! Sometimes, there are a lot of things that can happen that we don't plan for or don't expect. Our world, in Minecraft and in real life, can get really busy really fast. When that happens, it can really affect how we pay attention and how we feel it in our bodies. Taking a moment to step back, reset, and refresh can really make a big difference."

One of the group members, thinking ahead, asks, "What if we log in and it's still glitching?"

"That could definitely happen. Let's make a plan about how we can figure this out."

By naming and identifying for myself the intensity and experience of what was happening I could provide an opportunity for the group members to be curious if those experiences were happening for themselves (building interoception) and then model ways to regulate that intensity so that we all would not be acting out with an unhelpful behavior as a way to cope with the distress of this incredibly frustrating situation. Taking care of myself by modeling the option and benefit of stepping away and tending to what I needed to do helped give permission for the group members to do the same (coregulation). This led one of the group members to suggest the idea of refreshing the world, which can also be a helpful strategy to use outside the game.

After taking care of myself and supporting the group through my own experience, I then had more availability to consider the setup that might have been happening. In this example, the excessive spawning of a specific mob (the Iron Golem) was an intentional command given by one or more group members. While it is uncertain to know exactly who was doing this, the impression is that I was being setup to experience chaos and extreme unpredictability, tapping into the developmental task of asking, "Is the world okay?" For many children who come to our play therapy practices, learning how to navigate unpredictable situations and environments is quite common. Depending on the goals and history of the group members, I would track and consider this in future sessions.

Clinical Vignette 2

A child is playing in Survival mode. They have been away from their base, hunting for certain minerals, and the sky has begun to darken. As night approaches, threatening mobs will emerge. I hear a sense of urgency in their voice when they exclaim that they have to head back to safety before it turns dark and the attacking mobs spawn. I see that their body in real life is jerking quickly, mimicking the movements of their character on the screen. They do not make it in time, and mobs begin to appear. "Nooooo!" they scream out as they are getting hit by arrows from nearby skeletons. A baby zombie is at their feet, and they are holding their breath as they balance surviving both threats.

As you observe this gameplay, it could be easy to get distracted with problem-solving. Is there an impulse to want to help them with a strategy? Perhaps there is a desire to bring your game character toward the attack; to save your client from losing all their heart health and facing defeat. This child may have a history of breaking down when defeated and acting out in significant ways when overwhelmed. This could be part of their presenting concern for therapy, and you might want to prevent this from happening in the session. Perhaps this might even be a part of your own history – in the past, there might have been a younger sibling you played with, and your role was to help them get through the more difficult parts. This might have led them to learn how to play better by watching how you would handle the challenging situations. These thoughts and non-conscious impulses could be the countertransference dynamic that arises for the play therapist even in an interaction that seems as simple as playing Minecraft.

A clinician in this example might engage by helping the child focus on their experiences as their character is under attack, saying the following: "I noticed your voice changed when you realized it was getting dark. It sounded alarmed and urgent. I can see how your body is moving as you work your way back to the base." Then, as the threat of the attack happens, one might say, with an intensity matching that of the child's, "I can hear how upset you are! There are skeletons around you, and a baby zombie is getting after your feet. I noticed you held your breath as you were fighting them off!" Both of these interventions offer observations and reflections that draw the potential connection between what was happening for the child in the game and how it might have impacted their feelings, emotions, and physical engagement.

Another therapeutic response in this example can further bring the clinician into the experience with the child by naming how the game play is affecting them: "Oh wow, I noticed I held my breath for a moment when I heard you say it got dark. I felt a little nervous and worried that we might not get back to base in time." Responding to the moment of attack, one might acknowledge the intensity ramping up, "Ahhh, my stomach just tightened up; my whole body is tense. I'm taking a big breath with you."

How the clinician says this is not as important as the approach. Whether I was observing the child's game or playing in it myself, the technique is the same. Rather than rushing in to save or assist, I was helping the child become aware of how their body was responding. At first glance, it can be recognized how their body is responding to the game, but really, what is being observed is how their body responds to a moment of surprise, adversity, and an experience of things not going exactly as planned. What exceptional skills to learn!

Notice what it might feel like in your own body to be a part of that game. What happens for you when you hear the child's surprise that it has become night, and they have gotten distracted, and realize they are too far from their base? What is it like for you when you hear that they recognize they are in danger and are being attacked? Does your experience change based on whether they are well-equipped with items to protect themselves and are managing the battle easily? Are you hopeful that they might overcome the threat and manage it safely, or are you concerned that they might be defeated?

Being in the game in this way can be powerful and effective for the child, and it is not easy for either the child or the play therapist. Engaging in this way means seeing the game through the child's eyes, experiencing the stimulation and activation through their perception of what is happening. It also means placing aside the personal aspirations one might have for oneself. The task is to relate to the game with part of your felt sense and awareness in the digital world that is presented to us, while another part is focused on the play therapist's experience with themselves and the child in real life. To grow, develop, and heal, the child needs both from us.

Clinical Vignette 3

We are playing together in Survival mode, and I notice the child has been taking more risks; bravely moving towards hostile mobs that they feel empowered to take on, and playing longer into the more threatening stimulation of the night. Each challenge stimulates their nervous system, and I can see their body responding in ways that alternate between acceleration (tension) and then rest (focused and present). After a few close call battles, these challenges begin to take a toll on their Window of Tolerance. I notice more time staying tense – I can see it in the client, and I can feel it for myself! I notice they only have one and a half hearts left, and I take a big breath in. The client escalates, and while continuing to look at their screen, they blurt out: "Can we switch to Creative? Can we switch to Creative? I only have one heart left!" I can hear the fear in their voice, and the pleading tone wants me to jump in and save them.

I take a big breath with an audible exhale and acknowledge the intensity, "Yes, this is so scary right now. I can feel how intense this is. You've been battling for a long time. I'm right here with you, and we can certainly switch back to Creative, or if you need my help, I can help too ..." Reminding them they can also ask for help from me in the game, I pause, waiting for their decision. A moment later, they respond, "Oh! We can just go back to our beds at the base!"

Together, we turn and run, find our beds chosen with our favorite colors, and enable the sleep function, turning night into day. This gives us control over our experience of stimulation and allows our characters to rest, reset, and recharge – both in the game and in real life.

This example demonstrates how the client was actively working within their WOT, in terms of the amount of stimulation they could handle at that moment. The "setup" quickly moved from the developmental task of "Am I okay?" to the chronologically congruent task of "How well can I do it?" They became aware of when it was too much and recognized when they were at their threshold, making real-time decisions about what was needed for them. We were playing collaboratively in a manner that was congruent with the developmental theme of the "setup."

It would have been okay if they chose to switch to Creative mode, changing the gameplay to non-threatening and avoiding any danger in the moment. In fact, they might have done that many times before. In this example, I followed their lead and did not rush to save them immediately.

Discussing this scenario also assumes a clinical history and treatment plan where the child was benefiting from working toward staying in Survival mode and not switching to Creative when things got hard, as they may have in previous sessions. They might have also been working on asking for help from others. My response as an intervention was to bring awareness to their feelings and body, letting them know I heard the request, and also reminding them that there are other options for help. Tracking where they were in their WOT gave me the impression that they were not quite at the threshold to switch immediately, so there was a moment of pause to encourage in-the-moment reflection. In this example, it worked, and I could imagine the client and me talking about how close we came to being defeated, how intense it was, and how things feel so much better after sleeping through the night and starting fresh with a full heart health bar.

This is also a moment when I bridge what is happening in the game to a real-life experience that could be useful away from screens and gameplay, as explored further in Chapters 9 and 14. The client was very aware that their heart health bar was running low. This means that if they sustained any further damage, they would be defeated, and there would be significant consequences, such as losing their inventory, having to respawn, and experiencing the complex emotions that come with that outcome. The client was aware of this and chose to go to their bed to rest and recharge (as a helpful workable solution) rather than switching to Creative, which would have left them disappointed that they did not make it through a full session in Survival mode (perhaps perceived by the client as giving up).

Looking Ahead

The decision to think of and choose a solution that offers the opportunity to rest, reset, and recharge is incredibly helpful for our clients in real life. There are many instances where the children we work with encounter the equivalent of low-heart health bars in real life. Maybe it is at the end of the school day or after coming home from a long day playing with friends. Sometimes it can even happen in the morning if a lot of things go sideways right from the start. Using a moment in the game, such as the one above, can be a powerful way for the child to begin to connect the concepts of what takes a toll on their WOT and what is needed to bounce back. It is also very possible that this example could have gone sideways. The client could have been defeated, shut down, or escalated further from the disappointment and anger of the loss. Chapters 10 and 11 will delve further into what is happening in those moments and how we can support clients when they experience significant emotional responses.

By being aware of how playing Minecraft can stimulate emotions and elicit bodily responses in the play therapist, relational and interpersonal interventions can be applied to help the child learn more about themselves and manage their experiences in the moment. This paradigm shift presents an opportunity for the play therapist to coregulate with the child in moments of activation, stimulation, and distress that can occur while playing the game together. In a clinical or therapeutic setting, the approach to playing Minecraft is not to assist the child in achieving success in the game; rather, it is to bridge their experience of interacting with the game to their experience in the outside world. This concept will be further explored in the chapters ahead, with a focus on strategies for how parents can support their children in understanding these game dynamics and how they can be applied to situations outside the game.

The current era of scientific research in the fields of interpersonal neurobiology, Polyvagal theory, emotionally focused parenting, and depth of play therapy interventions and theories has shifted the paradigm for understanding how children's bodies learn, grow, heal, and play. That is what makes the Fourth Guiding Principle so powerful. Even though the child may think that we are just playing Minecraft together, the play therapist knows that we are connecting to something much deeper and more powerful than playing a game for fun.

Helpful Tips

1 **Shared Embodied Experience (Principle 4):** The play therapist must be fully engaged in the child's game experience, understanding that anything in the game – from technical lag to intense mob spawning – can activate somatic responses (e.g., tension, fuzzy brain, stomach dropping) in both participants.
2 **Building Interoception:** The clinician uses their own experience and the game's cues to help the child become aware of their internal physical and emotional sensations. Identifying and naming these sensations models the skill of interoception, which can support children in recognizing their needs and finding ways to meet them.
3 **Coregulation Model:** By verbally naming their own physical and emotional activation during gameplay (e.g., "My arms were so tense," "My stomach just tightened up"), the therapist engages the child's prefrontal cortex, modeling self-reflection and providing a regulated nervous system for the child to "borrow."
4 **Expanding the WOT:** The therapist's regulated presence during distressing moments (like hostile mob attacks or game freezing) provides the co-regulatory resource needed to help the child manage activation and expand their WOT. The game's natural cycles, such as the shift from threatening night to safe daylight in Survival mode, naturally facilitate this WOT work.
5 **Mindfulness and Grounding:** To maintain the regulated presence required for coregulation, clinicians must develop and utilize mindfulness (to observe feelings) and grounding skills (to modulate internal activation) as a routine clinical practice. This intentional focus is what transforms the session from casual play to a valuable therapeutic intervention.

Reflection Questions

1 What feelings might come up for me (e.g., boredom, urgency to "do something," confusion), and how could those feelings be valuable clinical information about the child's internal world?
2 What personal mindfulness or grounding practice would I need to strengthen to reliably remain a regulated presence for a child during the most chaotic and dysregulating moments of their Minecraft play?

References

Atlas, G. (2023). *Emotional inheritance: A therapist, her patients, and the legacy of trauma*. Little, Brown Spark.

Axline, V. (1947). *Play therapy: The inner dynamics of childhood*. Houghton Mifflin.

Delahooke, M. (2022). *Brain-body parenting*. HarperCollins.

Dion, L. (2018). *Aggression in play therapy: A neurobiological approach for integrating intensity*. W.W. Norton & Company.

Finch, E. (2021). Therapeutic adventures in Minecraft. Playmode Academy; *BACP Children, Young People & Families*. https://playmodeacademy.org/resources-and-publications/featured-article-in-bacp-journal

Freud, S., Breuer, J., Strachey, J., Freud, A., & Richards, A. (2001). *The standard edition of the complete psychological works of Sigmund Freud*. Vintage.

Geltner, P. (2006). The concept of objective countertransference and its role in a two-person psychology. *The American Journal of Psychoanalysis*, *66*(1), 25–42. https://doi.org/10.1007/s11231-005-9001-3

Gobbel, R. (2023). *Raising kids with big, baffling behaviors*. Jessica Kingsley Publishers.

Kennedy, B. (2022). *Good inside: A guide to becoming the parent you want to be*. Harperwave.

Landreth, G. L. (2012). *Play therapy: The art of the relationship* (3rd ed.). Routledge.

Mahler, K. J. (2016). *Interoception: The eighth sensory system: Practical solutions for improving self-regulation, self-awareness and social understanding of individuals with autism spectrum and related disorders*. Aapc Publishing.

Perry, B. D., & Szalavitz, M. (2008). *The boy who was raised as a dog and other stories from a child psychiatrist's notebook: What traumatized children can teach us about loss, love, and healing*. Basic Books.

Porges, S. W. (2011). *The polyvagal theory: Neurophysiological foundations of emotions, attachment, communication, and self-regulation*. W. W. Norton & Company.

Siegel, D. J. (1999). *The developing mind: How relationships and the brain interact to shape who we are*. Guilford Press.

Siegel, D. J. (2012). *Mindsight: Change your brain and your life*. Scribe Publications.

Siegel, D. J. (2018). *Aware: The science and practice of presence: The groundbreaking meditation practice*. Tarcherperigee.

Siegel, D. J., & Bryson, T. P. (2021). *The power of showing up: How parental presence shapes who our kids become and how their brains get wired*. Ballantine.

Wonders, L. L. (2025). *Mindfulness-based play therapy: A transtheoretical and neurobiological approach to psychotherapy with children and families*. Taylor & Francis.

Young, H. (2025). Exploring the potential of Minecraft to embody the therapeutic powers of play, acting as a core agent for change in the play therapy process. *British Journal of Play Therapy*, *19*(1), 47–59.

Chapter 7

Practicing Positive Endings (Principle 5)

A parent calls to inquire about play therapy for their child, who experiences tantrums at home when asked to do things they do not want to do, such as getting off screens. After hearing their concerns, I suggest playing Minecraft together during the play therapy sessions as an intervention to address the child's emotional distress. The parent reports that having to stop playing Minecraft and other video games is one of the things that causes the tantrums. I share more information about how I would work with their child, how I can support them as a parent, and my belief that what happens in the play therapy space can be translated into addressing distress at home.

The parent is skeptical, "But won't playing the game together make them even more upset when they have to end after your session together?"

I share that I understand the concern and am aware of the activation this can create for the child. I certainly do not want to contribute to a problem or make things more difficult. Playing together intentionally is also what makes the work so powerful. Offering hope, I share a piece of the fifth guiding principle of using Minecraft in play therapy: "How we end together in the session is practice for how they can end at home."

A common concern I hear about using Minecraft in play therapy is the belief that children may already be spending "too much time" on screens and digital devices. Many parents consider scheduling a play therapy session as a break from screens and their child's video game usage. Introducing Minecraft as a play therapy intervention can lead parents to feel frustrated that the very support they are seeking might be keeping their child stuck in the problem they are seeking help to alleviate. Parents are not the only ones with this concern; many play therapists may also express similar concerns: does staring at a screen together, while spending time with the child in a way intended to be therapeutic, only reinforce a growing problem with screens and gaming?

DOI: 10.4324/9781003614784-9

This concern is valid and is echoed in the literature. As Finch (2022) notes,

> It's important to recognize that using a particular video game in sessions might not be suitable for all children. For example, if the child has been struggling with coming off a game to take part in other activities at home, they may struggle with the end of counselling sessions.

I agree with the first part of this observation but propose a different clinical conclusion. Where Finch sees a child's struggle to end the game as a potential contraindication for its use, I see it as the precise indication for a targeted therapeutic intervention. The conflict that arises for parents and therapists is understandable, given that many professionals working with children may also be parents themselves, navigating their own challenges with screen time at home. As discussed in Chapter 6, this dual identity is a potent source of countertransference, where a clinician's personal struggles can surface in the therapeutic environment.

Rather than avoiding the game because a child struggles to end it, this book argues for leaning into that very struggle as the core of the clinical work. This chapter introduces the reader to the Fifth Guiding Principle: how the game ends in session is practice for endings and transitions outside of the play therapy space. The child's difficulty in transitioning away from the game is not a reason to exclude it from therapy; rather, it is a very workable and attainable clinical goal we are seeking. To effectively leverage this goal, we must first deepen our understanding of why these endings are so challenging for children.

Therefore, play therapists and parents are provided with an understanding of how to support the children in their lives when they are caught between recognizing the benefits of Minecraft play and acknowledging the distress that it can cause when it is time to end. By intentionally focusing on the challenging experience of ending the game, play therapists help the child learn and adapt to new ways of tolerating endings and navigating transitions. When considering playing and ending the game together, a child holding the other controller intuitively finds Minecraft to be a therapeutic space for them; they just need a little help to understand it better. We do this not by avoiding the point of conflict, but by making it the focus of our therapeutic intention.

Challenges with Ending the Game

Chapters 8 and 9 address broader strategies for adults and nuanced considerations around screen time; this chapter focuses on a common concern I hear from caregivers: the challenge they encounter at home is the difficulty the child has when being told to stop playing. When I hear this, I lean even further toward recommending Minecraft for our sessions, as this challenge identifies a workable, attainable clinical goal: practicing positive endings with the game.

As discussed in Chapters 5 and 6, when the child begins playing Minecraft, they have already entered into an experience that can be highly activating and stimulating. Not knowing when or how the game will end adds elements of potential distress that players implicitly know. Some children may have an unspoken perception of how they want the game to end, such as reaching a specific achievement or stopping only once a building goal has been met. Perhaps they plan to finish an elaborate build that takes over an hour, or maybe they are waiting for their friends to log on and help them. These are all possibilities for what the child might consider when deciding how long they want to play or what it might take to end the game feeling satisfied for the day. From that perspective, it is understandable that requests or hard stop boundaries from well-meaning adults can evoke strong emotions.

Children may also be holding onto experiences and feelings of endings from earlier in the day or week that did not go well. Perhaps recess ended early or stopped abruptly for an unknown or unexplained reason. Maybe they had to miss a sporting event over the weekend and had not realized how upsetting it was for them. There could be a long list of disruptions that lead them to feel more sensitive about finishing their Minecraft game for the day. These examples identify the impact of endings on the child's Window of Tolerance (WOT) and how some days could go more smoothly than others. A history of endings and transitions can be collected from families during the initial intake session, and caregivers can also inform the play therapist before a session if there was a noticeably hard ending or transition prior to the meeting. Holding these experiences in mind is essential because the inevitable transition off Minecraft at the end of their play therapy session can be activating and also a rich opportunity for repair.

Ending Minecraft in the Play Therapy Session

Using Minecraft in the play therapy session helps the clinician bring awareness to the experience of ending the game while actively working to expand the child's WOT. How we end the game in the session is practice for how the child can end the game at home. This practice helps the child learn more about themselves in all experiences of endings, including awareness of the thoughts, feelings, and body reactions that all occur when the game has to end. The opportunity for coregulation between the play therapist and child, and working with the big emotions of disappointment and frustration that can arise, provides a new experience in expanding the child's WOT, which can then be applied outside of the play therapy session and into everyday situations at home. The focus on practicing positive endings in this chapter considers how play therapists can work with the gameplay of Minecraft in a play therapy session, with attention to the specific experience of ending the game and setting a reasonable, achievable expectation for the client.

Clinical Vignette 1a

A parent schedules an intake session to see if Minecraft therapy would be a good fit for their child. The child loves playing video games, especially Minecraft, and has typically been resistant to trying therapy. When they were told that there was a play therapist who also played Minecraft, they seemed a little interested, perhaps even skeptical, about whether they would be able to play during the session. The family is pro-video games and understands that their child is getting to do something they like; the parent also acknowledged that they played video games when they were younger. It is emphasized that their child's response to the game is causing distress.

One of the primary concerns reported is that the child becomes highly dysregulated when asked to leave the game for dinner and often disrupts family dinner time by shouting and throwing things, requiring support from parents and drawing attention away from the dinner table. The family has tried timers and reminders, and both have been met with irritation and frustration from the child. When discussing the idea of playing Minecraft together in therapy, the parent hesitates, offering the observation that the child also has trouble getting off the game during playdates and when leaving a friend's house.

"Won't this just upset them even more when they have to stop playing with you?"

This is a valid concern, and the hesitation to consider whether playing the game together is the best way to meet their needs is understandable. Therapy can be a significant financial investment, and it requires a substantial amount of time and commitment to schedule and attend therapy sessions. The goal and aspiration for the child to end the game and join the family at dinner, or to be able to leave a playdate without a struggle, is a valid and understandable goal for a family to achieve in seeking play therapy. It is also attainable when we consider using Minecraft in therapy to practice positive endings.

What makes Minecraft therapeutic and relevant to working toward this goal is that the clinician is playing with a different intent than what might happen with two peers at a play date or when the child is lost in the game, right as food is being served on the table. Holding a dual focus on both being immersed in the game experience and connected to the pacing and flow of the session, clinicians can follow the steps outlined in the previous chapters to make endings more manageable and less overwhelming. This includes the process of: bringing awareness to the child's experience, working with their WOT, and offering the coregulation needed to eventually make smooth transitions from a fun play session to connected moments with others that involve less struggle.

The Role of the Play Therapist

At the start of each play therapy session, the therapist can be transparent in identifying all of the time boundaries and ending limits. This can remind clients how much time they have to play together and that they will receive "time remaining" announcements as they approach the end. The play therapist can also ask if there is a specific way the child would like to end the time together. Intentional preparation for the ending can also include inquiring what their goals are for the session: do they have an idea of how they want to play? Do they know what they want to work on for that specific day? These goals can be repeated back to the child to let them know that they are heard and that their ideas are taken seriously.

It also serves as a reminder for the play therapist to acknowledge throughout the session's progression. Often, after considering their goals for the session and hearing them repeated back, the child might change their mind about how they want to end. In this case, the process of reflective insight is already happening. Their perception of how they want to spend their time is changing, and they have a different idea of what it might be like to end given their new revised goal.

During the first couple of sessions, an ending time for the gameplay can be set earlier than the session's ending time. Knowing that endings can be particularly challenging for the client in this vignette, the play therapist can allocate more time to validate the difficult experience and coregulate together. As they track the child's experience of this, the ability to tolerate endings further into the end of the session is considered progress, as their perception of what the ending will be like becomes more predictable. When this happens, their ability to tolerate the emotions grows, and their WOT expands.

Clinical Vignette 1b

The play therapy session is scheduled for 50 minutes, but I set the time boundary with the client for 40 minutes of playing Minecraft together. I let them know that I will be giving reminders along the way as time passes. We discuss goals for what they would like to achieve in the game and how they would like to end on that particular day. The client decides that the goal is to play in Survival together and start a new game. Starting from the beginning, they informed me that they wanted to mine, craft weapons, and build a base. I ask how they want to end when our time is up, and they say that they want to sleep in beds so they can set a spawn point for the next game (that means when we log in at the start of our next session, we will pick up right where we left off). We discuss adding beds as another goal, so that it is not something the client requests frantically when our ending time approaches.

We begin playing in the new world, and along the way, I make observations of how much time has passed. As the session progresses, I acknowledge that we only have 10 minutes left. While they have been crafting weapons, we still do not have a base or beds yet. The child says it is "fine" and we can do it before we end.

I give the 5-minute heads up.

I can feel my own anxiety and tension emerge as I do not think we will have time to do everything, and I know that it will be hard for both of us, as I want them to be happy, and it is so hard to stop when they are disappointed.

Then it is time to end the game.

The child begs and pleads for just one more minute; they say they have to do just one more thing. Knowing that I have ten minutes remaining, I agree to the request. I notice their tense body language, and their breathing is more rapid; they are becoming agitated and appear unable to cope with this abrupt ending. I start validating how hard endings are and how hard it is not to reach a goal.

"It is disappointing that we did not get everything done that we wanted to." It hurts to end, and I name that.

The child asks for "thirty more seconds." I hear the emotions in their voice building. "I wish we could have more time and we have to end here." I exit and save the game as disappointment, anger, and sadness fill the room.

We still have five minutes left in our session time, and we sit together in the presence of the big feelings. I am rocking back and forth, soothing the distress in my body and taking big breaths with slower exhales.

"I know how hard this is," emphasizing the word know as it truly is hard for me as well.

"I just needed thirty more seconds!" the child responds.

"There were so many things you wanted to do today! I really wish we could have done all of them together." Both are true statements that I hope will help the child turn inward towards their experience.

"Then why didn't you just give me thirty more seconds?" The child is trying to reason with me, which can be a distraction for the big, unpleasant emotions underneath the reason.

"It is so hard to end when there is more to do. I can imagine you're upset, and it feels really yucky to end like this." I resist the urge to explain why I did not give 30 more seconds or try to reason, and instead, I stay with the emotion, considering it from their perspective. "You got so much done, and there is also so much more to do, and it doesn't feel good to stop there."

I observe the child sigh and put their controller down. My best guess is that they have felt seen and understood. With this in mind, I provide a narrative overview of everything we set out to do, what was accomplished, and what remains for the next session.

"We had a lot of goals set for today. Playing a new Survival world, mining from the beginning, and making weapons. We wanted to make a base and beds, but then time went by SO FAST!" I intentionally emphasize the passage of time as a way to plant seeds for the dual experience of being in the game and being in the room together. "Then we had to end, even though you were not ready, and there was still so much to do. That didn't feel good, even when we knew it was going to happen."

I see the child nod slowly.

The nod confirms that I understood how hard it was for them in that moment. Observing this gives me the green light to move towards problem-solving and plant seeds for what to do when this happens next time. "We might have a hard time ending when we meet next time - I wonder what we can do together to help make it feel easier?"

"Well, if I could have more time, then that would be better."

"Yes! More time would be so helpful. Today, I gave you a heads-up when we had ten minutes left. Would you like more time than that?"

"Maybe you can let me know when there are fifteen minutes left?"

> *"I can absolutely do that. And what if everything doesn't get done in that amount of time?"*
>
> *"I'll let you know what I absolutely need to get done, and then we can end it."*
>
> *"That sounds like a great plan. I know it was hard to end, and I'm glad you could tell me about it."*

Sometimes it does not go as smoothly as this example, and that is okay. Every child starts from a different place, but they all share the desire to be seen and understood in their distress. If there were still big emotions happening, or it looked like they were shut down from the ending, then I would skip the narrative overview and problem-solving piece and help them regulate by continuing to let them know I see and feel them. If the session time ran out, I would connect with the adult who accompanied or supported the child at the start of the session and help utilize their presence to coregulate with the child. This is also where play therapists can use all the other tools from their toolbox to support their clients in the ways they know best. The critical piece is not to give up and to consider how continuing to play the game is holding valuable information about the child's perception of the experience of being immersed in something they enjoy and having to end.

Other Ending Interventions

The Subjective Units of Distress Scale (SUDS) and mindfulness activities can be used at the beginning of a session to help the client become intentionally aware of the digital space as described in Chapter 4. There are also ending interventions that can be used to transition the child back toward the physical space outside of the game. There are many different ways play therapists may choose to transition out of a session with intentional care, such as offering transitional objects, collecting artwork to bring home, or washing hands and resetting a part of the room. I typically choose between two interventions that, in my experience, have blended well with the use of Minecraft: returning to the use of the SUDS check-in from the beginning of the session and/or a personalized ending routine, either in person or over the screen.

As described in Chapter 4, SUDS are often used in therapy as a cognitive, self-reflective intervention that invites the child to consider their level of activation or worry at the beginning and end of the session. In the interest of practicing positive endings, I use the assessment not only to help the child consider how they are entering the gaming space in that moment, but also to provide an opportunity for them to reflect on how they feel after their time playing the game.

What is most important about using this intervention is that it provides an opportunity for self-reflection at the end of the session, playing Minecraft in an intentional way. This is helpful when there may be a hard ending to the time together, while there had also been fun and enjoyable moments while playing. Rather than the child getting stuck in the complex feelings of not wanting to end, the SUDS check-out offers the opportunity to recognize that the hard feelings can also exist with the positive feelings of what they did accomplish and were able to finish.

The SUDS check-out offers a self-reflective ending, while engaging in an interpersonal ending ritual provides a relational closure to the session, bringing the experience of gameplay in the Minecraft world back to the shared experience of the child and the play therapist outside the game. Finch (2022) recommends taking a screenshot of the client's character in the game with the clinician, or even planting a tree in their world as a reminder of the time spent together.

I build upon this concept of a shared ritual by translating it from a digital symbol into a direct, physical interaction between us. One thing I offer clients is the option of a customized ending handshake, which we choreograph together. This could be an elaborate series of movements or a simple high-five, knuckle-bump, or wave. Some may decline at first but later revisit the invitation after more trust and rapport have been built; others might want to do it right away or offer alternative suggestions, such as trying a dance move together or following other prompts. Following the theme of being intentional about how we, as play therapists, end the session, it is not important to me what is chosen – or if anything is chosen at all – but that the child is aware that there is closure to that moment in time and a new experience will follow in the next meeting.

What Comes Next

At the beginning of the next session with the child, I revisit what happened previously, reminding them of our time agreement, reflecting on how hard it was to end last time, and how I can help them prioritize importance. The strategy of replaying what happened to shape a narrative and revisiting it later is inspired by the approach of "name it to tame it" (Siegel & Bryson, 2012), which builds reflective insight and awareness. This process can occur over multiple sessions, and it is a strategy shared with parents to use outside of the session. A key distinction is that we revisit the distress of the ending and explore different ways to manage it when the child is out of the moment and the distress has passed. Yalom (2002) refers to this approach with adults as "striking when the iron is cold" (pp. 121–123), and it also applies here to working with the big, hard moments with children. Finding ways to solve the problem after the intensity of the issue has passed can provide the child with more options to consider possible solutions. The brain science behind this will be discussed more thoroughly in Chapter 10. What aligns this strategy with the Seven Guiding Principles is that the child is not just receiving time remaining reminders, but also receiving reminders of the feelings and body responses – building interoception, increasing the WOT, and being helped to problem-solve after they are felt, seen, and heard. Ultimately, this practiced awareness of navigating endings in the therapeutic relationship directly builds the child's capacity to manage transitions and endings in their daily life at home.

Looking Ahead

The work of managing endings extends beyond the session itself. We must also help children and parents navigate the transition to what happens after the game is over, where unacknowledged emotions often surface. There may be instances in which ending the game is not difficult, but unacknowledged emotions are often involved with what happens after the game is over. This could encompass a wide range of things, including but not limited to: challenges at school, transitioning to bedtime, difficulty sleeping, overstimulation from the environment, and/or anxiety about the activity that follows. It is widely understood that parents and caregivers are also exhausted and distressed. There are many families with other siblings who have needs and busy schedules, requiring adjustments for all family members. In some instances, a child who struggles to end a game may be missing the engagement provided by the game, online players, or the play therapist. Having the transition time at the end of each session provides more opportunities for the play therapist to assess what might specifically be the game-related distress of ending, or perhaps anxiety manifesting from the unknown of something that comes next.

These concepts will be explored further in Chapter 9, which discusses how clinicians can help parents apply these strategies to turn successful endings in the playroom into successful outcomes at home. Chapters 10 and 11 offer information about the child's developing brain and its impact on the perception of self when relating to endings, while Chapter 12 emphasizes the importance of processing endings in the grieving process.

Helpful Tips

- **The Fifth Guiding Principle:** It states that a child's difficulty in ending the game is not a reason to avoid using Minecraft in therapy; instead, it is the exact sign for a targeted therapeutic intervention. How the game ends in session is meant to serve as practice for endings and transitions outside of therapy.

- **Acknowledge the Reasons for Distress:** The child's strong emotions around stopping play are understandable, as they may be holding onto an unspoken perception of how they want the game to end (e.g., completing an elaborate build or achieving a goal) or are reacting sensitively due to previous negative endings or disruptions experienced earlier in the day or week.
- **Use Endings to Expand the WOT:** By intentionally focusing on the challenging experience of ending the game, play therapists help the child learn to tolerate endings and navigate transitions. Working with the disappointment and frustration that arise provides a new experience that expands the child's WOT, which can be applied to everyday situations.
- **Establish Intentional Boundaries:** At the start of the session, the play therapist can be transparent in identifying all time boundaries and ending limits. They can also proactively inquire about the client's goals for the session and ask how the child would like to end their time together, incorporating these goals into the session plan.
- **Coregulate the Distress:** When big emotions (like disappointment or anger) surface at the end of the game, the clinician must resist the urge to reason or explain the boundary. Instead, the therapist can validate how hard endings are and remain present to coregulate the distress, only moving toward problem-solving or narrative reflection once the big emotions have passed.

Reflection Question

1 What is my own typical reaction to a child's protest or disappointment (e.g., guilt, rigidity, avoidance), and how might that reaction help or hinder my ability to be a coregulating presence during an ending?

References

Finch, E. (2022). *Thinking of using video games therapeutically?* Association for Counseling and Therapy Online. https://playmodeacademy.org/resources-and-publications/thinking-of-using-video-games-therapeutically

Siegel, D. J., & Bryson, T. P. (2012). *The whole-brain child: 12 revolutionary strategies to nurture your child's development, survive everyday parenting struggles, and help your family thrive*. Scribe Publications.

Yalom, I. (2002). *The gift of therapy: An open letter to a new generation of therapists and their patients* (pp. 121–123). HarperCollins.

Chapter 8

Working with Parents, Caregivers, and Families (Principles 6 and 7)

A parent and adolescent are working together to strengthen their relationship. The adolescent enjoys gaming and finds it soothing and empowering, as they have control over everything that happens in their Minecraft world. However, their parent does not like them playing video games, which, from their perspective, is an unhealthy distraction that promotes laziness, apathy toward real-life activities, and causes more distress when the game doesn't go their child's way.

During our work together, I meet with the parent and adolescent separately, aiming to bridge the gap in how they listen and respond to each other. The parent reflects on their teenage years and the rules, expectations, and judgments they experienced as a teenager. We also discuss their thoughts and judgments about their teen's video game playing. In sessions with the adolescent, they share different perspectives and experiences, describing how the game helps them feel confident and proud, and how it allows them to connect with friends at school over a common interest.

As the sessions progress, both the parent and adolescent become willing to listen to each other's perspectives. Collaborative conversations help them clarify their concerns and worries. Together, they can reach agreements that make sense to both of them. What began as addressing challenges with video games and Minecraft eventually led to conversations that fostered more connection in their relationship.

At the beginning of my career, I trained at a nonprofit community bereavement center that served families grieving the loss of loved ones. The clinical team employed a family systems model, dividing family members into developmentally specific groups so that each could process their grief in an age-appropriate manner before coming together with a shared language and understanding (Griese et al., 2018). This approach facilitated communication during a time of isolation and highlighted the importance of honoring both individual and relational experiences within the family system.

This early experience profoundly shaped my understanding of family work. It showed me the immense value of giving each member space to

DOI: 10.4324/9781003614784-10

process their individual experience before reuniting, leading to greater empathy and connection. This framework was further developed through my training in Attachment-Based Family Therapy for Depressed Adolescents (ABFT), which operates on the belief that strengthening the parent-child relationship is the primary protective factor for an adolescent in distress (Diamond et al., 2014). ABFT employs a task-based model that includes individual sessions for the adolescent and parents, the latter often involving exploration of their own intergenerational attachment patterns, before bringing the family together to repair ruptures and collaborate on a new path forward (Diamond et al., 2014). Training in this model developed my understanding of not only parent-child attachment patterns but also the benefits of exploring intergenerational attachment patterns between parents and their parents, thereby increasing awareness of current relational dynamics within the family (see also Saltman, 2020; Siegel & Hartzell, 2004).

I have carried this foundational belief, that healing happens by understanding the different parts of the system, into my work with using Minecraft in play therapy. It is not unusual for families to have a love/hate relationship with video games. This dynamic is part of a larger pattern. Research indicates that up to 80% of parents report struggling to engage in play with their children (LEGO Australia & Playgroup NSW, 2025). The very nature of digital media engagement often exacerbates this struggle; studies show that "solitary media use (by the parent or child) can disrupt ongoing parent-child interactions and children's play" (Kirkorian et al., 2025). Children may feel that their play is unfairly judged, while parents often worry about the developmental impacts and struggle to set clear boundaries. These conflicts are frequently complicated by parents' own histories with video games, leading them to project past experiences onto their child's present reality. Notably, research confirms that confrontations about screen time can disrupt positive parent-child interactions (Wisniewski et al., 2025). This chapter provides a pathway through this common struggle, exploring how the use of Minecraft in play therapy can also reach parents and caregivers at home, positively shifting these dynamics away from solitary use and confrontation toward collaborative connection.

This chapter examines how clinicians utilizing Minecraft in play therapy can help families positively shift their family dynamics. Focus is given on helping parents explore their assumptions about gaming, understand how their own upbringing influences their view, and ultimately use the game as a tool to increase connection with their child. The benefits extend beyond the therapy session and seamlessly fit into creative ways parents can connect with their child outside of the game time as well.

Clinical vignettes and family-level strategies will illustrate how to translate the in-game playing mechanics and experiences into coregulating coping skills that build secure attachment-building moments in daily life. The Seven Guiding Principles will be referenced throughout, with specific attention on Principle 6: parents and helping adults can support their child in having a therapeutic experience with Minecraft at home by being curious and learning about the game together.

A Family Systems Lens: Helping Parents Explore Their Own Relationship to Gaming

A starting place when working with parents or caregivers is to help them explore their thoughts and feelings related to gaming in general. This can begin with an inquiry into their history with gaming. Similar to the clinicians reading this book, some parents seek us out due to their personal experience playing Minecraft and other games. Some have no history with video games and are just now becoming familiar with the current generation of online game play, including all the advancements that make the games so immersive. To help facilitate a reflective process during an initial intake with parents or caregivers, clinicians may ask questions such as:

- **Did you play video games as a child?**

  If you did, were your parents or family members supportive of that interest?
  Were those positive memories from when you played?
  Did you think of the game even when you were not playing?
  Was it hard to stop playing?

- **Did your parents or siblings play with you?**

  If they did, what was that experience like?
  If they did not, was there a desire that they would have?

- **Were you ever proud of your accomplishments while playing?**

  If so, did you tell your parents? How might they have responded?

- **Did you ever feel guilty, judged, or ashamed when playing?**
- **Looking back, do you wish you had spent a different amount of time playing (more or less)?**
- **If you did not play, did you feel left out or different from your peers who might have been playing?**
- **What are your thoughts about games now?**
- **Are there specific things you worry about in your child's experience that may be similar or different from your own?**
- **How do your experiences and opinions of gaming influence your current parenting style?**

Depending on the answers to these questions, clinicians will gain insight into what the parents are bringing to their relationship with the child and their experience with the game. These are also questions that parents may not have previously given thought to. Considering these questions can help validate for the child that their interest in the game may be a complex part of their life that is hard to express fully. Adults giving attention to the depth of these questions can reflect the commitment they are making to understand the importance of Minecraft in their child's life. Conversations about earlier developmental experiences for the parents can also be activating, and it is essential to honor and respect parents' wishes regarding their level of desire and autonomy, whether or not they choose to delve deeper. Regardless of the answers, the questions serve as another way clinicians can reference the Second Guiding Principle, recognizing that the therapeutic benefits of the game begin for the family even before it is used in sessions.

Caregivers and Minecraft: The Past and Present

A parent's reaction to their child's Minecraft play is rarely simple. It is a nuanced response woven from threads of their own childhood, their deeply held values, and their legitimate concerns for their child's present-day well-being. Our role is not to assume the origin of their view, but to approach it with curiosity, understanding that it may be shaped by a combination of intergenerational patterns and contemporary reasoning.

For some parents, their stance is unconsciously informed by their own developmental experiences. A parent raised to prioritize tangible achievement over leisurely play might struggle to see the value in a digital playroom. Another, who found solace and connection in games, may be more likely to embrace their child's interest. As Siegel and Hartzell (2004) note, how parents make sense of their own childhood experiences and explore these histories can foster self-awareness, thereby enhancing their relationships with their children by separating their own past from their child's present experience. Furthermore, some parents might experience a strong emotional reaction that can be triggered explicitly as their child reaches the same age at which they themselves had pivotal (whether positive or painful) developmental experiences. Unmet needs from a parent's own adolescence can feel intensely reactivated in the present-day relationship (Atlas, 2022).

Simultaneously, we must honor that a parent's perspective is often firmly rooted in thoughtful, present-day considerations. These are not reactions to be analyzed away, but valid positions to be respected. Protective factors parents may be considering when demonstrating resistance or reluctance to games like Minecraft may include: following pediatric guidelines on screen time; protecting their child from online risks like cyberbullying or inappropriate content; prioritizing other developmental needs like physical activity, academic work, or offline social interaction; responding to their own observations of their child becoming dysregulated or obsessive after playing (see Chapters 9, 10).

The clinical task is to hold space for all of these truths at once. We can gently explore a parent's history with questions such as: "What was your relationship with games like at your child's age?" not to pathologize their response, but to uncover hidden scripts that might be influencing their reactions. This mentalizing process (validating their concerns while inviting them to see the game through their child's eyes as a world of creativity, problem-solving, and connection) is the foundation of collaborative work (Fonagy & Allison, 2014). Ultimately, our goal is to help parents make conscious, intentional choices about their child's interest in Minecraft and how they relate to it together. This process can be guided by both their values and a deeper understanding of their child's inner world.

Reframing the Child's Interest in the Game: What We Know As Clinicians

The Seven Guiding Principles provide clinicians with a framework for moving beyond seeing Minecraft as "just a game" to recognizing it as a world of opportunity for expressing identity, initiating developmentally appropriate play, exploring emotions, practicing competence and agency, using it as a coping tool, and finding social connection. As children have demonstrated since the game's release, Minecraft is far more than it seems on the surface. The widespread popularity of the brand means it serves as a shared cultural language. At the same time, its open-ended, sandbox nature allows it to become a deeply personal world where core emotional developmental needs can be expressed (see Chapter 5.) Clinicians can communicate this deeper perspective as a powerful intervention of psychoeducation for parents seeking to connect with their child over the game.

When a child says they've been "mining for diamonds all afternoon," they are sharing a story of perseverance toward a valuable goal. When they are devastated after "losing their whole inventory," they are expressing a real sense of loss and wasted effort. These are not trivial moments; they are the emotional core of their experience.

Caregivers who understand this can shift their perspective on how their child might be responding. A parent's question can then move from "Can you please stop talking about the game?" to a more connecting inquiry: "I see how hard you worked for those diamonds; you were really dedicated! What makes them so important to you?" or "Losing all your items when you are so far from your base is so frustrating! What's the plan to get back what you need?" This Minecraft-informed approach uses the game as a conduit to deeper conversations and emotionally attuned parenting.

Helping Parents Feel More Empowered to Listen When Children Talk About the Game

For many children, their digital world in Minecraft is a core part of their identity, yet it is a part they often feel they have to defend or hide from adults. The simple, yet profound, act of a parent moving to the position of a curious witness can be transformative. This shift communicates that they are interested in the child's world and that the child's passions are worth their time and attention. This non-judgmental observation makes a child feel that their interest is seen and understood, validating an aspect of their experience they may fear is dismissed.

This approach is grounded in the work of John Gottman on emotion coaching and is a core tenet of models like Attachment-Based Family Therapy (ABFT). It is particularly powerful for repairing ruptures where a child seems closed off, isolated, and only interested in the game, or when they express feeling profoundly misunderstood about what this activity means to them. The goal is not for the parent to become an expert on the game, but to become an ongoing learner about their child's experience of the game. This reminder of the First and Third Guiding Principles relieves the pressure on parents and caregivers to have all the correct answers (something that feels like a finite and exhaustive resource) and replaces it with the power and abundance of curiosity. Clinicians can share the following guidelines to help parents avoid the common traps of invalidation, dismissal, or unsolicited problem-solving, and instead, open a pathway to connection:

- **Lead with Curiosity:** Before speaking, observe. Notice their body language, tone of voice, and reactions to events on the screen. Ask yourself, "What emotion might they be experiencing right now?"
- **Reflect and Label:** Offer gentle observations to help them build their capacity for self-reflection. Use statements like:

  "Your voice got really quiet; I'm wondering if you're feeling disappointed?"
  "I can see you sitting up so straight; you seem really proud of what you just built!"
  "It looked like that was really frustrating. Did I get that right?"

- **Validate the Experience:** Prioritize understanding over correcting. Even if the reflection is not perfectly accurate, the attempt itself builds a connection.

While the triggers for these conversations may be in-game events, the relational guidelines can also apply to non-game-related moments. The healing occurs in the relational proximity that follows. As Siegel and Bryson (2012, 2018, 2021) and Gobbel (2023) emphasize, this process actively builds the neural pathways for emotional communication and interoception, helping the child learn more about themselves while they are playing the game (see also Chapter 6.) This style of engagement mirrors the therapeutic relationship, further validating the clinical work we are doing with our clients while offering parents a tangible strategy to continue that work away from the appointments. This is the foundation for the Sixth and Seventh Guiding Principles: that parents can support therapeutic experiences at home through curiosity, and that the benefits of this connection extend far beyond the game itself.

Clinical Vignette

Inspired by this new way of understanding Minecraft, a parent begins to read about the game's various elements and watches YouTube videos of other players. One night, the parent notices that their child has been quiet and not very engaged. They had gotten into an argument together earlier and agreed to revisit the conversation when things cooled down. The adolescent went to play Minecraft, and the parent decided to approach them to circle back on the disagreement. However, before approaching, they reflected on the previous conversations with their therapist, and the parent decided to do something different. Instead of seeing the game as a problem in that moment, they moved toward expressing interest in it, hoping it will help the teen open up.

As the parent sits down, the teen says, "I'm just about to fight the Ender Dragon. Will you watch me?"

"Sure," The parent is nervous. They have no idea what that means. Things are moving all over the screen. Some are familiar, while others are entirely new. The parent notices how determined their child is, making small noises of effort and exertion.

"YES! I DID IT! I FINALLY DID IT!"

"I'm not sure what you did, but I can tell it's a big deal! I can see how hard you were working, and I can tell how proud you are!"

"This is the first time I've ever defeated the Ender Dragon." There is a slight pause, and the adolescent's voice softens. "Thank you for giving me a moment to finish playing. I'm really happy that I did that."

"I'm excited I got to see you do that. I'm proud of you for sticking with it and not giving up."

"I'm glad you got to see me do it, too."

"I can imagine you're really energized from all that pressure, and I know we have that thing to talk about from earlier today. Would you like to go for a walk together, shake off some of this energy, and talk more about where things went sideways today?"

"Yeah, okay, we can do that."

In this vignette, the parent is bravely taking the therapist's suggestion and trying to find a moment to connect with the adolescent's interest in the game, even though there are other things to discuss. By prioritizing the child's interest in that moment, the parent communicates that they understand how significant it was for them. For the teen, it was a powerful moment for their parent to see them do something they were good at; to show them that they were working really hard on something and that their dedication had paid off. Their pride in defeating the Ender Dragon for the first time was not only for the accomplishment in the game but also for the experience of being witnessed by their parent.

The vignette concludes with the parent acknowledging their collaborative agreement to work through an incident that occurred earlier in the day. It is presumed in this scenario that the teen agreed to going for a walk with their parent because they felt seen and heard, opening up their capacity (and Window of Tolerance) to talk about the hard stuff. After having a moment of success and accomplishment, they could then put everything aside and listen to what their parent had to say.

The invitation to walk is also a strategy for coregulation, as both the teen and the parent would be moving their bodies together while processing the more challenging topic of conversation. Furthermore, the side-by-side, relational proximity of walking together can be perceived as less confrontational than standing across from one another. Because the teen felt seen and heard in the prior moment, they could set aside everything else and listen to what their parent had to say on a topic entirely unrelated to Minecraft.

It is also understood that not all engagements will proceed in this manner. Children will not always have a successful moment or an easy transition, and it cannot be assumed that even the pride of being witnessed will lead to a willingness to revisit a conversation about when something did not go well. As clinicians working outside the heat of the moment, it can often be easy to offer suggestions and have the perfect script of how to respond – and then assume everything will go as planned.

I have made that mistake.

Clinician parents know that this is not the reality and that there are many other complicating factors at play within a family system. The intent of discussing strategies and sharing potential scenarios, such as the one above, is to provide parents with an alternative course of action to choose from, instilling the hope and possibility that things can go differently, even if it takes one hundred tries. Chapter 9: Promoting a Healthy Relationship to Screen Time and Game Play offers a deeper look into how to work with the big upset when things go off-script.

The Power of Joining the Game: Building Attachment and Connection

Clinicians can empower parents by guiding them through a paradigm shift, where they take on the role of the child being the expert. Parents are encouraged to acknowledge that their child is the expert on the game and to embrace the dynamic that the child can become the teacher. Heitner (2016) acknowledges the relational benefits of parents and children playing together, while also recognizing the obstacles many parents might have to overcome in learning about the technology. For parents who feel hesitant or unsure about where to start with Minecraft specifically, Heitner (2016) encourages them to begin by simply watching YouTube videos of gameplay or talking to other parents for ideas to build their curiosity and confidence before diving in.

To begin, therapists can suggest tangible starting points, such as having the parent hand the controller to the child for character creation, allowing the child to guide the choices for the parent's character. This act serves as a profound physical metaphor for the desired shift in roles. Once in the game, clinicians can remind parents that the primary focus is on collaboration rather than competition, with the goal of fostering connection. Embracing a non-directive approach at home can take the pressure off the parent or caregiver, who no longer have to learn a multitude of game mechanics, and they can direct their attention toward the choices and decisions their child makes. This also puts the parent in the role of coregulator as they help their child regulate in-game distress through the shared experience of being in the game together.

For parents who are drawn to more directive strategies, clinicians may suggest engaging in any number of collaborative projects, such as building bases, safe places, treehouses, pirate ships, castles, roller coasters, parkour courses, or tunneling through caves. Taking on a supportive role in Survival mode by gathering resources, keeping watch for mobs, and being available to help if the child requests it is another way to achieve a more task-oriented goal while playing. For advanced insight, consider guiding a parent to join their child on a public server. This can provide a unique window into the child's online social world and serve as a catalyst for crucial conversations about online safety. It is essential to note that while this chapter emphasizes connection through collaboration, there can also be therapeutic value in structured competitive play, such as asking the child if they want to play "Easy, Medium, Hard, or Insanity Triple Plus?!" as explored in Chapter 10.

The language used during gameplay is another critical coaching point. Clinicians can help parents reframe their questions, moving from generic inquiries like "What are you doing?" to those that demonstrate curiosity about the child's internal experience, such as "What was the hardest part about building that?", "What are you most proud of today?", or if there were any challenging parts, "Did you notice if you got really tense during those stressful moments?" Asking questions about the child's character can initiate robust dialogue, giving the child permission to share aspects of their sense of self that might not otherwise be communicated. For a deeper understanding of the clinical importance of identity expression, clinicians can direct parents and caregivers to Chapter 4.

Last, referencing the Second Guiding Principle, clinicians can remind parents that the therapeutic relational work begins even before the game starts. Discussions between parents and their children about when they might play together, for how long, and what they might want to do during the game are themselves exercises in collaborative problem-solving, goal-setting, and completing objectives together. Further discussions can include whether the time is spent with the entire family or if a specific child is seeking individual connection with caregivers. Clinicians can further remind parents and caregivers that there is no single right way to structure this time and that an unsuccessful session is not a failure but instead serves as constructive data for the relational process and future planning. There will always be another chance to do things differently.

Having Fun While Playing Minecraft Together

Clinicians can also help parents understand the distinction between the deeply therapeutic skills and work that occur during play therapy sessions (discussed throughout this book) and recreational play, which is simply for fun. While clinicians must be intentional about avoiding their own agenda during sessions, we can encourage parents to give themselves permission to play for fun and show up authentically. Contrary to the Third Guiding Principle, which is intended as a reference for play therapists, children often crave the genuine engagement that arises when the adults in their lives let their guard down and have fun. Gobbel (2023) advocates for opportunities for shared fun as a way of building relational bonds, as playful interactions can be profoundly tender moments that strengthen the attachment relationship. Furthermore, when a parent authentically models a range of emotions such as excitement, disappointment, frustration, and joy, they provide a powerful live demonstration of emotional regulation and expression for their child.

Even in this play-focused mode, clinicians can remind parents to remain attuned to opportunities for connection and encourage them to notice their child's body language, facial expressions, tone of voice, and physical movements during play. We can teach parents to reflect the emotions they observe gently, along with the in-game moments that may have prompted them. A practical coaching tip is to suggest parents imagine the experiences through the "perspective of the child." For example, while destroying a mob may be trivial for the parent, it might represent a significant moment of pride and competence for the child. This attuned presence and understanding, even during play, communicates to the child that they are seen and that their interests are important.

Of course, perfect presence is an unrealistic ideal. This is the perfect context to introduce parents to Donald Winnicott's concept of the "good-enough mother" (Winnicott, 1953) or, more contemporarily, the "good-enough parent." This theory relieves parental pressure by valuing a parent's reliable, imperfect presence, which provides a comforting space for the child to experience their own successes and disappointments. When moments of distress inevitably arise during play, clinicians can frame them not as failures but as powerful opportunities. Coach parents to first show understanding of the child's feelings and then, if appropriate, to share a brief, relatable story of a time they faced a similar challenge, either currently or at a similar age. This strategy helps the child feel normalized and validated. If a parent struggles with this, these dynamics can be processed in parent-only sessions. A final, practical tip is to guide parents away from asking "*why*" something happened (which can feel interrogative) and toward "*what*" questions (e.g., "What was the hardest part?", "What happened that was so upsetting?"), which foster collaborative reflection.

Translating Game Mechanics and Skills into Family Coping Strategies

Engaging parents and caregivers with the game becomes a natural transition to having a shared understanding, reference, and language of Minecraft dynamics. Just as clinicians may do in their sessions, parents can be coached in translating in-game concepts into coping skills and strategic approaches for managing the distress that arises in everyday life. Questions such as: "How is the stress of homework deadlines like the night closing in on you in Survival mode?", "How can we 'respawn' and try again after a tough day?" can be a powerful way to give insight into possible coping and regulation strategies while speaking their language. The following is a list of ideas that feature common elements of playing Minecraft and how to translate them into family-level coping strategies:

- **Timers:** Minecraft has a natural day cycle with a gradual sunrise that signals the start of a new day. For family members who struggle to get out of bed in the morning, "Sunrise" alarm clocks can be a fun way to help wake up, stimulating the cycle of a Minecraft world.
- **Backpack Inventory:** Every player in Minecraft has an inventory of nine items that they can carry and easily access throughout their journey. This can be translated to an actual backpack that holds nine intentional items for children to carry, helping them through challenging moments and making them feel powerful.
- **The Safe Space at Home:** Building a safe space in the game keeps the player protected from all the dangers of the Minecraft world. Collaborating on a special place at home that honors family members' agreements provides an opportunity for needs to be voiced, heard, and discussed.
- **Healing Potions:** Invisibility, speed, sleep, strength – Minecraft has a potion for that! Reframing hydration, nighttime relaxation teas, and nutrient-dense drinks as healing potions can be a fun way to help children connect how they feel to what they put in their bodies.
- **Character Skins:** Designing one's character is a fun, powerful, and expressive experience. Reframing getting dressed into character design can help the child consider what makes them feel powerful, and in what situations they may feel powerless and need more armor.
- **Mining IRL:** Minecraft primarily features a first-person view of mining. For children who have difficulty transitioning from the game, holding a phone in video mode can replicate the appearance of the Minecraft first-person screen view in real life. Children can explore both inside and outside the home as they "mine" blocks with their hand and arm viewed over the screen.
- **Health Bar and Food Bar:** The ten hearts and ten drumsticks are critical indicators of health and energy. Families can discuss what depletes both health and energy, and what replenishes them.

The Power of Parents Joining a Session: Caregivers as the Most Important Coregulator

While coaching parents to play at home strengthens connection, the most powerful interventions often happen when the clinician actively guides the family's interaction during sessions. In this context, the therapeutic potential of Minecraft shifts from merely fostering connection to actively repairing the core relational ruptures that drive family conflict. Family sessions offer a structured yet adaptable platform for this work, enabling families to transition from observational or parallel play to a shared, emotionally attuned experience.

The clinician can facilitate this shift through key interventions. The most effective is to have the child act as a guide, leading caregivers on a tour of their therapeutic world. This serves as the initial application of Principle 6, as families experience the connection that comes from playing the game together with the child, with the clinician modeling a helpful way of engagement.

Beyond guided tours, joint family builds like a "Family Safe Space" or a shared "Worry Box" make abstract ideas tangible. The build process itself becomes a live metaphor for the family's interpersonal world, where the clinician can observe and intervene in real-time communication and problem-solving patterns.

This in-session work serves as the training ground for the family's most essential skill: coregulation. The clinician's primary role shifts from being a game facilitator to acting as an attachment coach, guiding the parent on how to stay present and regulated alongside their child, in moments of dysregulation. We are not just creating a virtual safe space; we are cultivating a relational safe space. The therapist models, mentors, and prompts the parent in real time, empowering them to become their child's primary coregulator. This meta-skill transforms the Minecraft session from a simple, fun activity into a model for secure attachment.

This work of establishing the parent as the child's primary coregulator is the ultimate expression of Principle 6 and the chapter's main goal. It builds the relational safety needed for a child to apply the skills learned while playing Minecraft in sessions to a wide range of relational experiences at home with their parents and caregivers. This secure, coregulated foundation is the essential prerequisite for the deep processing that follows, and it is the very mechanism that activates Principle 7; ensuring that the benefits of this work extend well beyond the therapy session and into the child's daily life. The detailed vignette in Chapter 13 will illustrate exactly how this foundation takes place from the session to the home.

Helpful Tips

- **Begin with Individual Sessions:** Start family intervention by meeting with the parent and adolescent separately. This allows each member to process their individual histories and perspectives, such as intergenerational attachment patterns and past judgments about gaming, before collaborative reunification.

- **Model Principle 6 to Foster Connection:** Actively apply Principle 6 by modeling non-judgmental curiosity in-session. Have the child act as the expert and guide, for instance, by leading a tour of their therapeutic world, to build a relational connection.
- **Empower the Parent as Coregulator:** The ultimate goal is for the clinician to coach the parent on how to stay present and regulated alongside their child, thereby empowering the parent to become the child's primary coregulator.
- **Guide Parents to Reflect Emotion:** Coach parents to shift their questions from generic inquiries (e.g., "What are you doing?") to those that reflect and label the child's in-game emotional state (e.g., "That looked really frustrating" or "You seem really proud!").
- **Apply Principle 7 Through Skill Translation:** Help families translate in-game concepts (e.g., "Healing Potions" for healthy hydration or "respawn" for trying again after a tough day) into shared, real-world coping strategies and language.

Reflection Question

1 Reflecting on my current caseload, which family might benefit most from having their conflicts over gaming reframed as opportunities for connection, and what one initial question could I ask the parent to begin exploring their own history with games?

References

Atlas, G. (2022). *Emotional inheritance: A therapist, her patients, and the legacy of trauma*. Little, Brown Spark.

Diamond, G. S., Diamond, G. M., & Levy, S. A. (2014). *Attachment-based family therapy for depressed adolescents*. American Psychological Association.

Fonagy, P., & Allison, E. (2014). The role of mentalizing and epistemic trust in the therapeutic relationship. *Psychotherapy*, *51*(3), 372–380. https://doi.org/10.1037/a0036505

Gobbel, R. (2023). *Raising kids with big, baffling behaviors*. Jessica Kingsley Publishers.

Griese, B., Burns, M., & Farro, S. (2018). Pathfinders: Promoting healthy adjustment in bereaved children and families. *Death Studies*, 42(3), 134–142.

Heitner, D. (2016). *Screenwise: Helping kids thrive (and survive) in their digital world*. Taylor & Francis.

Kirkorian, H., Barr, R., Coyne, S. M., Munzer, T. G.-C., Paulus, M., & Thomason, M. E. (2025). Digital media, cognition, and brain development in infancy and childhood. In D. A. Christakis & L. Hale (Eds.), *Handbook of children and screens* (pp. 13–30). Springer. https://doi.org/10.1007/978-3-031-69362-5_3

LEGO Australia & Playgroup NSW. (2025). *The BIG Start report: Parent-child play in Australia*. https://www.playgroupnsw.org.au/wp-content/uploads/2025/03/BIG-Start-Report-2025.pdf

Saltman, B. (2020). *Strange situation: A mother's journey into the science of attachment*. Ballantine Books.
Siegel, D., & Hartzell, M. (2004). *Parenting from the inside out*. Thorsons.
Siegel, D. J., & Bryson, T. P. (2012). *The whole-brain child: 12 revolutionary strategies to nurture your child's development, survive everyday parenting struggles, and help your family thrive*. Scribe Publications.
Siegel, D. J., & Bryson, T. P. (2018). *The yes brain: How to cultivate courage, curiosity, and resilience in your child*. Bantam.
Siegel, D. J., & Bryson, T. P. (2021). *The power of showing up: How parental presence shapes who our kids become and how their brains get wired*. Ballantine.
Winnicott, D. W. (1953). Transitional objects and transitional phenomena: A study of the first not-me possession. *The International Journal of Psychoanalysis*, *34*, 89–97.
Wisniewski, P., Park, J., Badillo-Urquiola, K., Gabrielli, J., Doty, J. L., & Hartikainen, H. (2025). Moving beyond fear and restriction to promoting adolescent resilience and intentional technology use. In D. A. Christakis & L. Hale (Eds.), *Handbook of children and screens* (pp. 403–410). Springer. https://doi.org/10.1007/978-3-031-69362-5_55

Chapter 9

Promoting a Healthy Relationship to Screen Time and Game Play

The integration of video games like Minecraft into play therapy presents a unique dialectic: a tool powerful enough to foster therapeutic growth in session can be the very source of familial conflict at home. This chapter explores how clinicians can navigate this paradox. As described throughout Section 2 (with the framework of the Seven Guiding Principles), the intentional therapeutic use of Minecraft can bring deliberate awareness to in-session play, such as tracking the passage of time, celebrating met goals, and collaboratively planning for future sessions. Therapists use the game to expand the child's Window of Tolerance (WOT) and fundamentally reshape their relationship with the experience of playing the game. The ultimate goal is to translate this healthier engagement into the home environment, transforming screen time from a point of contention into a positive experience for the entire family system. Chapter 8 works toward this goal by providing parents with strategies to connect with their child in new ways, primarily by encouraging them to play together.

However, this therapeutic approach often conflicts with the very valid concerns parents and educators bring to us. In a world saturated with screens, their questions are not only common but necessary: "How much screen time is too much?" and "Aren't we trying to get them off screens?" Adults worry about eroded social skills, exposure to violence, and the looming threat of what researchers often term problematic interactive media use (PIMU), a concept preferred over the imprecise language of "gaming addiction" (Knibbs, 2025; Marciano et al., 2025). When a therapist then introduces a screen into the sacred space of therapy, it can feel like endorsing the very thing they are fighting against, potentially exacerbating dependencies.

These concerns are amplified for parents of children struggling with emotional dysregulation, for whom video games are often a known trigger for explosive emotions. The question, "Will playing this game in session make my child more dysregulated?" is a logical and critical one. While Chapter 10 details the clinical approach for working with the emotional

DOI: 10.4324/9781003614784-11

dysregulation that arises while playing Minecraft, this chapter directly addresses the parental fear that we are, by focusing on a digital game, causing more screen-related challenges. Furthermore, families may seek this specific modality out of both curiosity and apprehension. Introducing a popular, enticing video game prompts pressing practical questions: What ages is this appropriate for? What constitutes a healthy engagement with screen time? How does a family determine what healthy gaming habits look like for them?

This chapter will address these valid concerns head-on by providing clinicians with the evidence-based frameworks and practical strategies needed to answer parent questions, set effective boundaries, and ultimately leverage the in-session use of Minecraft to promote a balanced and healthy relationship with technology within the family system.

Developmental Considerations for Playing Minecraft

Parents and caregivers of children new to Minecraft often ask about the recommended age, which is reflected in the official ratings of PEGI 7+ in Europe and E10+ (Everyone 10+) from the Entertainment Software Rating Board (ESRB) in North America (Minecraft Staff, n.d.). In practice, however, children much younger than these ages often express a strong desire to play. In fact, the PEGI 7+ guideline aligns with my observations in practice, as it is not unusual for seven-year-old clients to already be playing. Age-related interest before the recommended guidelines is not just anecdotal. According to Bickham et al. (2025), studies indicate a substantial prevalence of Minecraft play among middle childhood, starting as young as age six. Additionally, Knibbs (2025) references the ability of a five-year-old to watch a Minecraft build tutorial and replicate it in their own game. This common scenario means that for many families, the focus is less on adhering to the age guideline and more on managing the screen time that accompanies their child's early interest.

Screen time recommendations are similarly fluid and must be adapted to the individual needs of each child and family. For example, the Mayo Clinic (2024) and the American Academy of Pediatrics (as cited in Santos et al., 2022) recommend that children aged 2–5 have no more than one hour of supervised screen time per day. For children aged 5–12, drawing on 2016 advice from the Council on Communications and Media, cited by Santos et al. (2022), excessive exposure is often defined as more than two hours of combined daily screen time. However, experts note that rather than applying universal rules, families should manage screen exposure based on their specific circumstances (Mayo Clinic, 2024; Santos et al., 2022). This individualized approach has become notably more complex since the pandemic increased both the availability and necessity of screen-based activities. This reality fundamentally challenges the utility of a rigid time-based approach. The Ministry of Health, Singapore (2025), for instance, captures this nuance by specifying that its two-hour guideline applies only to screen time unrelated to schoolwork, forcing families to distinguish between the quality and purpose of screen engagement, which is precisely the shift in thinking experts now advocate.

Considerations around screen time are further complicated when children use Minecraft in their play therapy sessions, as this therapeutic use might be accounted for within total daily usage limits. Acknowledging this nuanced complexity, experts suggest shifting the focus from the quantity of time spent on screens to prioritizing the content, context, and quality of engagement (Barr et al., 2020; Mayo Clinic, 2024; Reich et al., 2025). Focusing on the quality of a client's experience when using Minecraft in a session is a key aspect of the Seven Guiding Principles, where the framework emphasizes the intentional engagement of the play therapist being present in the game with the child. The clinical orientation held by the therapist in sessions can be applied outside of the session, where the utility and guidelines around screen use can be assessed through the lens of quality and intentional engagement.

Knibbs (2025) argues that the complexity of the situation is obscured by ill-defined terms like "screentime" and "gaming," which lack adequate contextual clarity about the content or specific behaviors involved. In this light, fixating on total screen time becomes a distraction, as it ignores the crucial distinction between mindless engagement and what is truly enriching, such as the educational and therapeutic contexts of the modern era. Knibbs (2025), drawing on the work of Jocelyn Brewer, advises that a more valuable approach is one of "digital nutrition," which focuses on the quality of engagement and personal nourishment technology provides, rather than simply counting minutes. This paradigm aligns directly with the Seven Guiding Principles; the third principle emphasizes that play therapists orient to the game from outside a casual gaming experience, ensuring the time spent in session is not like consuming empty calories, but instead is a therapeutically nourishing experience designed to foster emotional growth.

Navigating Parental Concerns Specific to Minecraft

Other concerns that arise when considering a digital modality such as Minecraft include how to contextualize the violent or aggressive aspects of gameplay, questions around PIMU, the dangers of being in online environments, and the potential for isolation. These are valid concerns when working with clients in session and when they are playing at home. The framework of the Seven Guiding Principles provides a foundation for skillfully working with these dynamics when with the play therapist: violent and aggressive aspects of gameplay can be showing us more about the child's experience of the world while also providing opportunities for coregulation (Chapters 5 and 6); practicing positive endings addresses challenges with PMU (Chapter 7); clinicians protect the child's privacy in the digital environment (Chapter 18); playing together and with peer groups prevent an isolating experience (Chapter 15). Parents and caregivers can trust that the clinical and therapeutic use of Minecraft can alleviate many initial worries; however, there may also be concerns about what happens when those dynamics arise at home.

Contextualizing Minecraft Violence

Objective observation of Minecraft gameplay can understandably raise concerns about violence, given the inclusion of weapons used for both protection and aggression. However, the game's blocky aesthetic, lack of blood, and accessibility of a "peaceful mode" make its violence qualitatively different from the graphic realism of games like *Call of Duty*. This distinction is critical. Adopting a "digital nutrition" framework requires us to explore precisely what constitutes violent play so that families can make informed decisions.

Violence in video games can be assessed through the media content coding Likert scale provided by Common Sense Media (Coyne et al., 2023). The authors note that games are graded on a scale of 0–5; non-violent games, such as *Boggle* or *Bejeweled,* score a 0, whereas games like *Grand Theft Auto* and *Call of Duty* score a 5. Common Sense Media gives Minecraft a score of 2 out of 5 for violence from or against players, animals, and hostile creatures (Chapman, 2017). The lower rating is attributed to the fact that there is no blood or graphic gore and that the accessibility to peaceful mode provides an option that significantly reduces the violent characteristics.

Associated Risks

The relationship between violent video game exposure and adolescent aggression is not universal but is instead highly dependent on individual risk profiles. Research utilizing an eight-year longitudinal design has demonstrated differential susceptibility, identifying distinct adolescent classes based on aggression trajectories and contextual factors (Coyne et al., 2023). The adolescents most vulnerable to increased aggression from violent game play were a minority (13%) characterized by pre-existing high aggression, high depression, symptoms of Internet Gaming Disorder, and a specific physiological profile of low stress reactivity. For a larger, moderate-risk group (37%), violent game play was associated with escalating aggression, particularly when combined with poor self-regulation, though this was mitigated by high parental media monitoring. Conversely, for two other classes, one with multiple external risk factors (e.g., poverty, family stress) and another with high protective factors (e.g., high socioeconomic status, low family hostility), exposure to violent video games did not confer a substantial additional risk. It was, in some high-risk cases, even associated with decreasing aggression. Therefore, the risk is not inherent in the game itself but in the complex interplay between game exposure and an adolescent's individual disposition, mental health, and family environment.

These results, combined with Minecraft's inherently lower violent content score, suggest that the game's aggressive elements are highly workable in a therapeutic context when adolescents are also supported by the helping adults in their family and community systems. The key factor is not the game itself, but the presence of supportive adults in the adolescent's family and community systems who can provide context and guidance. Utilizing the Seven Guiding Principles in sessions and adapting them for home, clinicians and families can transition from a position of anxiety to one of empowered management, equipped with a practical framework to navigate the child's experience with the game.

Problematic Interactive Media Use and Internet Gaming Disorder

Even after guidelines regarding the nuances of screen time, concerns of problematic interactive media use and internet gaming disorder lie heavily on the minds of everyone caring for youth. Research by Coyne et al. (2023) and Thorell et al. (2024) converge on a fundamental principle: understanding Internet Gaming Disorder (IGD) necessitates moving beyond simplistic metrics, such as screen time, to a nuanced, multifaceted assessment. Both sources firmly situate IGD within a differential susceptibility framework, emphasizing that individuals vary significantly in their vulnerability to developing problematic gaming behaviors (Coyne et al., 2023; Thorell et al., 2024). This perspective is critical because, as both reviews highlight, IGD is rarely an isolated condition. The disorders consistently co-occur with other clinical factors, with Coyne et al. (2023) identifying a specific "High Gaming, High Aggression" profile characterized by high IGD symptoms and depression, while Thorell et al. (2024) corroborate that aggression and emotional distress, like depression, are frequently significant covariates in the relationship between digital media use and other conditions.

A key distinction between the sources lies in their specific evidentiary focus, yet their conclusions strongly support each other. Coyne et al.'s (2023) longitudinal findings, which used a measure adapted from DSM-IV pathological gambling criteria, offer empirical evidence of how IGD appears in high-risk adolescent groups. Thorell et al. (2024) expand on this by explicitly acknowledging IGD's status in the DSM-5 as a condition needing more research and by outlining its specific diagnostic criteria, such as tolerance and withdrawal. Moreover, Thorell et al. (2024) bolster the case for a multifaceted approach by directly comparing screen time to problematic use, concluding that links between IGD and issues like ADHD symptoms are stronger than those with screen time alone. Ultimately, the sources collectively make a convincing case that clinical focus should be on the symptomatic behaviors and related risks, rather than just the amount of time spent gaming.

The classification and understanding of gaming disorder continue to be hot topics among clinicians and researchers, mainly because of significant ambiguities in terminology. As Knibbs (2025) points out, terms like the World Health Organization's "gaming disorder," the NHS's "gaming addiction," and the academic term "gaming dependency" are frequently used interchangeably to describe all types of gaming, leading to confusion for both professionals and the public about what really constitutes a disorder. This debate is fueled by applying diagnostic criteria (often based on substance misuse) to an activity that does not follow a predictable addictive pattern and can serve as a way to cope maladaptively, avoid situations, or even build positive social connections. Knibbs (2025) also argues that the line between pathological gaming and dedicated, career-focused activities like esports is very blurry, creating a "catch-22" where the same activity is linked in some studies to increased depression and anxiety, and in others, to their reduction. As a result, Knibbs (2025) concludes that the evidence is mixed at best and calls for more rigorous research and standardized terminology to clarify these complex issues.

Heitner (2016) adopts a gentle, collaborative approach when considering the impact of gaming, acknowledging that a deeper examination may be necessary if the interest in the game leads to overwhelming stress, interferes with homework, other hobbies, and family interactions. In short, she encourages families to ask, "Does it take more than it gives?" A practical assessment question to consider would be: "Did this change after spending time with the game, or was it happening before?"

Ultimately, these necessary perspectives lead clinicians and families to reconsider the value of quality over quantity. This can be an easy decision, as the quality of time spent playing Minecraft has already been recognized as beneficial in numerous ways, as noted in this book. However, it is not unusual for parents and caregivers to express concerns about their child's interest in Minecraft, which they may fear could lead to isolation. This concern, however, often stems from a misunderstanding of Minecraft's potential as a profoundly social universe, using the child's comfort with screens as a point of possible connection.

Minecraft as the Child's Social World

Research demonstrates that the social value of digital play extends far beyond the therapy room, directly countering concerns that gaming can lead to isolation. In a study directly relevant to fostering family connections, Choo et al. (2013) examined the use of Minecraft, combined with Skype, for maintaining long-distance relationships. Their findings revealed that combining collaborative play in Minecraft with synchronous video communication provided significantly greater benefits for feelings of "togetherness" compared to using a video call alone. This empirical evidence powerfully supports the clinical aim of using Minecraft to strengthen relational bonds as discussed in Chapter 8. It suggests that the game's creative, collaborative environment serves as a shared "third space" that enriches communication, providing a tangible model for how the co-play strategies encouraged in therapy can translate into meaningful connection within a family system, whether members are in the same room or separated by miles. The specific focus on utilizing a video conference service, such as Zoom, further validates the social and relational benefits children receive when using telehealth for Minecraft in play therapy.

Digital Literacy and Awareness

A consistent thread in digital literacy guidance, from Heitner (2016) to Knibbs (2025), is the call for parents to transition from anxious monitors to active, confident mentors. This paradigm shift from being "screenworried" to "screenwise" (Heitner, 2016), involves moving beyond restrictive monitoring toward active co-engagement and curious, non-judgmental dialogue about the child's online modus operandi (Knibbs, 2025). Both experts posit that parents need not be technical experts but rather "enthusiastic tour guides" (Heitner, 2016) who provide crucial wisdom about relationships and ethics. This mentorship is operationalized through practical strategies, such as Heitner's (2016) "greenlighting" process for new apps and Knibbs' (2025) "connected parenting" (CPR) model for setting boundaries, all while acknowledging that technology companies exploit innate child vulnerabilities (Knibbs, 2025). The core, enduring tenet is that fostering healthy digital engagement depends less on technical savvy and more on committed, relational mentorship.

Practical Strategies for Managing Minecraft Use at Home

A common question for parents and caregivers is how to help children transition or "get off" the game when needed. Even families that support technology and Minecraft may face increasing struggles when asking their child to put down the game for dinner or other family or life commitments. This may have been even more difficult during the shift to post-pandemic lifestyles, as children adjusted to relying more on screens and then having to step away to return to in-person learning and social activities. These transitions can also be confusing, since much school learning happens on screens, and social playdates often involve digital games. The following strategies aim to turn these potential conflicts into opportunities for connection and growth.

A fundamental approach to managing digital play is to adopt a framework that encourages connection rather than conflict. Knibbs (2025) presents the CPR model, which stands for Consistency, Persistence, and Resistance, as a guide for connected parenting, specifically designed to address challenges such as excessive technology use. In this model, Consistency is not about strict rules, but about a child-centered approach where limits are based on a clear, internalized set of values and implemented with understanding, providing the safety of predictable boundaries. Persistence involves maintaining these boundaries with empathy, recognizing a child's frustration while calmly keeping the limit. Last, Resistance means calmly enduring the unavoidable boundary testing, which ultimately reinforces a child's sense of safety by demonstrating the predictability of their world. Children and adolescents will test boundaries like someone might push against a restraining bar on a rollercoaster. Once they trust that it is there and will not move, they can feel safe engaging in a scary or unfamiliar task. Together, this CPR method helps parents build the trust and open communication needed to effectively manage Minecraft time agreements, shifting away from an authoritarian or overly permissive style and promoting household harmony (Knibbs, 2025).

This supportive mindset can be applied in the moment using an approach based on the ACT model of therapeutic limit setting (Landreth, 2012). This three-step process emphasizes connection and coregulation instead of punishment. First, acknowledge (A) the child's feeling or desire (e.g., "I know you're having a lot of fun building and don't want to stop"). Second, communicate (C) the limit clearly and calmly (e.g., "But our agreement is that game time ends at 5:00 for dinner"). Finally, suggest or target (T) an acceptable alternative (e.g., "You can either save your game now, or I can pause it for you in one minute"). By validating the child's experience while firmly holding the boundary, the ACT model helps reduce conflict and empowers children to internalize these limits over time, transforming a potential power struggle into an opportunity to increase their WOT. Ultimately, these strategies are not just about managing screen time; they are practical exercises in coregulation as described in Chapter 8, helping the parent and child build a stronger, more attuned relationship even during conflicts.

Beyond managing moments of conflict, the most effective approach is to proactively create a family media plan during a calm moment. To avoid battles over turning off devices, shift from a reactive, authoritarian stance to a proactive, collaborative one. The best strategy is to develop a family media plan together during a calm moment, not in the heat of an argument. Start by asking your child open-ended, curious questions like: "What do you think is a good way to end the game when it is time for dinner?" Work together to set clear boundaries, such as whether permission is needed for use, daily time limits, and a consistent shutdown routine, including a screenshot of where they left off as a reminder of what they will do when they resume, and having them share their three favorite moments from that play session. Building on the therapeutic closing rituals from Chapter 7, children could also have a deliberate ending handshake with their caregiver.

To help transition to the next activity, having a list of what comes next can create a sense of predictability and expectation, which can ease any distress that might occur. This might include a chart showing the times and descriptions of upcoming activities, or even a playful map with visual representations of appointments. These tools can also be used in Minecraft, where a book and quill serve as reminders for scheduling, or a tour of a village with user-made signs can represent more detailed itineraries.

When considering collaborative agreements with limits, Heitner (2016) suggests distinguishing between content limits and time limits. This acknowledges the different impact and engagement of Minecraft over other screen-based activities, supporting families in orienting toward preferred times for Minecraft play over other choices. For example, suppose a child wants to play for 30 minutes before dinner and has difficulty ending, in that case, the solution is to redirect them to watching a YouTube video that is under 30 minutes, reminding them that they can play Minecraft when there is more time for the game.

As described in Chapter 7, shutdown reminders may need to start before the desired ending, with small reminders provided along the way. Gobbel (2023) suggests that parents view this approach as "scaffolding," where a child may initially require more support and then have that support gradually removed as they adjust to the changes. Agree to try this plan for a week, then review it to discuss what worked and what needs improvement. Support this shift by co-creating a list of fun, non-screen activities (such as board games, walks, or cooking) to help make it easier to step away from the game (see Appendix B for a full list of Minecraft-informed, offline strategies that turn in-game strengths into real-world regulation). This collaborative process mitigates power struggles by fostering mutual respect and modeling responsible behavior, transforming a potential conflict into an opportunity for connection and problem-solving.

Looking Ahead

Guided by Principles 6 and 7, this chapter resolves the challenge of integrating Minecraft into therapy by addressing concerns about screen time through cultivating digital awareness and positive engagement with the game. This reframe, akin to "digital nutrition," allows clinicians to transform the use of Minecraft in play therapy from a valid concern of escalating a potential problem into a space for connection and growth.

The clinical understanding necessary to demystify issues like PIMU and contextualize perceived violence provides a guide for clinicians and caregivers in their choice to implement Minecraft in play therapy. Practical frameworks, such as the CPR and ACT models, transform potential challenges into action, turning limit-setting battles into predictable, regulating experiences that build a child's WOT.

A foundation of digital awareness enables the relational repair discussed in Chapter 8 as clinicians prepare for the most complex clinical work. The question is no longer if the modality works, but how its power is precisely applied.

Section 3: Clinical Applications and Special Focus Populations turns to this advanced work, demonstrating the model's robust versatility with clients experiencing significant emotional dysregulation, complex trauma, and unique developmental needs, among so much more.

Helpful Tips

- **Focus on digital nutrition, not just screen time.** Prioritize the content, context, and quality of a child's engagement with Minecraft over rigid, time-based rules.
- **Become an "enthusiastic guide," not a "screenworried" monitor.** Shift from restricting access to actively mentoring the child on ethics and relationships within the game.
- **Apply the CPR model (Consistency, Persistence, Resistance)** to establish predictable, child-centered boundaries that build safety and household harmony.
- **De-escalate conflict with the ACT model.** In the moment, acknowledge the child's feeling.
- **Clearly communicate the limit and target an acceptable alternative** to promote coregulation.
- **Co-create a family media plan.** Collaboratively establish shutdown routines (e.g., taking a final screenshot, sharing three favorite moments, or a special handshake) during a calm time, not during a conflict.

Reflection Question

1 What is one specific question I could ask a family to help them move from a debate about minutes of screen time to a conversation about the "nutritional value" of their child's Minecraft engagement?

References

Barr, R., Kirkorian, H., & Radesky, J. et al (2020). Beyond screen time: A synergistic approach to a more comprehensive assessment of family media exposure during early childhood. *Frontiers in Psychology*, *11*, 1283.

Barr, R., Kirkorian, H., Radesky, J., Coyne, S., Nichols, D., Blanchfield, O., Rusnak, S., Stockdale, L., Ribner, A., Durnez, J., Epstein, M., Heimann, M., Koch, F.-S., Sundqvist, A., Birberg-Thornberg, U., Konrad, C., Slussareff, M., Bus, A., Bellagamba, F., & Fitzpatrick, C. (2020). Beyond screen time: A synergistic approach to a more comprehensive assessment of family media exposure during early childhood. *Frontiers in Psychology*, *11*, 1283. https://doi.org/10.3389/fpsyg.2020.01283

Bickham, D. S., Cingel, D. P., Nathanson, A. I., Rose, C. A., Johnson, C. R., & Scharrer, E. (2025). Parenting and screens during middle childhood. In D. A. Christakis & L. Hale (Eds.), *Handbook of children and screens* (pp. 395–402). Springer.

Chapman, D. (2017). Parents' guide to Minecraft. Commonsensemedia.org. *Common Sense Media*. https://www.commonsensemedia.org/game-reviews/minecraft

Choo, A., Karamnejad, M., & May, A. (2013). *Maintaining long distance togetherness synchronous communication with Minecraft and Skype*. Games Innovation Conference, 2013 IEEE International. https://doi.org/10.1109/IGIC.2013.6659138

Coyne, S. M., Warburton, W., Swit, C., Stockdale, L., & Dyer, W. J. (2023). Who is most at risk for developing physical aggression after playing violent video games? An individual differences perspective from early adolescence to emerging adulthood. *Journal of Youth and Adolescence*, 52, 719–733. https://doi.org/10.1007/s10964-023-01739-0

Gobbel, R. (2023). *Raising kids with big, baffling behaviors*. Jessica Kingsley Publishers.

Heitner, D. (2016). *Screenwise: Helping kids thrive (and survive) in their digital world*. Taylor & Francis.

Knibbs, C. (2025). *Managing your gaming and social media habits: From science to solutions*. Routledge.

Landreth, G. L. (2012). *Play therapy: The art of the relationship* (3rd ed.). Routledge.

Marciano, L., Dubicka, B., Magis-Weinberg, L., Morese, R., Viswanath, K., & Weber, R. (2025). Digital media, cognition, and brain development in adolescence. In D. A. Christakis & L. Hale (Eds.), *Handbook of children and screens* (pp. 21–30). Springer International Publishing.

Mayo Clinic Staff. (2024). *Screen time for kids: How much is too much?* Mayo Clinic. https://www.mayoclinic.org/healthy-lifestyle/childrens-health/in-depth/screen-time/art-20047952?p=1

Minecraft Staff. (n.d.). *Minecraft Parents' Guide*. Minecraft.Net. https://www.minecraft.net/en-us/article/parents--guide-minecraft

Ministry of Health, Singapore. (2025). *Guidance on screen use in Children.* https://www.moh.gov.sg/others/resources-and-statistics/guidance-on-screen-use/

Reich, S. M., Aladé, F., Cingel, D. P., Takeuchi, L., Warren, R., & Uhls, Y. T. (2025). Media and parenting: Current findings and future directions. In D. A. Christakis & L. Hale (Eds.), *Handbook of children and screens* (pp. 379–387). Springer.

Santos, R. M. S., Mendes, C. G., Miranda, D. M., & Romano-Silva, M. A. (2022). The association between screen time and attention in children: A systematic review. *Developmental Neuropsychology*, *47*(4), 175–192. https://doi.org/10.1080/87565641.2022.2064863

Thorell, L. B., Burén, J., Ström Wiman, J., Sandberg, D., & Nutley, S. B. (2024). Longitudinal associations between digital media use and ADHD symptoms in children and adolescents: A systematic literature review. *European Child & Adolescent Psychiatry*, *33*, 2503–2526. https://doi.org/10.1007/s00787-022-02130-3

Section III

Clinical Applications and Special Focus Populations

Chapter 10

Working with Emotional Distress and Dysregulation

"Okay, I think I'm on board and ready to try this for my child. However, I have one more concern. When they play the game, they get very upset when they lose. If something doesn't go their way or if they die and can't find their stuff, they become really sad. It's not always like that, but sometimes they get so upset they don't want to play anymore. It breaks my heart to see because I know how much they love playing. They also experience intensely upsetting moments at school, and I worry that their reactions might be pushing friends away. Maybe that's something you can help with, too?"

"Yes! I can definitely help your child learn to better manage their emotions and reactions in more effective and less disruptive ways. We'll focus on how these issues occur at home and at school, but first, we'll start by understanding what happens when playing the game."

"Wow, that sounds perfect. I can see how your clients really love this approach. You mentioned earlier that you focus on what is happening in the game for the child and how it impacts their brain and body. Can you tell me more about that?"

"Great question. Understanding what is happening in the child's brain and body while they're playing is so important. Here is some information I've learned about the developing brain, the nervous system, and what happens when big emotions happen - even when playing Minecraft ..."

Many children who attend play therapy are identified by their parents or caregivers as experiencing emotional distress and dysregulation that affect their relationships at school and home. Due to Minecraft's stimulating gameplay, symptoms of distress and dysregulation can become manageable during the session as the child engages with the challenges in the game. Opportunities to practice naming emotions, identifying needs, asking for help, and using coping skills learned through coregulation can occur as early as the initial moments of starting the game.

If there are issues with the hardware and technology, or even resistance to meeting with the therapist, we can begin to apply an approach

DOI: 10.4324/9781003614784-13

that helps name the emotions that arise, validates the child's experience, and offers our presence, grounding, and coregulation to help them move through the distress. The support provided to clients in these moments can begin to establish an accessible, internal template for navigating moments of distress outside of the playroom – even if the starting point is with challenges before the game is played. This is another benefit of the first four guiding principles.

Other workable moments that can occur during the session include instances when a client feels frustrated with the gameplay, mistakes that happen, dissatisfaction with choices made, interactions with other players or the play therapist, and at the end of the session when it is time to log off. These experiences create opportunities for the clinician to assess and work with the child's Window of Tolerance (WOT) while working with the child's nervous system activation as it is stimulated through the game.

This chapter focuses on children who struggle with emotional distress and dysregulation by bringing together the first five guiding principles discussed in the previous chapters. The guiding principles will continue to serve as helpful reminders throughout all the chapters in this section, as play therapists are encouraged to focus on what the child is experiencing and needing emotionally and relationally while playing Minecraft. Specific directive interventions are also provided in this chapter and throughout the other chapters in this section to support clinicians in working with the various clinical presentations that may arise for their clients. As play therapists consider what the child is showing us, their experience in the interactions, and how they can coregulate with the child, it is also important to consider brain development and the brain's relationship to the child's nervous system functions and WOT. This chapter will also focus on how the child perceives their environment and the impact this has on their brain and body.

The Developing Brain and Nervous System Function

To begin understanding what happens when children have emotional responses while playing Minecraft, it's helpful to start with a current understanding of brain and body development in children. When meeting with parents and caregivers for the first time, I present this information as an educational supplement that provides a framework for shared language and a mutual understanding of what might be happening in their child's brain and body during moments of distress. This also leads to understanding the appropriate expectations of what might happen in significant moments, which can later lead to problem-solving and the desired behavior. This language will also be helpful throughout the rest of this book, as these concepts will be referenced in the following chapters.

In *The Whole-Brain Child* (2012), Daniel Siegel and Tina Payne Bryson introduced clinicians to a three-part visual description of a child's brain by inviting readers to make a fist with their fingers over their thumb, representing the brainstem, midbrain, and prefrontal cortex. To help parents understand how these brain regions relate to their child's experiences, I simplify the anatomical language while preserving Siegel and Bryson's core framework. These three parts help illustrate key functions: the brainstem (our most primitive region) operates unconsciously, managing vital functions like breathing and reflexes. The midbrain serves as our survival center, constantly scanning for threats and triggering protective reactions. This is what Siegel and Bryson refer to as our "lizard brain." The prefrontal cortex (the last to develop, maturing into our late 20s) enables higher-order thinking like impulse control and problem-solving.

For children, this means their developing brain is still under construction, particularly in the logical "wizard brain" (prefrontal cortex) (Siegel & Bryson, 2012). While children can certainly solve math problems or create elaborate stories, their developing prefrontal regions remain vulnerable to being overridden by the more reactive midbrain, especially during moments of intense activation, such as when they are upset about having to end a Minecraft game or suddenly lose all their items in a battle. This explains why children often react impulsively rather than respond thoughtfully to challenges. While this is a developmentally normal process, understandably, it can frustrate parents and caregivers, especially when it comes to playing video games.

These brain systems work in connection with the autonomic nervous system (Porges, 2011). The midbrain-limbic system guides sympathetic (fight/flight) and parasympathetic (collapse/shutdown or connect) responses that keep us safe. Polyvagal Theory (Porges, 2011) clarifies these pathways as the sympathetic system, which drives behaviors associated with aggression through fight-or-flight responses, and the parasympathetic branch, which mediates either shutdown (dorsal vagal collapse) or social engagement (ventral vagal connection). Similar to Siegel and Bryson's "lizard brain" and "wizard brain," Robyn Gobbel (2023) uses animal metaphors such as the "owl brain" for the logical thought processes that occur in the prefrontal cortex, the "watch dog" for the fight/flight sympathetic response, and the "possum" for the shutdown of the dorsal vagal collapse. Making distinctions between the logical responses of the prefrontal cortex and the instinctual reactions of the midbrain-limbic system through the use of accessible metaphors helps make the complex nature of neurobiology more accessible.

Understanding these systems can reframe how clinicians and caregivers conceptualize what is happening in a child's brain and body when they play Minecraft. A child's nervous system might recruit hyper-aroused "watchdog" reactions (acting out to create safety) or hypo-aroused "possum" responses (shutting down when overwhelmed) as adaptive attempts to cope with perceived threats in the environment. While adults may not view the things that happen in Minecraft as a tangible threat to the child playing, it can certainly feel like a big deal for them. Readers may already be thinking of children in their lives who struggle with these different emotional expressions when something goes wrong in their Minecraft world, as well as at school and at home.

What can be taken away from this understanding is that children can have big, emotionally driven fight/flight or collapse/shutdown behaviors as reactions from events, situations, and general stimuli that override their thinking and decision-making skills in a way that is very different from an adult who has a developmentally larger capacity to think through situations. Mona Delahooke's book, *Beyond Behaviours* (2019), applies the theoretical frameworks from Polyvagal Theory and interpersonal neurobiology to clinicians and parents curious about their children's brain and body responses. Delahooke (2019) encourages clinicians and parents to consider the child's observable behavior as the tip of an iceberg. In other words, the visible behavior is just a small indicator of what is really happening beneath the surface. This analogy serves as a reminder to consider that children's behaviors, even while playing Minecraft, can also involve more complex activations that are less observable in the moment.

What Happens in the Brain and Body While Playing the Game

While playing Minecraft together in the play therapy sessions, therapists can observe, learn, and conceptualize what happens in moments where their clients are dysregulated so that they can help the child and their family learn more about how their brains and bodies work when in other challenging situations. A child's big reaction to something that happens in the game can be viewed as the tip of the iceberg, and our clinical approach in the moment can help go beneath the surface to become curious about what is happening underneath. During moments of high stakes and intense situations in the game, a child's brain and body can be on high alert as they prioritize what they want to accomplish. When something goes wrong, it can feel like something unsafe has happened, and their "lizard brain" and autonomic nervous system trigger a survival response. For adults watching a child play the game, it may seem like the child has been defeated and has to start again, but for the child playing, it can feel like the end of the world.

Recognizing how the brain develops and the functions of the three distinct parts can inform how clinicians relate to and conceptualize the child's experiences playing Minecraft. The Third and Fourth Guiding

Principles – playing to be in the experience of the game with the child and modeling how to work with the stimulation in the game to help the child learn more about themselves while playing – provide the ground for using Minecraft intentionally and clinically. As described in Chapter 6, interventions that occur through coregulation and help build interoception and increase their WOT are often the starting point for clients who are struggling with emotional distress and dysregulation. For these clients, we are likely to employ a non-directive play therapy approach, where we let the child's play and behaviors, rooted in dysregulated nervous system states, guide us in the session. In a non-directive session, the approach to one's interventions involves naming the emotions that arise, identifying what may be needed in the moment, and applying coping skills. This approach can help the child learn more about how their brain can stay present and their body stay grounded.

Other clients and perhaps many of the adolescents in one's practice may have a wider WOT. They can benefit from directive play therapy interventions that rely more on the prefrontal cortex to think through past problems and problem-solve upcoming scenarios that they already sense may be challenging. This can include discussing emotions that they can expect to encounter, identifying helpful peers and allies in distressing situations, and visualizing successful steps to problem-solve potential problems. For some adolescents, playing Minecraft serves as an entry point to building a positive relationship, allowing them to determine if they feel safe and can trust their clinician. In such situations, interventions may occur while playing the game and engaging in conversation, or more often, when taking a break from the game and having a deeper discussion, with the client using the controller as a fidget.

The following clinical vignettes will demonstrate examples of how these concepts might manifest during different moments of playing Minecraft, while considering the understanding of brain development and the stress behaviors that arise from dysregulated nervous system states. To begin, it will be helpful to reflect on a scenario that helps the reader consider the different responses children may have from adults due to their developing brains.

Working with the Child's Perception

The Second Guiding Principle in Chapter 4 orients the play therapist to the notion that clinical therapeutic work can begin even before the game is played. The chapter references the powerful exploration that can happen as players choose how they want to represent themselves through their character in the game, and the mindfulness interventions that can be integrated into the world. However, in some cases, the clinical opportunity to support moments of distress and dysregulation can happen even before the child logs into the game. The following vignette provides two examples that illustrate the differences between an adult's and a child's perception of the game, even when challenges arise at the beginning of the session.

Clinical Vignette 1a

As an adult, consider a situation where you have a scheduled time to play Minecraft online with your friends. You've had a really hard week, and you've been looking forward to this fun time where you can let everything go and shake off the stress you've been holding. You log in to your computer and start messaging with your friends, who are already logging in to the world. They are excited and interact with expressive emojis as you all are getting ready to play.

Take a moment to consider how you might be feeling: can you name the emotions to yourself? Can you identify what sensations arise in your body? Is there a specific moment like this that comes to mind? Now imagine how you might feel when you suddenly realize that you are getting error messages and cannot log into the game.

As your mind races, you come to the thought that your online account subscription may have expired.

Thinking quickly, you work through the steps in your head: you need to log into a different account, authorize passwords and verifications, locate your payment method, and resync your game and online accounts. In your mind, you can imagine this will take about 5 minutes at the most. You message your friends about what happened and let them know you'll be in the game shortly.

A similar scenario through the eyes of a middle-aged child who struggles with disappointment and behaviors rooted in dysregulated nervous system states can look very different.

Clinical Vignette 1b

As a middle-aged child, you have a scheduled time to play Minecraft online with your friends. You've had a really hard day at school: they did not have your favorite hot lunch, your best friend was out sick, and the substitute teacher didn't know it was your turn to take care of a class pet, leading you to miss out on one of your favorite class activities. Coming home from this crummy day, you've been looking forward to this fun time where you can let everything go and forget about all the things that happened. You log in to your computer and start messaging with your friends, who are already logging in to the world. You can sense their excitement in the messages, and they are getting ready to play.

Suddenly, you see error messages popping up on your screen saying that you are unable to connect to the world. You immediately begin yelling for the adult you're with that afternoon. When they come over, they seem confused and say that they'll have to look around a bit to see what went wrong. Your whole world feels like it is shutting down as the events of the day all catch up to you. Tears well up in your eyes, and feeling helpless and hopeless, you lie on the floor.

Many of the children who come to play therapy for emotional distress behaviors rooted in dysregulated nervous system states might have visible external reactions that are driven by an internal physiological response that perceives the stimulus in their environment as a threat. Children can exhibit a sympathetic fight-or-flight response, which manifests as anger and upset, often accompanied by tears of sadness for not being able to play and pleading with adults to fix the problem. In some situations, they may exhibit a dorsal vagal response, where their body's physiological freeze/collapse response leads to curling up and shutting down. They may not want to answer questions or share more about what happened because their physiologically distressed state makes it challenging for them to access the logical part of their brain. This can be frustrating for adults who want to help the child, ideally wanting to see their child in a ventral vagal state, where they are calm and collected and can use their prefrontal cortex to think through the following steps.

In the first example, the adult was able to access their prefrontal cortex as they felt the impact of the event and then thought through what they needed to do to resolve it and what would come next. Polyvagal Theory (Porges, 2011) explains how our nervous system automatically reacts to safety or danger. Feeling safe allows us to connect with others; feeling threatened triggers survival modes, such as fighting, fleeing, or freezing. When the ventral vagal system is active, one can feel safe enough to stay calm, connect with others, and think more clearly. In the second example, the child's behavioral response reflected their autonomic nervous system's reaction to a perceived threat – that they would not be able to play with their friends and that their hopes for the afternoon were ruined. Parents reading this might be able to relate to this experience, and play therapists may also think of clients who would respond similarly.

Suppose the play therapist was with the child in the second example. In that case, one might observe that the child has a limited WOT for accommodating distress, as their perception of safety was unable to handle the unexpected change. This can be conceptualized as a moment when the autonomic nervous system activates a stress response that prevents them from working through the problem-solving needed. Referencing the Developmental Tasks from Chapter 5, the child could be working through the setup of "Is the world okay?" triggered by the unpredictable nature of access to the game not being dependable.

As the process in the previous chapters demonstrated, the play therapist could coregulate with the child and bring the focus toward soothing the emotions related to the upset of not being able to play the game as they imagined. This approach could help the child feel safe as they move toward a ventral vagal state, where they can be grounded and connected with the play therapist and caregiver. As these moments continue to occur in play therapy, the child begins to develop a template for managing their distress in new ways.

Soothing, coregulating responses from the play therapist can be applied and accommodated to help the child take as much time as needed. During the initial stages of working with a client, it can take significantly longer for the child to return to their WOT, allowing them to be more capable of moving forward with the session. In some cases, helping the child soothe through the initial distress could be the whole focus of the session. If these disruptions continue in future sessions, a marker of progress can be how quickly the child moves through their distress and returns to their WOT.

Being with the child's experience of distress when playing Minecraft – even when it is at the start of a session when something goes wrong with the technology – also relates to the first guiding principle that the play therapist does not need to be a good player at Minecraft to relate and attune to the child playing the game. Even the clinician who is not skilled at playing Minecraft, or maybe even brand new to the game, can still help the child recognize their emotions, identify what they might need, ask for help, and apply the coping skills learned from coregulation in the moment. If the above example happened at the start of the play therapy session, the therapist would likely feel the emotions communicated by the child in the moment (the setup), they could coregulate together through the distress (Chapter 6 – The Experience of the Clinician) and begin working with the child's ability to hold and manage their bodies distress (building interoception and increasing WOT).

Considering the previous example, this is how a play therapist might respond from the framework of the Seven Guiding Principles:

Clinical Vignette 1c

"Oh no! This is so upsetting! I'm not sure what is going wrong with our game today. I can understand how sad and angry you must be." I pause and take a deep breath, releasing it with a big, audible exhale. "I can imagine how much you must have been looking forward to playing together today, and this was not how you expected it to go." I'm watching the child's body language; they may still be shut down, and that's okay. I may notice that they're rocking slightly or fidgeting as a way to self-soothe. This tells me that they are upset, but they can manage the distress caused by my emotional communication. I normalize the situation by adding: "These upsets can happen sometimes. There might be a small fix that can get us playing again in 5 minutes. I know it's not what you expected or wanted, and I hope we can get through it quickly."

Depending on the child's response, I may stay with their distress for a more extended period. In some cases, they may begin problem-solving or working with their parent or caregiver if they are online and need to resolve an issue on their end. If it looks like it may not be resolved quickly, and if the child appears to be moving from the shut-down dorsal vagal state into the connected ventral vagal state, I may choose to move forward by connecting with the child's wizard and owl brain by offering a small choice for the next step.

"It doesn't seem like we are going to be able to play right now. I know this is not what we expected, and I would still like to play together in another way if that's okay with you." I pause to observe their response. If there is a nod of the head or some affirmation, I will then offer two choices. "Would you like to play Uno together or Battleship?" These choices can be any number of options based on what is available in your practice or your history with the child.

The play therapist's response in this situation can take many different forms, depending on the child's level of distress, the rapport established between the child and play therapist, what happened earlier in the day or week, and the child's current WOT. Readers new to Minecraft may be concerned that there will always be disruptions with the technology or the hardware; that is not the case, and it is not what is intended to be demonstrated. This example begins to set the stage for how even introducing the notion of playing the game can create workable moments of therapeutic and clinical interventions for our child clients who may struggle with emotional distress and dysregulation. It has also been my observation, based on anecdotal experience, that our clients reveal to us what they need help with in their own unique ways; this often means that their most significant challenges will be present in the relationship from the outset.

Interventions for Expanding the Window of Tolerance

Chapter 6 introduced the importance of the therapist's awareness of themselves to coregulate with the child, helping to build the child's skills of emotional awareness and interoception while expanding their WOT. When clinicians play Minecraft with children, there are many ways they can intentionally support the client's WOT, either when the child's capacity has exceeded its limit or to help them recognize their own levels of activation. This can occur even at the beginning of the session or game, particularly when working with individuals who are experiencing distress and intense emotions.

Children who are initiating or joining a new Minecraft game encounter a moment that requires them to reflect on their WOT and capacity for challenge through the initial choice of whether they want to play in Creative or Survival mode. The child may not recognize this explicitly, but their preference to either explore a non-threatening world or immediately enter a world of danger is one way they are exercising control over the level of stimulation they want to feel and experience. A child who has already had a stimulating day may choose to find peaceful and relaxing moments while playing in Creative mode. In contrast, a child who chooses Survival mode understands that they will encounter moments of disappointment, frustration, and possibly even anger if things do not go their way.

One of the ways Minecraft implicitly supports children in practicing control over their WOT is through the wide range of customizable options available to them in their gameplay experience. Controlling in-game features such as the weather, teleporting to other players, and sleeping in beds to offset the nighttime invasion of mobs all offer children the opportunity to consider how much stimulation they want and how they might exercise external control to stay grounded in their gaming experience by staying within their WOT. Another point to consider is the level of difficulty clients might choose to play in Survival mode. Clients can choose between four modes: peaceful, easy, normal, and hardcore – each offering increasing levels of challenge and difficulty.

"Easy, Medium, Hard, or Insanity Triple Plus?!"

Just as the game offers features to help children control their level of stimulation, allowing the child to have control over the level of difficulty they experience while playing with their parent or therapist can also serve as a powerful relational intervention. This can be a paradigm shift for many play therapists and can raise meaningful dialogue about the benefits of intentionally "letting a child win" when they know an adult can beat them. Some adults will play as hard as they can against a child as a way to help the child learn to manage distress. While there can be benefits in a child having an authentic play relationship with adults in their lives, it may not be the best intentional therapeutic intervention, as it lacks the opportunity for the child to turn inward and build the insight and recognition needed to self-assess their WOT and then ask for what they need to manage their distress. An alternative to playing as hard as one can against the child is to ask the child how hard they want you to play. This can also provide clinicians with a directive intervention that also facilitates non-directive play.

This concept was introduced during my certification training as a Synergetic Play Therapist by my supervisor, Polly Douglass, who adapted the idea from Lawrence Cohen (2013). When playing Minecraft with a client, there are opportunities for them to challenge the play therapist directly. This could occur during building challenges, parallel play in Survival mode, or even player-versus-player battles that the client might initiate. In those instances, it was suggested to me that I ask the child how hard they would like me to play. I initially had reservations about this because I thought the child would know that I was letting them win if I played more easily than I typically would, or that I would defeat them quickly if I played skillfully, which might cause a big upset in the moment. What unfolded were natural and beautiful moments as my clients turned inward to assess their own capacity for distress on that particular day and moment, and then advocated for themselves with what they needed.

Providing the child the opportunity to reflect on how hard a challenge they were seeking in their play can also become a way to track progress. Clients who once asked for easy or medium difficulty when we played together might later be asking for hard, even though they may not be able to win or defeat me. However, their ability to cope with and manage the challenge serves as a way to increase their capacity to handle distressing challenges in all areas of their lives. Where a child might once have reacted to the stress of a challenging game with fight/flight (hyperarousal) or shutdown (hypoarousal), they can learn to stay grounded through the support of the play therapist. In these calmer moments, their "wizard" or "owl" brain (prefrontal cortex) can recognize the challenge and stay engaged in play, and even ask for different levels of difficulty in the challenge, if needed.

Recognizing Progress

Positive shifts, both relationally and in gameplay, can be observed as progress in the play therapy sessions when the child begins naming their emotions independently and then asks for what they need or implements coping skills on their own. The third case vignette in Chapter 6 provides the example of how a child was overstimulated by the challenges in the game, but then remembered they could control that stimulation by making it to their bed and sleeping through the night. Another example is the child who recognizes they are feeling frustrated and wants to take a break to play with something else in the room, then returns to the game a few minutes later. These new levels of awareness can lead children to notice their own levels of stimulation at home and, as the day progresses, the impact of events throughout the school day, and even as they look ahead to the weekend or long family outings.

Clinical Vignette 2

"I want to have a battle with you, but you can only use the weapons I give you." We are in Creative mode, and the client is dropping some items for me to add to my inventory before we switch to Survival. "Here, you can have a wooden sword and a shield."

I take the items offered to me and notice the client is beginning to equip themselves in netherite armor and a netherite sword – one of the strongest items in the game that could be used for battle. I am at a disadvantage, yet I also know that I could be more skilled at battle than this client. I offer them the choice of how hard they want me to play.

"Yes, we can definitely go into battle together! Do you want me to play easy, medium, hard, or INSANITY TRIPLE PLUS?!" I raise my voice and animate my expression as I describe the last level of intensity and challenge. The child laughs and immediately requests insanity triple plus.

"Okay, that means I am going to play as hard as I can - just like I am playing another adult."

We begin the battle, and as I suspected, I am dodging attacks and doing damage even with my wooden sword. I notice the child's non-verbal body language; their face is wincing, and they are pulling away from the screen. In a soft, timid voice, they say, "I mean easy…easy…I want you to play easy."

"Yes, absolutely!" I immediately stop attacking and expose myself to their attacks. Within moments, I'm defeated.

"YES!! I took you down! You really couldn't do much with that wooden sword and no armor." The client's body language

straightened up, and with the inflection of their voice, demonstrated pride and accomplishment.

"You totally knew how to defeat me! I felt so powerless with that wooden sword."

"Let's play again, but this time let's try medium."

We continue to play, and at medium intensity, I get a few hits in. The battle takes longer, and I notice the client holding their breath at times and then letting out big sighs. Eventually, they defeat me, and with the same pride and sense of accomplishment, they acknowledge that the battle took longer.

"Wow, that was intense," I add. "I'm going to take a break for a moment to shake off all the tension I was holding in my arms while we battled (prompting interoception, and the coping skill of progressive muscle relaxation.)

"Yeah, I was tense too. Hey, would you like to see my Pokémon cards?" (Adapting their own coping skill of taking a break from the stimulation.)

"I don't know a lot about Pokémon, so you'll have to teach me."

Clients who are working with exploring their WOT find ways to make the requests and adjustments they need to feel good and empowered in the moment. Although it appears that they are in a contest, it is not about winning or losing – it is about how they recognize the ability to turn inward and notice how much stimulation and challenge they can accommodate, and how to recognize when it is too much.

In the vignette above, when the child asks for the clinician to play "easy," what is really being communicated is that their WOT has reached its threshold. They are either about to have a hyperaroused (fight or flight) sympathetic response, or a hypoaroused (shut down or collapse) parasympathetic response. By asking to play "easy," they are finding a way to regulate the external intensity that they are being exposed to in the moment. This is also the beginning of how the child clients begin to explore feelings of confidence and mastery. Referencing the Developmental Tasks from Chapter 5, the child could be working through the setup of "How well can I do it?" initiated through a competitive play style.

For children who have big, distressing emotions, the impact of having reactive behaviors might lead them to feel insecure and insufficient. The next chapter builds on the information discussed and delves deeper into how to support children who suffer from negative self-talk and how to foster self-esteem during challenging moments.

Looking Ahead

Playing Minecraft with clients during their sessions naturally creates opportunities for moments in the game that can cause distress in the child. Those moments provide clinicians with the opportunities to work with the nervous system activation of physiological distress and the behaviors of the big emotions that arise as a protective strategy to soothe the distress, as they happen in real time. When the distress caused by the game activates a child, their brain and body are stimulated with the natural protective functions of their autonomic nervous system. For some children, there is a small capacity to handle and manage this distress. By playing Minecraft with the child, clinicians and caregivers can help increase the child's capacity to tolerate these intense moments by working within their WOT and helping them manage their activated nervous system. When these areas of focus come together, our clients who struggle with emotional distress and dysregulation can develop their ability to name their emotions, identify their needs, ask for help, find meaningful ways to cope, learn more about themselves, and, most importantly, have fun.

Helpful Tips

- **Therapeutic Focus on Dysregulation:** Minecraft sessions are intentionally used to work with moments of distress, as challenges within the game (like getting upset when losing items or encountering tech issues) provide opportunities to practice naming emotions, identifying needs, asking for help, and applying coping skills through coregulation.
- **Understand the Developing Brain:** Children's intense, impulsive reactions (e.g., frustration over ending the game) are understood neurobiologically: the developing prefrontal cortex (the logical "wizard brain") is vulnerable to being overridden by the reactive midbrain/limbic system (the survival center or "lizard brain").
- **Validate the Threat Perception:** The therapist must recognize that what happens in the game can feel like "the end of the world" to the child, triggering an autonomic nervous system survival response (fight/flight or shutdown), even if it doesn't appear as a tangible threat to the adult.
- **Coregulate to Expand the WOT:** The primary clinical response to a child's activation is to use the clinicians regulated presence to coregulate the distress, helping the child move toward a connected ventral vagal state. This process intentionally works with the child's nervous system to expand their WOT for challenging moments.
- **Empower Control over Stimulation:** Clinicians can use directive interventions, such as asking the child to choose the level of challenge (e.g., "easy, medium, hard" for a battle) or allowing them to control

customizable features (like Creative vs. Survival mode), enabling the child to self-assess their capacity for distress and advocate for their needs.

Reflection Question

1 Think of a client who becomes easily frustrated. What is one customizable game feature (e.g., difficulty mode, or competitive challenge) I could proactively offer them control over to help them practice assessing their own capacity and advocating for their needs before they become dysregulated?

References

Cohen, L. J. (2013). *The opposite of worry: The playful parenting approach to childhood anxieties and fears*. Ballantine Books.

Delahooke, M. (2019). *Beyond behaviours: Using brain science and compassion to understand and solve children's behavioural challenges*. John Murray.

Gobbel, R. (2023). *Raising kids with big, baffling behaviors*. Jessica Kingsley Publishers.

Porges, S. W. (2011). *The polyvagal theory: Neurophysiological foundations of emotions, attachment, communication, and self-regulation*. W. W. Norton & Company.

Siegel, D. J., & Bryson, T. P. (2012). *The whole-brain child: 12 revolutionary strategies to nurture your child's development, survive everyday parenting struggles, and help your family thrive*. Scribe Publications.

Chapter 11

Negative Self-Talk and Building Self-Esteem

Parents of the child I am about to meet with have mentioned in their intake that their child suffers from low self-esteem and negative self-talk. When things get hard for them, they tend to make negative statements about themselves, often expressing self-hatred and believing they are bad. In the initial session with the parents, they elaborate on how the child is not bad or inadequate at all. However, any attempts to remind them of how much they are loved and all the things they succeed at are met with resistance and a doubling down on their negative beliefs.

During my first session with the child, they requested to play in Survival mode, and when creating the game, they turned off the "keep inventory" setting. A feeling of discomfort arises in my stomach as I recognize this game setting as a way of playing with high pressure and high risk. I reflect on my conversation with the parents during their intake and their concerns about the child's negative self-talk. I draw attention to my concern and name my own fears.

"Wow, this is going to be intense! I'm actually not very good at Survival mode, and I'm already feeling worried that I'm going to have a hard time in this world if I lose my inventory and have to look for it each time." That statement is true for me, and I quickly shift side-to-side in my seat to shake out some of the tension of the anxiety.

"I'm really good at Minecraft, so I'm not worried. I even want to have my own YouTube channel."

After the first day cycle of mining for materials, they are defeated, lose all their inventory, and spawn far away from where they died. They immediately put their controller down and fall to their side in a fetal-like position. I hear murmurs that they are "so stupid, can't do anything right, and hate everything" that they do.

A child's experience of the world is so small, yet their minds are full of imagination, creativity, and endless possibilities. This is a strength that many adults cherish in children and may not want to lose in themselves; however, this can become a disruptive challenge when the child's imaginary

DOI: 10.4324/9781003614784-14

perception of themself bumps up against the natural boundaries and consequences of the world around them. An endless imagination can create narratives about who the child "should" be or what they "should" be able to achieve, creating narratives that are too big to attain. Nowhere is this collision between a child's ideal self and their lived experience more immediate and visible than in Minecraft, where an imaginative vision can be thwarted by a misclick, a creeper explosion, or the simple limitations of a skill still in development. This gap between imagination and reality can leave the child with feelings and sensations that are much too difficult. Negative self-talk or self-aggressive statements can occur when a child's experience of big, upsetting feelings becomes too much to handle, and their brain tries to take over with an idea or fantasy of themselves that overrides the feeling of the distressing emotion. In many cases, it becomes more manageable for the child to punish themselves for not meeting their idealized sense of self, rather than staying with the deep, intense emotion that lies underneath their fantasy.

The experience of the child's external reality colliding with the child's ideal perception in the moment creates a jarring conflict of mind and body that can feel like an aggressive attack on oneself. Thinking, verbalizing, and believing negative statements about oneself can be a non-conscious way to find power and control over an uncomfortable experience while also directing the focus of the experience from the sensations in the body to the more workable and tolerable aspects of one's imaginative mind. A shift in perception of oneself that results in negative self-statements and low self-esteem can be an indicator that the child is in a self-preservation, protective mode. Referencing the framework of the Polyvagal Theory (Porges, 2011) as described in the previous chapter, the autonomic nervous system drives hyperaroused or hyporaroused behaviors based on how the child's nervous system perceives the stimuli in their environment. In the example at the start of the chapter, the child's nervous system unconsciously perceives losing as a threat, and the protective behavior is expressed through both self-aggressive statements and physical shutdown.

For play therapists and the families they are supporting, reframing the negative self-talk from a system of belief toward a strategy of protection and feeling something different than what is happening in the body, can be an empowering way to deactivate the charge and impact of hearing a child make hurtful statements about themselves while also guiding the helping adults toward affirmation of the child's experience. Utilizing the approach of naming emotions and identifying the feelings underneath them, growth-oriented statements can be offered as a cognitive coping skill to help the child *feel into* their experience. When the child begins to feel into their emotional experience, they can then shift their previous cognitive coping strategy of negative self-talk into a new way of understanding how they relate to big emotions in challenging moments. It is from this place of felt understanding, rather than cognitive correction, that authentic self-esteem can begin to grow. This approach can be a powerful intervention that offers the opportunity to be utilized when playing Minecraft in conjunction with the framework of the Seven Guiding Principles.

It can be easy and natural for helping adults to challenge negative self-talk and offer counter statements and observations immediately. Of course, we do not want the child to feel angry at themselves, to hate themselves, and to believe that everything that goes wrong is their fault. As adults, we know those negative beliefs are not true, and we can understand what a hurtful experience that is for a child to feel. We may even have our own history with low self-esteem and negative self-talk, and we knowingly do not want that pain for the children in our lives. It is normal for adults and parents to offer opposing statements, deny the "truth" the child believes, provide compliments, and offer plenty of counterexamples. This is so natural because, in many cases, they are likely all true – the child is being overly hard on themselves, and there are plenty of counterexamples one can offer in hopes of easing their hurtful emotions. Where this strategy falls short, however, is that while those actions help relieve and soothe the pain of the experience for the adults, they continue to leave pain with the child, as it is not witnessing and validating the physiological truth of the experience in their own body.

Working with Negative Self-Talk and Building Self-Esteem

Clients that we see in play therapy may be coming in specifically to work on decreasing negative self-talk and increasing self-esteem. Parents may identify these issues during the initial intake sessions, or they may arise alongside other clinical goals the child is working on. In other cases, it may not be on the parents' radar, and it may be something that we, as clinicians, observe during the session while playing Minecraft together. As the previous chapters have made clear, children play Minecraft because it involves choices, interactions, and ways to express themselves that are meaningful and important to them. When something is so significant in a child's life, it can be normal for pressure and expectations to build up until they become overwhelming. So, when does negative self-talk and low self-esteem become a clinical focus of the treatment plan? The indicator I look for when assessing the impact of these dynamics, whether in an intake or during gameplay, is how the pattern of negative self-talk and low self-esteem affects the child's autonomic nervous system and their ability to remain engaged in the game experience.

Clinical Vignettes

Consider the clinical vignette at the beginning of the chapter, where a child initiates a potentially challenging session. This may lead the child to become self-critical and shut down, as indicated by the dorsal vagal response that can occur when they are outside their Window of Tolerance (WOT). Now consider the next situation that could arise with a different client:

A child is working on a build in Creative mode. While they are building, they tell you about their friends at school and a new friend they have just met. Halfway through the session, the child says, "I'm horrible at this - this looks really bad. My friend Alyssa can build these so much better. She showed me one like this in her world, and it's just way better."

"What do you like better about hers?"

"Well, she is really good at using redstone and builds different types of doors that can move with a lever."

The child is saying all this while they're continuing to build. They stay engaged in the dialogue, and it's observed that they take deep breaths along the way, pausing to make eye contact at times, and even commenting on what I am working on.

As the time is nearing the end of the session, they say, "Actually, this looks pretty good. I tried to make a red stone door here, but I want to spend more time on it next time."

These two examples are drastically different and yet not so far off from what therapists might encounter in their sessions. Working with these situations can be challenging because there is often an overlap between typical emotional developmental milestones that the child is working through and the larger clinical issue of avoiding feelings and experiences of disappointment, frustration, sadness, and anger. The primary strategy in both examples is to expand the child's WOT to withstand the experiences they are having so that they can stay grounded and cope, coregulate, or self-soothe through their experience. Offering validation, normalization, reflective statements, "name it to tame it" responses (Siegel & Bryson, 2012), and growth-oriented statements can all help the child reduce the impact of their negative thoughts while increasing their emotional awareness and capacity to navigate challenging moments.

Part of the difficulty for play therapists in working with these clinical issues is that a conflict of confidence, worth, and self-image all become part of what the emotionally developing child encounters during the natural development of their pre-teen years. Referencing the Developmental Tasks introduced in Chapter 6, children between the ages of 7–11 enter into the emotional task of asking "how well can I do it?" (L. Dion, personal communication, March 11, 2020). That reflective self-assessment acknowledges a normative emotional developmental lens that focuses on the type of achievement throughout a child's experience. Building the self-assessment skills of reflection and critique of one's own effort is an essential pathway to identity formation, particularly during the pre-adolescent and adolescent years, when the developmental task of "Who am I?" is addressed.

The challenge with this task is when the child's sense of self-assessment comes into conflict with unintegrated experiences from the earlier stages of "Is the world okay?" and "Am I okay?" The combination of "How well can I do it" and "Am I okay" creates a new threat to the nervous system, rooted in a perception of being unsafe when a child's effort and accomplishment come into question. The child's experience of self-judgment and criticism activates increased autonomic arousal, which can be perceived by that child as a threat to their experience in the world. This chain of events is demonstrated in the case vignette at the start of the chapter.

"Shoulds" and Unmet Expectations

Feeling unsafe in moments of perceived or self-prescribed criticism can also be activated by the threat of "shoulds" that the child experiences (Dion, 2018). The internal or external pressure of comparison or drive to be perfect or better can create unmet expectations and feelings of something that "should" be different for the child. The challenge of self-perception becomes an internal conflict for the child, regarding who they should be and how they should act. This distress can often activate the autonomic nervous system, creating a physiological response as the child seeks to manage the internal conflict. It is not uncommon for children in these scenarios to either feel internalized pressure from what they think others expect from them, or they may begin to craft their own comparisons to the experiences of others or an idealized self. This can escalate the autonomic nervous system as their reflexive reaction to want to be different or perform differently feels confusing based on what they know or see to be true from their perspective.

When the adults who care for these children understandably approach the negative self-talk as "not true," it creates a further sense of division within the child who is really trying to come to terms with their feelings of disappointment. Even if the child comes to believe the "truth" of the adult, the feeling of the experience in their body may still be present and can be even more likely to surface when inevitably triggered again.

This is not to say that we agree with the child – the nuance of a helping approach is to support the child in reducing the fear around the stimulation, sensation, and experience of all the emotions that are activated in their body when they are disappointed, frustrated, sad, and angry about what happened. When those big feelings become approachable, the child can then move toward utilizing cognitive awareness and strengths that provide upper-level reasoning. As a child continues to develop these skills, new situations can be met with recollections of when the moments of negative self-talk were not true. This also leads to the possibility of reflecting on the effort and persistence needed to reach past goals and considering what current outcomes would be more in line with what the child imagined. The sequence decreasing the negative self-talk and building self-esteem is possible when the child's autonomic nervous system is soothed – what Porges (2011) identifies as the ventral vagal state – allowing space for the prefrontal lobe to interact and engage in new helpful ways (what Siegel & Bryson (2012) and Gobbel (2023) respectively call the "wizard brain" and "owl" brain). In these instances, the prefrontal lobe of the adult can be borrowed to help the child think through and apply the concept of a growth mentality in future situations.

How This Happens While Playing Minecraft

Working with these dynamics in a Minecraft session requires the clinician to keep in mind the goal of expanding the child's WOT to tolerate and be with big emotions that arise when they may be disappointed, frustrated, sad, and angry. This can be approached by providing validation, normalization, reflective statements, "name it to tame it" responses (Siegel & Bryson, 2012), and growth-oriented "and" statements, such as "I know this is really hard AND I know you can do hard things." Play therapists may utilize this approach multiple times during a session or throughout a course of therapy. It can also be offered to parents as a strategy to practice at home when the child is playing Minecraft, other video games, participating in sports, working on school projects, or doing household chores.

Supporting the Child to Build Self-Esteem

The child in the first vignette at the start of the chapter is having a much different experience than the child in the second. At the start of the game, the first child is represented with internal pressure to take chances in their gameplay by intentionally choosing a high-consequence difficulty setting. There is also the external comparison that the child may hold to idealized players, such as social media influencers and YouTube gamers, whom they aspire to emulate. When the child is defeated and inevitably set back by losing their inventory and having to respawn a large distance away from their items, it becomes too overwhelming, and they respond with a hypoaroused, collapse-style presentation, indicating they are outside their WOT.

They begin to cope with this experience through the negative self-talk of saying that they are "stupid, can't do anything right, and hate everything" that they do. This is the challenge that the family is seeking support for, and through the stimulation and activation of gameplay in Minecraft, it can become workable in the moment. In moments such as these, the natural instincts of adults could be to dismiss the child's statements. It would be common to respond with "No! That's not true! You are not stupid, and there are many things you can do. Remember how much fun you had playing with your friend last week. They thought you were pretty good, didn't they?" Rather than dismiss the experience they are verbalizing by trying to disagree, it can be more helpful to validate the emotional feelings underneath the negative statements. This approach provides the play therapist the opportunity to speak directly to the child's emotional brain that perceives their loss as a threat to their identity, thus activating their nervous system in an unhelpful way.

> *"Oh no, that was so devastating," I say this in a soft, soothing tone of voice. "There was so much pressure to get through this first night without losing everything. I can absolutely see how sad and angry this makes you." (Bringing in emotional language to try and help the child connect to their emotional experience.)*
>
> *"I just hate it. I can never do anything right." The child mumbles this as their body language keeps them turned away from me.*
>
> *"It really feels that way, doesn't it? When something goes wrong, it's like nothing can ever go right." (Continue to acknowledge and recognize their perception and feeling of the experience.)*
>
> *I pause, and the child is silent. I decide to keep going.*
>
> *"I know you must really hate it when that happens, and I can understand how it feels like nothing goes right. I could see how hard you were working to battle those mobs." (Beginning to affirm their personal effort and the progress that was being made.)*
>
> *"I was SO close. If only that baby zombie didn't sneak up on me from behind!" The child rolls their body forward and is sitting up. They look more grounded and focused again. I decided to move forward with normalizing their experience and bringing in a growth mentality perspective.*
>
> *"Ugh! Those are SO annoying. It's almost impossible to see those coming, and I bet they get a lot of players. It's really crummy that you were defeated on that first night, and I could see how much progress*

you were making. The game can be really hard, and it can be really fun when you make it through those hard sections. It might take a couple more tries, and it will feel really good when you get to where you want to be. Would you like to try it again?"

The second case vignette is provided to represent what I believe is normative in the child's exploration of "how well can I do?" The language and self-talk of the child, who is dissatisfied with their build and compares it to a peer's, may be hard to hear; yet, the child is reflecting on the aspects of their peer's work that they feel drawn to. This child is also bumping up against the "Who am I?" task and seeking acceptance, exploring the comparative questions of how they might fit in with others. Their body language, as observed, communicates that they are grounded, connected to their experience in the game, and able to maintain a relationship with the therapist. They may not be satisfied with what they are building, but they do not feel unsafe or threatened by that experience of dissatisfaction.

Revisiting Principle 1 and the Role of Skill

Play therapists who lack skill in the mechanics and strategies of the game provide opportunities to model for their clients how to ask for help, accept defeat, learn new things, and acknowledge the dual experience of not playing well and also having fun anyway. In the first clinical vignette, another aspect of the child being defeated and losing their inventory was that it presumably happened to me as well. Another way of approaching that situation could be to highlight my experience of being disappointed that I was defeated, lost my inventory, and still had fun:

"I had a feeling this was going to be really hard for me. I am not a very good Survival player, but even when I lose, I am still having fun. Even though I've respawned so far from my items, I want to keep trying because I know that one of these times I am going to get it right. You made it a lot further than I did. I'm learning a lot from how you are approaching the game, and I'll try to do some things differently the next time."

The framework of the Seven Guiding Principles is that when the clinician remains focused on the stimulation in the game while staying connected and aware of their relationship with the child, meaningful clinical interventions can occur. Play therapists new to Minecraft, working with children who struggle with negative self-talk and low self-esteem, can utilize their own lack of skill in the game as a means to help empower their clients to reflect on aspects of the game where they excel. Children can take on the role of being the expert and benefit from the sense of accomplishment and confidence that arises when they have the opportunity to share their knowledge with interested adults as demonstrated in Chapter 8.

Clinicians who are skilled players also provide a valuable resource for the clients. As mentioned in Chapter 10, they can help the child moderate the challenge of playing together by asking how hard the child would like them to play. In this case, skilled players can provide an increasingly challenging experience as the child may choose to continue scaling the difficulty higher throughout their sessions. Players who understand the learning curves, challenges, and dedication required to become proficient and advance to higher levels of the game can provide specific, growth-oriented statements and reflections that resonate with the diverse needs of each client.

Regardless of the clinician's skill level, it is vital to remember that playing Minecraft provides endless opportunities for upsetting and discouraging events to occur: being defeated quickly by mobs, accidentally falling from high places, glitches that disrupt gameplay, feeling unlucky with opportunities in the game, elusive achievements that cannot be met, and many other circumstances. For the clients who struggle with negative self-talk and low self-esteem, these distressing moments can be triggers that cause the clients to feel poorly about themselves and want to give up. It can be heartbreaking to witness, and yet, as described throughout this chapter, it provides the play therapist with opportunities to work with those challenges in the moment.

Looking Ahead

This chapter provided a framework for working with negative self-talk and building self-esteem as a specific goal identified by the parents of caregivers of clients we may see. Working with these dynamics while playing Minecraft together is the first step, as it helps clinicians witness how the child becomes triggered, notice how their nervous system responds, and begin to coregulate with them in the moment. These intentional, clinical experiences create new moments of growth and acceptance for the child as they learn to become more tolerant of the distressing feelings associated with their negative self-talk and become grounded in a way that enables the prefrontal cortex to consider new ways of framing their experiences.

However, the work does not stop here. Teaching these skills and new ways of responding in the moment to the parents and caregivers who are with the child when negative self-talk presents at home is an essential part of the child's growth in building their self-esteem. Clinicians can direct parents to Chapter 8, which provides information on a family systems approach that coaches caregivers on similar ways to respond and emphasizes the importance of initiating family gaming sessions when activation occurs.

Helpful Tips

- **Protective Mechanism:** Negative self-talk is a self-preservation, protective mode that occurs when the child's nervous system unconsciously perceives failure (like losing inventory in Survival mode) as a threat, often leading to physical shutdown (dorsal vagal response) and self-aggressive statements.
- **Ideal vs. Reality Collision:** Negative self-talk is fundamentally rooted in the jarring conflict between a child's imaginative ideal self (what they "should" be able to achieve) and the natural boundaries or consequences of their lived experience, which is made immediate and visible by setbacks in Minecraft.
- **Validate Emotion, Not the Belief:** Clinicians should resist challenging or correcting the child's negative beliefs (e.g., "You are not stupid"). This approach only soothes the adult's pain and fails to validate the child's physiological truth.
- **Refocus on Underlying Feelings:** The effective therapeutic strategy is to validate the deep, intense emotions (such as sadness, anger, or devastation) that lie underneath the negative statements, helping the child connect to their emotional experience rather than their cognitive distortion.
- **Expand the WOT:** The primary goal is to utilize these distressing moments in the game to coregulate and soothe the child's nervous system into a ventral vagal state. This intentional work expands the child's WOT, allowing their prefrontal cortex to engage in reflective thinking and build authentic self-esteem.

Reflection Question

1 When a child says, "I'm so stupid for losing everything," what is a validating response I could offer that acknowledges the intensity of their feeling (e.g., devastation, anger) without agreeing with or correcting their negative self-judgment?

References

Dion, L. (2018). *Aggression in play therapy: A neurobiological approach for integrating intensity*. W. W. Norton & Company.

Gobbel, R. (2023). *Raising kids with big, baffling behaviors*. Jessica Kingsley Publishers.

Porges, S. W. (2011). *The polyvagal theory: Neurophysiological foundations of emotions, attachment, communication, and self-regulation*. W. W. Norton & Company.

Siegel, D. J., & Bryson, T. P. (2012). *The whole-brain child: 12 revolutionary strategies to nurture your child's development, survive everyday parenting struggles, and help your family thrive*. Scribe Publications.

Chapter 12

Grief and Bereavement

A child is grieving the death of their parent who died approximately 6 months prior to entering therapy. The surviving parent has reached out for grief support and reported the child has worries about starting school again in the Fall, has had trouble adjusting to their new home, and has appeared shut down when talking about the deceased. They also note that the child has been playing Minecraft in isolation at home and they are wondering if playing Minecraft in therapy would offer anything different.

"I can understand how concerning it is to see your child isolate while only finding solace in the game."

"I don't mind that they are playing but I just want to be sure that they can grieve in a healthy way and not get stuck in their grief when they are older."

"It makes sense that they are finding comfort in Minecraft. There are a lot of things they can control in that world that can help with feelings of chaos from the outside world."

"Hmm, there were a lot of circumstances around the death that even I have had a hard time making sense of."

"If you're willing to try it out, the difference with your child and I playing Minecraft in session is that we will intentionally process aspects of the death and their grief that they may not have worked through yet. Minecraft helps with this because we are starting in a world they already know and are familiar with."

"That sounds interesting and I know they would be interested in that. Can you tell me more?"

"Absolutely!"

Grief is a universal human experience, yet it uniquely and profoundly affects millions of children worldwide. Children experience grief as a response to loss on multiple levels, from the effects of macro-level tragedies like wartime trauma and natural disasters to the death of a family member, friend, or pet. They also grieve profound changes in their daily lives, such as changing schools, losing friendships, or feeling disconnected from their community. By the end of 2024, over 43 million children

DOI: 10.4324/9781003614784-15

were forcibly displaced from their homes due to conflict and persecution (United Nations High Commissioner for Refugees [UNHCR], 2025). Over the past six years (2016–2021), 43 million children were internally displaced by weather-related disasters, such as storms and flooding (United Nations International Children's Emergency Fund [UNICEF], 2023). While children grieve many types of loss, this chapter will focus primarily on bereavement, the grief experienced following the death of a significant person.

Before the COVID-19 pandemic, an estimated 140 million children globally were orphans, having experienced the death of at least one parent (Hillis et al., 2021). Within the United States, the 2025 Childhood Bereavement Estimation Model indicates that 6.4 million children will experience the death of a parent or sibling by age 18 (Judi's House, 2025). Despite its prevalence, the needs of grieving children are frequently overlooked or misunderstood by the very systems designed to support them, including schools, community groups, and even close family and friends. This oversight is further complicated when caregivers seek support and are met with frameworks that pathologize grief. The emotions, thoughts, and behaviors of grieving children, which can be normative stress responses to loss, are often compared to clinical criteria for anxiety and depression, creating confusion and concern for the adults caring for them.

Grief and the ways individuals and communities mourn, celebrate, or remember the deceased vary across cultures worldwide. Some choose to mourn and grieve in solitude, while others rely on the strength and support of their communities. Some may celebrate the deceased through vibrant ceremonies, while others still follow a path of remembrance by not acknowledging names or identities. As this is written from my own personal cultural background and in reference to the clients who enter my practice, the information presented in this chapter is centered around the specific lived experience of my White, heterosexual, cisgender male American identity. Clinicians approaching this work from diverse identities are encouraged to adapt the concepts presented here to align with their own personal, cultural beliefs, and rituals, as well as those of the clients they serve.

In the United States, there has been an increase in grief support camps and organizations to support children and families who are grieving to try to meet the immense need validated by the data from current studies, such as the Childhood Bereavement Estimation Model (Judi's House, 2025). Appropriately, these camps and organizations focus on play therapy modalities to help children express their grief in meaningful ways. The familiarity and accessibility of Minecraft provides an entry point for promoting a healthy grief process throughout the child's development while offering the flexibility and nuance needed for play therapists and their clients to express themselves through creative, dynamic play. This chapter aims to provide an overview of what clinicians might observe in children who are grieving and inspire ways to integrate contemporary interventions for children who are grieving into Minecraft gameplay. Therapists anywhere in the world can adapt their current interventions or utilize the ones offered in this chapter for any and all children seeking to express and integrate their experience of grief and loss.

The Impact of Grief and Loss on Children and Adolescents

This chapter recognizes grief as the personalized, individual response children have to the death of a significant person in their lives. This includes the full-body and mind experience that validates all the thoughts, emotions, sensations, and behaviors that arise in youth who are grieving. Grief is commonly referred to along with the process of bereavement, which is more recognized explicitly as the objective state of loss, versus grief as the subjective response children experience. This chapter focuses on grief as it is related to the death-loss of a significant attachment figure, such as a family member or friend; however, the grieving process can also be activated from the emotional void that emerges through the loss of a family dynamic, home, pet, friendship, community, and so many other places or items of comfort and safety.

Disenfranchised Grief

Children and adolescents may also experience disenfranchised grief where a loss is not recognized by one's community, such as when there is a conflict of social or cultural norms, or when there is no opportunity for ritual or closure (Doka, 1989). Clients may present with disenfranchised grief following the death of a celebrity, prominent athlete, entertainer, or a lesser-known member of their community, such as a student they might not have known very well. Furthermore, disenfranchised grief can present in complex family systems where different relationships to the deceased may be present, or for members of the LGBTQIA+ communities who may not feel validated or supported in their relationship.

The death of the young adult Minecraft influencer Technoblade catalyzed a potent experience of disenfranchised grief for an entire generation of youth. His death from cancer was announced by his father in a video posted to his channel, which garnered over 87 million views (Technoblade, 2022). For many children, he was a daily companion and a symbol of resilience. Yet, their profound sense of loss was often minimized or misunderstood by adults who failed to recognize the significance of a parasocial relationship.

His death created a critical therapeutic opportunity to validate this often-invisible grief and use it as a gateway to help youth navigate universal themes of mortality, cancer, and loss through a shared cultural touchstone.

Neurobiological Impact

Children who are grieving experience a loss of safety and predictability in their world as the impact of loss generates questions of what comes next. The experience of loss creates a new template for the brain and body that the world can be unpredictable and unknown. This new experience of uncertainty can trigger autonomic nervous system activation as a child's neuroception, or their subconscious detection of safety or threat, heightens, altering their perception of the world and driving the fight, flight, or freeze survival responses clinicians may observe as outward behaviors in children who are grieving (Porges, 2011). The newly heightened nervous system responses can reduce a child's Window of Tolerance (WOT), leading play therapists to be tasked with simultaneously working with the topics presented in Chapters 5–11. Children grieving a significant loss are confronted not only with the absence of a special person or significant relationship in their life, but also with the space of navigating how to move forward and how to make sense of the unknown.

Common Grief Reactions and Developmental Differences When Grieving a Death

Common grief reactions clinicians may expect in their clients include emotional, cognitive, and physical expressions. Children may express feelings of sadness, despair, and sorrow as well as shock, disbelief, and numbness. These experiences can be present alongside relational dynamics of yearning, longing, and deeply missing the person who died. Other common emotional reactions include anger, irritability, and frustration, as well as anxiety, fears, and worries concerning safety or the future. Feelings of confusion, insecurity, guilt, remorse, shame, and powerlessness can also be present. From a cognitive perspective, children may be preoccupied with constant thoughts and memories of the death or the person who died. It is also common to experience believing the person who died is still present, which can involve hearing, seeing, feeling, or smelling the person, or having vivid dreams about them. Other thoughts include worries about one's own health or the health of another loved one, confusion and disbelief about the finality of death, or even thinking that the death was somehow their own fault. Difficulty making decisions is frequently reported, along with insecurities, lowered self-esteem, or reduced self-confidence, and impaired memory and concentration.

Physically, responses to loss may include frequent illness or a variety of physical complaints such as stomachaches, headaches, an increased heart rate, tense or sore muscles, and unexplained body aches and pains. Children may also experience a loss of energy, fatigue, or conversely, a feeling of being on edge. Difficulty relaxing or feeling calm and regulated are also common nervous system body-based reactions. For many children, the intensity of these grief reactions typically diminishes gradually over the first six months to a year following the death, and it is also recognized that there is no distinct timeline for processing one's grief. Integrating Minecraft into play therapy interventions for children who are grieving can be a powerful way to work with the big emotions that arise, process memories, reframe their relationship to worries and distressing thoughts, and improve their relationship to themselves and others.

Developmental Differences

Developmental differences in how children understand and react to death are helpful for play therapists to consider when utilizing interventions with Minecraft with children of different ages. Children aged 6 to 9 can likely understand that death is permanent and irreversible, though they might worry that their own thoughts or actions caused the death. This presentation is similar to the experience younger children may have, where the notion of magical thinking might lead them to believe they caused the death in some way or that their person can come back from the dead. In both cases, reactions could include confusion, increased fears or worry, sleep and eating difficulties, restlessness, clinginess, and regressive behaviors. Age-appropriate reactions for children 6 to 9 can consist of initial denial or disbelief, anger, irritability, physical aches, difficulties with schoolwork, anxiety, and attempts to conform with peers.

Neurotypical 10–12-year-olds can fully understand death's concrete and irreversible nature. They may exhibit initial shock, denial, anxiety, anger, aggression, distrust, feelings of guilt or remorse, and a curiosity or fascination with death. Adolescents 13 years and older tend to possess a complete adult understanding of death, including the ability to process abstract and spiritual meanings if that corresponds with their personal beliefs and worldview. Their responses may encompass intense sadness, depression, anger, irritability, distrust, feelings of guilt, remorse, shame, non-compliance, risky behaviors, and prolonged sleep problems or fatigue.

When Grief Evolves Over Time

The diagnosis of Prolonged Grief Disorder (PGD) provides a clinical framework for identifying grief that remains highly disruptive and impairs a child's functioning 6 to 12 months after a loss (Schuurman & Mitchell, 2020). However, this model faces significant criticism. Critics contend that PGD is a socially constructed, scientifically unproven idea that applies ethnocentric timelines to a natural process (Schuurman & Mitchell, 2020). From this perspective, expressions of grief are not abnormal symptoms but adaptive coping mechanisms, and children possess an inherent ability to recover healthily from loss when given adequate relational and sociocultural support.

Despite the importance of this debate, play therapists must remain vigilant in distinguishing between typical grief and clinical risks. Therefore, they should perform risk assessments, safety checks, and consider referrals if clients display more concerning behaviors such as severe depression, self-harm or suicidal thoughts, reckless or illegal actions, an inability to function at school, or persistent issues with eating or sleeping that affect health. Additionally, ongoing post-traumatic stress symptoms related to the death, such as increased arousal, intrusive thoughts, nightmares, or avoidance that interfere with a healthy grieving process, signal the need for developmentally appropriate, trauma-specific interventions. Chapter 13 provides guidance on supporting clients who have experienced trauma, as these resources may be necessary if these concerns persist.

Experiences of grief and loss can induce a range of disorienting emotional and cognitive responses, including anxiety, fears, worries about safety or the future, confusion, insecurity, and feelings of powerlessness, alongside difficulty making decisions and a sense of impaired self-confidence. In contrast to these often unpredictable and overwhelming feelings, the inherent gameplay in Minecraft provides the child a stable entry point into a world that is safe and predictable due to their individual level of control in the game. This environment can offer a vital sense of agency and security, countering the feelings of powerlessness and insecurity that are often associated with grief. By providing this consistent and controllable space, Minecraft may offer respite, a sense of calm and regulation, and a secure outlet that mitigates the potential for grief to interfere with normal functioning or development, particularly when children navigate intense fears or anxiety following a loss. Even without prompt or encouragement, a child playing Minecraft may already be processing their grief by finding respite in this safe space, effectively engaging in self-soothing and regaining a sense of stability when their real world feels disrupted.

This chapter offers examples of how Minecraft can be creatively used to help children cope with grief over a death, a pet, or other major life events like divorce, family separation, moving, or saying goodbye to something meaningful. Based on directive play therapy techniques, suggestions will be provided to help clinicians recognize their client's interest in Minecraft while guiding therapeutic activities that foster growth and healing in the child's grieving process.

Integrating Minecraft into Processing Grief: Directive Interventions

When offering directive interventions, it is essential to determine whether the child prefers to have their Minecraft worlds saved with the clinician or create a world on their own account to continue working on at home. Some clients may require multiple sessions to work on their builds and appreciate having a safe container in which to focus solely on emotional work during their play therapy appointments. It is not uncommon for children who are grieving to move back and forth between processing their grief and then focusing on something else. This process is known in the grief community as "puddle jumping." Additionally, it relates to Stroebe and Schut's (1999) Dual Process Model of Coping with Bereavement, which acknowledges that children experience both pain and healing simultaneously. An example of this would be if the child begins to build an area that serves as their chosen memorial space, but then decides to embark on a quest for a seemingly unrelated purpose. While this may appear to be a distraction or avoidance, it can also be a natural way for the child to work through their grief process, and it is another great indicator that they are attuned to their own WOT (see also Chapter 6).

Other children may become attached to this novel approach of using Minecraft to process their grief and want to integrate it with their gameplay at home. Having the child create a world on their personal account would be a preferred option in this case, so they can have access to it whenever they like. This can also create opportunities in future sessions for them to share the meaningful additions that they worked on between appointments. Access to a child's Minecraft builds at home can also be a natural conduit for family-level discussions and play sessions.

It is recommended that caregivers are made aware of the importance of keeping any specific builds a child holds in their world private from others who might be playing at home. The experience of someone altering, modifying, or destroying something a child worked so hard on that carries personal and therapeutic meaning can be accidental and unintentional, but also devastating. One can imagine the disruption that would ensue if a sibling or another player at home did not understand the significance of a build and decided to use it as a fun target to test their new explosive cannon launcher.

Acknowledging the Impact of Grief

The following directive interventions demonstrate how to apply these concepts in practice. Rather than clinical vignettes, they are presented as examples of the direct, empathetic dialogue a clinician can use.

The Grief Cave

Imagine that your grief lives in a cave, taking the form of mobs in Minecraft. Mobs can take on a lot of different behaviors: they can be aggressive, assertive, sneaky, and some, like the Iron Golem, may even leave you alone until you agitate them. Peaceful mobs, such as villagers, can be friendly and may want to interact in helpful ways, like offering to trade items.

Grief can be like that, too. Sometimes it can feel intense and overwhelming, and its presence is always there. Other times, it may seem like it's not even around until something reminds you of it. Grief can also bring up fond memories that we want to hold onto, and recalling them can be helpful when we are deeply missing someone or something special to us.

What does your grief cave look like? What are the mobs you would include that remind you of your grief? Are there any special items you want to include in your grief cave that remind you of how to manage the different reminders of grief?

Lighting a Torch: The Grief Cave Memorial

Sometimes it is hard to talk about the person you are grieving. You know they are gone, you think about them, you miss them, and you might want just to do something else. The Grief Cave Memorial is perfect for those kinds of days. Find a hidden cave somewhere in a biome you won't get lost in. At the entrance of the cave, place a chest. In the chest, you can hide torches or lanterns. On days when you just want to let your person know that you are thinking of them, you can go to the cave, grab the lantern from your chest, and place it somewhere in the cave, lighting up the darkness. At the end of our session, you can go back to the cave and place it back in the chest.

> *"But what if I want to keep it burning even when we are not playing?"*
> *"You can do that too! You can leave the torch up for as long as you want."*
> *"And what if we move to a new biome really far away. Can I light a campfire instead? In case we can't find our way back?"*
> *"Yes! A campfire is another great way to let you and your person know that they are on your mind while we are playing."*
> *"Maybe a glow stone too!"*
> *"Great idea! What other items would you want to use?"*

Grief Waves

Grief can be like experiencing the waves of the ocean. Sometimes they can be powerful and overwhelming. At other times, they can be gentle, maintaining a distance between each other. There are also the waves we can see coming and the waves that take us by surprise and wash over us from behind.

Grief waves we might anticipate include birthdays, holidays, and other meaningful events when we know we are missing the person or part of our life we are grieving. The grief waves that we do not see coming could be the moments when we are surprised by a memory or a reminder (maybe something that pops up on social media). This could also be the many different things that activate memories, such as hearing a specific song, eating particular foods, smelling something that evokes memories, or even passing by a place that holds meaning.

In Minecraft, items like water and lava can be powerful representations of how grief waves can signal something coming up or be upsetting when they take us by surprise. How could you create something that uses water or lava to show all of the things you might expect to face in your grief? What would you need to make it through those moments and obstacles? If you are caught by grief waves that you do not see, how could you stop the waves or the flow of the water or lava? What would help keep you safe?

Remembering the Person and Relationship

Once a child feels their grief has been acknowledged and validated, the therapeutic work can naturally expand to focus on the relationship itself. The next set of directive interventions supports this shift from the pain of loss to the comfort of memory.

Building a Memorial

Building a memorial space is a helpful intervention for children who are grieving, as it provides a dedicated outlet to acknowledge, represent, and share meaningful memories associated with their grief. Minecraft offers a way to do this that connects the child to their grief by turning inward to identify significant moments and memories, while also finding ways to externalize and express them within the game. There is no right or wrong way to approach creating this kind of build, and it can evolve and change over time as their grief does. Children inspired by their memorial builds may also want to share photos and videos, sentimental objects, and clothing items, and tell stories that help them actively engage with their grief. As with all therapeutic work in Minecraft, it's not about the game itself; it's about what the game brings up in the relationship among the child, the play therapist, and other helping adults in the child's life.

For clients who might not immediately engage with a direct prompt to build a memorial, clinicians can use a classic family systems activity, adapted by Ellie Finch (2021a) for Minecraft from in-person methods using stones. In this activity, the client is asked to choose a block to represent themselves and place it in a tree, explaining their choice, before adding blocks for each family member around it. For clients grieving a family member, this can naturally lead to processing their grief and serve as a transition into building a memorial and sharing memories (Finch, 2021b).

Sharing Memories

If a child appears to struggle with memories, it may be helpful to have a preparation session with the parent or caregiver before the meeting to discuss how memories are addressed at home. A child who has experienced a significant loss when they were at an age of unconscious memories can still benefit from identifying a connection with the things or people that might have been special to the deceased or important in their life. Many children enjoy hearing about memories and stories that occurred before they were born. Although the child may not have been alive at the time, it can still be soothing and meaningful for them to hear stories about the person they are grieving and feel closer to them in their absence.

The more you learn about the child and the family, the more suggestions you may have to initiate a meaningful build, or also notice how the child's grief is being remembered. *The Invisible String* discusses the connection between two people when they are not in close physical proximity (Karst, 2001). Reading this book together with a child and discussing ways their invisible string is represented in the world can also be a helpful intervention.

Staying Connected

The Invisible String (Bibliotherapy and Directive Intervention)

The Invisible String (Karst, 2001) is a book about staying connected to the people and things you love, even when they are far away. This book addresses a range of different losses and can be read as an adjunct to the intentional grief work in Minecraft. To facilitate the invisible string build, a child can use a colored block of their choice to connect to the different people, places, or items that are meaningful to them. Other creative ways for children to connect with their significant memories could include using doors and levers to activate water, red stone, railways, and more. As with all uses of Minecraft, the clients will be the best teachers and resources for what is both fun and meaningful to them.

Journaling with Book and Quill (Memorial Add-On)

Similar to journaling, writing things down in Minecraft and keeping them private can be a meaningful way for clients to remember the person they are grieving. It also offers a space to collect new stories to cherish and to revisit the stories of the deceased when they feel nostalgic. Using the book and quill, clients can write down memories they do not want to forget, such as what the person looked like, what they enjoyed doing, and funny stories they recall. Clients can be encouraged to write whatever comes to mind and feels significant to them. When finished, they can store it securely in an Ender chest, in their memorial space, or in another safe location.

Processing Changes

Children may also want to explore the changes that happen following a death or a significant life event or transition. Grieving a death, a family separating, moving, saying goodbye to a friend, or going to a new school can all be ways in which situations prompt a grief process. Clients in these scenarios may want to explore their experiences in the past, present, and future. Similar to sand tray prompts, children can utilize the open world dynamic of Minecraft to build before and after representations that help them to tell the story of what was important in the past and what fears, anxieties, worries, or excitement they have about the future and what will come next (see Chapter 13 for more about directive interventions with changes).

Integrating into Their Life Moving Forward

As children navigate their grief process, they may be drawn to directive activities that help them explore where they find meaning in their lives moving forward.

As I Grow Activity

The As I Grow Activity, adapted from the Judi's House (Griese et al., 2018) *Pathfinders* curriculum is a way for children to acknowledge the past, present, and future of their lives. Building a system of roots beneath a tree can represent all the people, places, and events that have helped shape who they are today. The tree's trunk can represent all the hardships and adversities they have had to overcome. Just as a tree may have carvings, scratches, and limbs missing on its trunk yet remain rooted, grounded, and strong, children may also have similar experiences that were hurtful but helped shape who they are. The branches of the tree can represent the present: their current growth and connection to move upwards toward the future. The leaves and outer edges of the tree can represent their future hopes and dreams; the things they want to achieve in the short and long term. This could be getting a driver's license or having a family of their own.

Clients can assign meaning and significance to different blocks used for various parts of the tree, using the book and quill to ensure they do not forget what each one represents. Signs can also be hung or posted to describe meaningful areas. Clients are encouraged to be as creative and expressive as they would like; pushing the bounds of the exercise can inspire new ways to talk and reflect on experiences. For clients who feel less creative or inspired, finding an established tree in a biome and discussing its different parts can be just as meaningful (see also Grounding and Mindfulness Skill in Chapter 13 for additional ways to incorporate this activity).

Looking Forward

The above directive interventions illustrate how clinicians can help their clients process and manage their grief. These interventions can also be adapted for non-death losses, such as pet loss, divorce or family separation, moving, ending a friendship or romantic relationship, and even saying goodbye to something meaningful, like school or peer communities. The next chapter will explore ways to support children when their grief and loss experiences exceed their ability to heal and show up as trauma symptoms. Children may experience trauma not only related to the experience of a death but also from circumstances leading to the loss of a home, safety, or community. These situations involve significant grief due to loss and separation, often worsened by other crises that may lead to trauma reactions. This is especially relevant for clinicians working with children affected by war, conflict, natural disasters, or other frightening events like school shootings and gun violence.

Helpful Tips

- **Intentional Therapeutic Processing:** While children may already play Minecraft for solace, the key difference for grief counseling is the intentional processing of the death and grief within the game, using a world they already know and are familiar with as a starting point.
- **Addressing Loss of Control:** Minecraft provides a stable entry point into a world that is safe and predictable due to the child's individual level of control, which helps counteract the feelings of powerlessness and chaos often associated with grief and loss.

- **Reframing Grief as Fluid:** In the therapeutic context, grief is often characterized by "puddle jumping" or the Dual Process Model, where children naturally move back and forth between processing their grief (e.g., building a memorial) and focusing on something else (e.g., embarking on a quest). This is recognized as a natural way for the child to work through grief and attune to their own WOT.
- **Validating Other Losses:** Minecraft offers an opportunity to validate experiences of disenfranchised grief and other losses, utilizing the game as a gateway to explore universal themes of loss.
- **Directive Interventions for Specific Focus:** Directive interventions, such as the Grief Cave Memorial (using torches as moments of remembrance), Grief Waves (using water/lava to represent anticipated and surprising moments of grief), or Building a Memorial, to help children externalize, express, and integrate their experience of grief and loss.

Reflection Question

1 Considering the "puddle jumping" nature of grief, what signs would I look for in a session to know when a child is moving from their "loss orientation" (e.g., building a memorial) toward a "restoration orientation" (e.g., going on an adventure), and how would I support that natural rhythm?

References

Doka, K. J. (Ed.). (1989). *Disenfranchised grief: Recognizing hidden sorrow.* Lexington Books/D. C. Heath and Com.

Finch, E. (2021a). *How does counselling using Minecraft work?* Counselling-Directory.org.uk; Counselling Directory. https://www.counselling-directory.org.uk/articles/how-does-counselling-using-minecraft-work

Finch, E. (2021b). Therapeutic adventures in Minecraft. Playmode Academy; *BACP Children, Young People & Families*. https://playmodeacademy.org/resources-and-publications/featured-article-in-bacp-journal

Griese, B., Burns, M., & Farro, S. (2018). Pathfinders: Promoting healthy adjustment in bereaved children and families. *Death Studies*, *42*(3), 134–142.

Hillis, S. D., Unwin, H. J. T., Chen, Y., Cluver, L., Sherr, L., Goldman, P. S., Ratmann, O., Donnelly, C. A., Bhatt, S., Villaveces, A., Butchart, A., Bachman, G., Rawlings, L., Green, P., Nelson, C. A. III, & Flaxman, S. (2021). Global minimum estimates of children affected by COVID-19-associated orphanhood and deaths of caregivers: A modelling study. *Lancet*, *398*(10295), 391–402. https://doi.org/10.1016/S0140-6736(21)01253-8

Judi's House/JAG Institute. (2025). *Childhood bereavement estimation model.* https://judishouse.org/research-tools/cbem/

Karst, P. (2001). *The invisible string.* DeVorss Publications.

Porges, S. W. (2011). *The polyvagal theory: Neurophysiological foundations of emotions, attachment, communication, and self-regulation.* W. W. Norton & Company.

Schuurman, D. L., & Mitchell, M. B. (2020). *Becoming grief-informed: A call to action*. Dougy Center: The National Grief Center for Children & Families. https://www.dougy.org/assets/uploads/Becoming-Grief-Informed_A-Call-to-Action.pdf
Stroebe, M., & Schut, H. (1999). The dual process model of coping with bereavement: Rationale and description. *Death Studies*, *23*(3), 197–224. https://doi.org/10.1080/074811899201046
Technoblade. (2022). *So long nerds* [Video]. YouTube. https://www.youtube.com/watch?v=DPMluEVUqS0
United Nations High Commissioner for Refugees. (2025). *Global trends: Forced displacement in 2024*. United Nations High Commissioner for Refugees.
United Nations International Children's Emergency Fund. (2023). *The climate-changed child: A children's climate risk index supplement*. UNICEF.

Chapter 13

Minecraft as a Container for Trauma Processing

A client attends their third play therapy session after losing their home in a devastating fire. The parents reported that the child has not discussed the event since and has been isolated, withdrawn, and explosive over issues that do not seem to match the intensity of their reactions. We log into the game together, and the child immediately asks if they can continue working on their build. The world is saved on the Minecraft account associated with my practice and remains private and confidential; it was named "The Before Times."

Minutes into the session, as they fly around the perimeter of the house they are rebuilding, they start to tell me a memory of how their friends used to play in the yard together during the summers. "It was a really special place," they say.

I notice the tone of their voice drop; it sounds sad but also inviting. I ask if they want to tell me more, and they say, "Yes."

Dropping blocks from their inventory in front of me, they ask if I can help them work on the next part.

"Can you help me build my room? I want to show you what my old room used to look like. It was really pretty cool."

Children globally face a growing risk of exposure to potentially traumatic events, which can profoundly disrupt their emotional and psychological development (Child Mind Institute [CMI], 2022; National Child Traumatic Stress Network [NCTSN], 2023). Clinicians are acutely aware of the large-scale catastrophes that can affect the children who come into play therapy, including wartime tragedies, environmental disasters, gun violence, and so many other unexpected events that shatter communities and disrupt the sense of safety for the children within.

This type of trauma is widespread. Large-scale studies coordinated by the World Health Organization indicate that a majority of children and adolescents globally may experience at least one potentially traumatic event by the time they reach adulthood (Kessler et al., 2017; World Health Organization, 2022). Storms and flooding were the primary accounting factors for 95% of recorded internal child displacements, totaling 43 million between 2016 and

DOI: 10.4324/9781003614784-16

2021 (United Nations International Children's Emergency Fund [UNICEF], 2023). Over 43 million children were forcibly displaced from their homes due to conflict and persecution by the end of 2024 (United Nations High Commissioner for Refugees [UNHCR], 2025). Furthermore, approximately half of all children in the United States (about 35 million) are reported to have experienced at least one traumatic event before age eight (Bartlett & Steber, 2019).

Other traumatic events children may be processing in play therapy may include witnessing or being involved in accidents, peer bullying (both in-person and online), and interpersonal violence from within the family (including various types of abuse and domestic violence). In some circumstances, the sudden loss of a significant person, or the unexpected death of a pet, can be deeply traumatic, particularly if the death was violent or the child was exposed to distressing details (Alvis et al., 2022). For young children especially, a sense of security is closely tied to the safety of their primary caregivers or safe adults in their lives, making tragic events even more unsettling (CMI, 2022).

Building on definitions established by the International Society for Traumatic Stress Studies (ISTSS), the Substance Abuse and Mental Health Services Administration (SAMHSA), and the National Child Traumatic Stress Network (NCTSN), Bartlett and Steber (2019) characterize childhood trauma as an actual or threatened adverse event that causes emotional distress and overwhelms a child's ability to cope. Experiences such as those listed above can often trigger intense emotional and physical reactions that may linger long after the event has passed (NCTSN, 2023), further impacting the children's brains and bodies, which may lead to sensitized responses to typical daily interactions (Perry & Szalavitz, 2008; van der Kolk, 2014). Children might feel extreme fear, powerlessness, or panic, along with physical symptoms like a racing heart, nausea, or loss of bodily control.

Due to the reactivity of a child's nervous system, children often unconsciously seek ways to gain control and feel safe in their environment. When children are unable to defend themselves or rely on others for protection, the overwhelming nature of these reactions can leave a lasting impact (Bartlet & Steber, 2019; NCTSN, 2023). As these experiences can disrupt a child's sense of safety and stability, a play therapy intervention such as Minecraft can address and alleviate the core symptoms of trauma by providing options for both client-led and structured experiences that rebuild a sense of agency and control.

Minecraft as a Safe Environment

The initial invitation to play Minecraft together in the therapy space provides a powerful entry point for exploring control and safety, leading to opportunities for expressive and healing play. As discussed in Chapters 5 and 6, clients can use the game's elements to reveal their internal world.

At the same time, the play therapist coregulates during moments of autonomic nervous system activation heightened by trauma. Using Minecraft in this way helps create a safe digital world, serving as a ventral vagal anchor (Porges, 2011) amid distress (see Chapter 10). The game establishes a purposeful container, enabling children to confidently manage their symptoms with the understanding that they have coping tools and can take a break when necessary (see also "puddle jumping" in Chapter 12).

This sense of safety stems from the game's structure. Children play freely and creatively within the fixed boundaries of the digital world, which promotes predictability through expectations of gameplay. Accessible, user-controlled mechanics offer a high level of control, allowing children to create a safe experience by managing day-night cycles, weather, and even making enemies "peaceful," all while maintaining the joy of exploration and imagination.

For some children, however, the expansive nature of the world can be overstimulating. In these instances, the clinician can provide additional containment by prompting builds on a limited landmass, such as a seed for an island world or a flat world surrounded by a wall built by the clinician before the session (Finch, 2022). This offers the freedom of creativity within a more immediately secure space with visible boundaries.

Even within a tailored environment, potentially triggering elements may arise. Therefore, a final, critical layer of safety involves modifying specific auditory and visual factors, such as weather, darkness, or character mortality (e.g., playing in Peaceful Mode), to fit the child's unique triggers and Window of Tolerance (WOT) (see Chapter 6). This requires careful clinical attunement; for example, in his work with children who are refugees and war survivors, Oleksii Sukhorukov notes how the sound of thunder could be mistaken for shelling (personal communication, September 9, 2025). In those instances, weather elements can be turned off and further adjusted to meet the clients' needs. Through these layered adjustments, the digital world becomes a truly customized and secure therapeutic container.

Age-Related Reactions to Trauma and the Appeal of Minecraft

According to the National Child Traumatic Stress Network [NCTSN] (2010), a child's reaction to traumatic experiences and how they express their distress largely depend on their age and developmental stage. The NCTSN fact sheet acts as a resource for anyone working with children to recognize how children and adolescents might respond to traumatic events.

- **Younger children** (preschool and early school-age) often experience feelings of helplessness and pervasive fear, yet struggle to articulate their

emotions. Their distress may manifest as a regression in acquired skills, such as independent sleep or toileting, or through repetitive play.
- **School-age children** frequently exhibit persistent concern for their own and others' safety, and may be preoccupied with their actions during the event. They may feel guilty or ashamed, experience sleep disturbances, difficulty concentrating, or engage in reckless behaviors.
- **Adolescents** tend to be self-conscious about their emotional responses, which can lead to withdrawal from friends and family. They may harbor feelings of shame, guilt, or fantasies of revenge, which can sometimes lead to self-destructive behaviors or a fundamental shift in their worldview.

This information is not only critical for clinicians who may be unaware of a child's potential exposure to traumatic events, but also for the caregivers and systems providing care for children outside of the play therapy room.

Community Appeal

Support from family, healthcare providers, schools, and the community is vital in helping children navigate the emotional and physical challenges that follow a traumatic event (NCTSN, 2010). As the previous sections and chapters have demonstrated, intentional Minecraft gameplay and awareness of the safe and regulating nature of the game can be a powerful way for helping adults in various roles and settings to support children in their communities who may have been impacted by traumatic events. This is a crucial recognition, as it can be assumed that children will likely be playing the game outside of the play therapy appointments as well. The Seven Guiding Principles provide a supportive framework that can be helpful for clinicians to share with the community members supporting children as the potential pressure to "get it right" can be relieved with the assurance that helpers do not need to be good players (Principle 1), the availability of the game is helpful in itself (Principle 2), and that the child's play is a healing expression (Principles 3 and 4).

Appeal for Children

For young children, accessing Minecraft intentionally can create opportunities for play and creative self-expression, providing a healing release of distressing emotions without the need for explicit discussion (see Principle 3 of the Seven Guiding Principles and Chapter 5: Being in the Game). School-age children can benefit from the opportunity to identify, name, and express their fears, sadness, and anger in the familiar, predictable environment of Minecraft's digital world. The option to have structured play through directive interventions or for the child to lead the play through non-directive engagement positions Minecraft as a unique intervention that meets the child's therapeutic needs while maintaining the flexibility crucial for managing trauma symptoms. This approach can be initiated in the clinical space of a play therapy session and then further developed as the child practices skills learned in the session at home and with the support of a caregiver (see Principles 4, 6, and 7 of the Seven Guiding Principles; Directive Interventions and Case Vignette below; and Chapter 18).

A Bridge for Adolescents

Adolescents may choose to have more open and relationally-focused discussions about the impact of a traumatic event as their brain development leads to making meaning, creating a coherent narrative, and relying on the therapist for reflective thinking (Siegel, 2014). This developmentally appropriate style of processing creates an opportunity for clinicians to provide psycho-education interventions, helping the client understand their symptoms of emotional dysregulation and related behavioral changes (NCTSN, 2010). In these instances, clinicians playing Minecraft with adolescents may find that the processing that occurs is mainly verbal. At the same time, the gameplay serves as a secure, transitional object (Winnicott, 1953) that helps the teen stay connected to their process while also managing their WOT through the stimulation of the game (see Chapter 8; Siegel, 1999).

The Importance of Trauma-Informed Care

Exposure to traumatic events can significantly jeopardize a child's development and long-term well-being, necessitating a trauma-informed approach from clinicians (Bartlett & Steber, 2019). To mitigate these impacts, a framework focusing on resilience and trauma-informed care (TIC) is crucial. Bartlett and Steber (2019) describe resilience as the positive adaptation that occurs despite adversity, shaped by the interaction of biological, psychological, social, and cultural factors within an ecological framework (for the original discussions of resilience, see Masten, 1994 and Southwick et al., 2014, as cited in Bartlett & Steber, 2019).

This model recognizes influences at the individual, family, school, community, and cultural levels, which present both risk and protective factors. While factors like poverty increase risk, extensive research has identified the consistent presence of a sensitive, nurturing adult as a powerful protective factor that can restore safety and help process events (see Perry & Szalavitz, 2008). TIC, a strengths-based approach, operates by integrating this understanding of trauma's impact into all aspects of service systems (Bartlett & Steber, 2019).

Building on the Substance Abuse and Mental Health Services Administration's [SAMHSA] concept of Trauma and Guidance for a Trauma-Informed Approach, Bartlett and Steber (2019) present the "Four R's" as the key elements of TIC. As outlined in their work, Bartlett and Steber (2019) describe the Four R's as the ability to:

- **Realize** the widespread impact of trauma.
- **Recognize** the varied symptoms of trauma (understanding challenging behaviors as adaptive responses).
- **Respond** by adjusting practices and environments to integrate trauma-informed knowledge and care.
- **Resist** re-traumatization of children and caregivers.

Evidence for TIC continues to grow, with promising initiatives showing improvements in clinician knowledge, skills, and reductions in children's post-traumatic stress symptoms (Bartlett & Steber, 2019). Effective implementation of TIC requires that clinicians complete comprehensive, evidence-based training on child trauma and commit to ongoing professional development. Furthermore, this work necessitates a continuing commitment to clinician self-care, as providers are highly susceptible to secondary traumatic stress (Bartlett & Steber, 2019). While a full review of specific trauma modalities is beyond this chapter's focus, clinicians are encouraged to seek training in established, evidence-based treatments such as Trauma-Focused Cognitive Behavioral Therapy (TF-CBT) and Eye Movement Desensitization and Reprocessing (EMDR), as well as the emerging and promising approach of Brainspotting. The foundational practice of trauma-informed play therapy (including Child-Centered Play Therapy and Synergetic Play Therapy) provides a critical lens for engaging children, and all approaches can be informed by a neurodevelopmental understanding of trauma, such as the Neurosequential Model of Therapeutics (NMT).

Building on the foundation of TIC, clinicians can implement the child's interest in digital gaming to connect in a novel and affirming way. While using Minecraft is not a formal component of standard TIC training models, trauma-informed play therapists can draw on their existing skill set to supplement their trauma work, incorporating both directive and non-directive interventions in Minecraft. As the previous chapters have illustrated, clinicians can use the Seven Guiding Principles to directly strengthen the adaptive trait of resilience, as described by Bartlett and Steber (2019).

Introducing Minecraft into Trauma Therapy: Clinical Applications

Implementing the Seven Guiding Principles

TIC provides the essential "why" and "what" for clinical practice as clinicians embrace the imperative to realize, recognize, respond, and resist re-traumatization. Yet, the "how" can remain elusive, especially when engaging with children and adolescents for whom traditional play and talk therapy may feel limiting or simply unapproachable. By following the Seven Guiding Principles, clinicians can effectively work with their clients to practice emotional regulation, explore narrative coherence, and experience interpersonal safety in real time.

The clinician's experience of being in the game with the child (Principle 3) and the coregulation of the play therapist to help build interoception and expand the child's WOT to stay present (Principle 4) can both be referenced as an underlying conceptual thread that is supplemented by the directive interventions below. The intentional awareness and practice of positive endings (Principle 5) are crucial for working with traumatized children to minimize unexpected environmental changes and to implement containment practices thoughtfully, as described below.

Caregivers of children who play Minecraft as part of a therapeutic, trauma-informed treatment plan can benefit from understanding how a child's relationship to the game can be helpful and how playing together can further support coping (see Clinical Interventions below and Chapter 18). Principles 6 and 7 serve as a reminder that the family system can be integrated into the child's experience of playing Minecraft outside therapy sessions, and that boundaries around the amount of time spent playing can help promote the use of Minecraft-informed coping skills in offline settings (see Chapters 8 and 9).

Directive Interventions

This section introduces activities that can serve as directive play therapy interventions in Minecraft. These interventions provide a compelling option for clinicians working with children and adolescents impacted by trauma as they provide safety, opportunity for process, and, most importantly, play. By adapting interventions commonly found in the beginning stages of EMDR into the client's digital world, such as grounding, resourcing, containment, emotional processing, and the practice of healthy coping skills, clinicians can address the core symptoms of trauma in an engaging, trauma-informed, and developmentally attuned manner. It is essential to note that while these interventions draw on EMDR-informed practices, they are not a substitute for formal EMDR training and certification. The interventions described here are applications of these principles in the context of Minecraft-based play therapy and can be safely utilized within the clinician's scope of practice.

Creating Safety: Grounding and Mindfulness Skills

While Chapter 4 introduced mindfulness as a tool for general immersion in the game, this section focuses on its specialized application as a directive, stabilizing intervention for children affected by trauma. Here, grounding and mindfulness are essential clinical tools for expanding the child's WOT and managing dysregulation.

Beginning with a foundation of grounding and mindfulness skills helps the child stay connected to the present moment by being aware of their body through their five senses (Schwartz & Maiberger, 2018). A child's ability to ground and stay present is a critical skill when they might begin to lose connection with their body due to trauma triggers or general overwhelm (Maiberger, 2009). The experience of playing Minecraft can be so quick and frantic that it is easy for children to lose focus on their real-life experiences. In these instances, the Fourth Guiding Principle serves as a framework for clinicians to use their presence in the relationship to support coregulation, helping children become more aware of their experiences while playing the game and manage potential distress. For further support, grounding interventions can be used to intentionally bring awareness to the solid connection between one's body and the earth, as well as the ground beneath them (Maiberger, 2009).

This does not have to be the physical earth, but it can be whatever helps the child experience the quality of a solid connection to what one's body is contacting (such as a chair, or even a bean bag cushion). Grounding and mindfulness practices can help intentionally slow down the experience at the start of a session or when entering a new world, using the game's stimulation and prompts to connect more deeply with oneself. This creates a dual awareness for the child, where attention is both on the game and toward themselves.

Play therapists can facilitate this by prompting their clients to imagine what it might feel like for their character to be standing on the ground in the game. Are they standing on grass, sand, or snow? Is there dirt under their feet? What would it feel like if their feet were bare? If their character is wearing armor, how heavy might it feel to walk? These questions can be revisited throughout the first session as brief grounding practices. This practice can also be adapted into other interventions, such as the As I Grow tree from Chapter 12. Clients who need more stable prompts to ground can be invited to imagine themselves as a tree in the game, perhaps one they built from the exercise or a random tree found in a biome. Activating "spectator mode" can even allow the child to digitally enter the tree and imagine their feet becoming its roots, and connecting themselves all the way down to the Bedrock.

After clients have practiced grounding, they can engage in a five-senses mindfulness exercise within the game. This mindfulness technique teaches the child to tune into their sensory experience in the moment by focusing on what is directly around them. Bringing attention to the game and the world around them, the client is prompted to name something they can see, touch, hear, smell, and taste. This is a highly effective method for children to practice further the skill of slowing down and bringing their attention to their full-body experience. Using grounding and mindfulness skills can help ease the distress that occurs when a child is outside their WOT and bring both the brain and body back into the present moment (see also Chapters 6 and 8).

Practicing these skills in the game can help make them more accessible to the child when they are away from the game. For example, using a real-life tree as a grounding support and bringing mindful attention to their experiences in different environments. This exercise can also be practiced at home and taught to parents and caregivers to do together as a family, both in and out of the game.

Building a Place of Safety and Empowerment

After the client has practiced grounding and mindfulness exercises, they can begin building a "safe place" as a resource for visualizing and internalizing states of calm, peace, and relaxation (Gomez, 2013). The "Safe Space" build is a fun intervention that can serve as a consistent starting point for new clients in the Minecraft world (Finch, 2021a, 2021b, 2022). It allows experienced players to showcase their skills and newer players to experiment, all while building trust with the clinician as they collaborate on creating a secure in-game location without immediately processing distressing emotions. For example, a child's safe space might be a small room with a chest of items, a hidden cave in a mountain biome, or an underwater structure that is far removed from other areas. The specific content is less important than the felt sense of safety it evokes for the child.

While this can often be a low-vulnerability intervention, clinicians should be prepared to adapt it to the client's needs. Some clients may struggle to identify safety and require multiple sessions to experiment with builds that work for them (Finch, 2024). For others, the terms "safe place" or "safe space" may not resonate in environments such as war zones under constant threat (Sukhorukov, 2025a). In these cases, clinicians can offer alternative descriptors such as ease, peaceful, calm, serene, or relaxing to find a word that prompts an internal sense of being okay (Maiberger, 2009).

One such adaptation is the "Happy Place," which serves as a gentler reframe. Shifting the focus from safety to joy can be particularly helpful for clients with a limited WOT for perceived threats. Here, clinicians guide clients to build based on what directly elicits feelings of happiness and positive affect. This could manifest as a vibrant garden with flowers and gems, a magical room with a jukebox and bookshelf, or an idyllic outdoor camping spot with a bonfire next to a body of water. The focus here is on referencing the positive emotion and feeling of joy.

For clients who need a sense of active strength, the language can be shifted toward empowerment. For example, Luke Blackwood, creator of *Legend Land* (see Chapter 20), suggests using the term "fortress" instead of "safe space," as this language can directly influence a client's felt sense of protection (Sukhorukov, 2025b). A fortress acts as both a retreat for relaxation and a symbol of strength, providing a powerful metaphor for resilience. A fortress might be a towering castle with high walls and a lava moat, a high-tech bunker sealed with pistons, or a mountain base with a single, easily defensible entrance. The key is that the child describes it as feeling strong, impenetrable, and under their control.

For children in contexts of active, ongoing threat, the concept of a "Fortress" can be further adapted into a "Place of Power." When considering the impact of working with children in war zones, Sukhorukov (2025a) uses the term "Place of Power" to acknowledge the threat children face. This intervention includes a pillar topped with a symbolic item that children could select to deposit into a "Chest of Power," physically externalizing their positive emotions (Sukhorukov, 2025a). The process of turning inward to identify a feeling of empowerment that is externalized in the chest further builds the child's capacity for self-reflection and interoception (see Chapter 6).

Working with Worries: Containment

Grounding, mindfulness skills, and access to a safe space (or alternatives) are initial tools for supporting traumatized children. Additional strategies, like containment exercises, can be beneficial when children experience distressing worries. Symptoms such as difficulty with eating, sleeping, anger, focus, poor impulse control, withdrawal, or relationship challenges can all show up as worries (CMI, 2022). Children might worry about recurring events, something bad happening to someone they care about, or disruptions to their routine or daily schedule, among many other concerns. Containment exercises can be introduced through in-game directive builds, helping children practice calming their worries. These techniques can also be adapted to rely on the child's imagination, enabling them to develop a portable skill they can use anywhere.

The Worry Box

A Worry Box is an intervention that serves as a tool for the child to help identify, name, and externalize the worries triggered by their traumatic experiences. To begin, children can be prompted to create a box or container that is large enough and secure enough to hold all of their worries. Children are asked to consider what material their worry box is made of, where they would like to build it, and how they would like to keep it secure. Ideally, this would be constructed away from their Safe Space to hold the intention and experiences of both separately. Similar to the Safe Space, the initial build of the worry box can be a fun and safe intervention during the early stages of the child's therapy, as it gives them complete control over the places and design elements of their world before they are prompted to explore further areas of distress.

As children begin to gain comfort with their play therapist, they can be prompted to explore the thoughts, feelings, or specific events and dynamics that they worry about. Mobs can be spawned or items can be dropped while in Creative mode to represent the elements of their worries. Children can explicitly share what certain items might represent, or they may choose to use an anvil and a name tag to assign words or phrases to their worries. After clients have established their worry box and added worries, it can be revisited throughout the session or at the beginning or end to determine whether new worries need to be added or whether old items that are no longer worrisome can be removed.

Book and Quill

Children who process through writing, or adolescents who journal, or who are more comfortable with the mechanics of text, a book and quill can serve as a private and safe container in the game. Similar prompts can be used as the worry box, yet the client has the flexibility to describe their worries in more detail through text. The book can be named and saved, creating a digital bookshelf of categorized worries. This supports clients in considering which worries might be grouped together and provides opportunities for therapeutic reflection on the areas of the child's experience that appear most distressing. After books are saved, clients can place them in a dedicated chest or bookshelf to further contain the distress.

For play therapists who use bibliotherapy in their practice, the book *Silly Billy* (Browne, 2006) can serve as an adjunctive support to illustrate the benefits and practice of sharing worries. The book tells the story of a grandmother who makes worry dolls for the child to whisper their worries to at night before falling asleep. Clients can spawn mobs within their worry box or dedicated worry container to represent their own version of the worry dolls. The practice of the mobs holding the worries can then be implemented at home, further bridging the experiences in the game to tangible practices outside of Minecraft.

Visualization

When clients do not have access to the game, clinicians can coach parents and caregivers to prompt the use of visualized reminders of their safe spaces or worry containers. Beginning with grounding and mindfulness skills, children can imagine what it would feel like to be standing or sitting in their safe space, taking in all five sensory experiences. If worries arise, they can imagine putting their thoughts and feelings in a jar and leaving it there so they do not come back to bother them (Gomez, 2013). Clinicians can practice these visualizations with clients at the end of sessions to contain the significant experiences that may have arisen during the play. It is critical to note if any of these exercises create more distress or if the child does not report positive experiences, in which case clinical consultation for the therapist is advised.

Emotional Processing

To assist in narrative exploration and creative expression in processing experiences of traumatic events, clinicians can combine bibliotherapy with Minecraft. Similar to using the *Silly Billy* for worries, the book *A Terrible Thing Happened* can be used to provide psychoeducation about the somatic impacts of witnessing a variety of traumatic events and how pushing feelings inside can perpetuate distressing emotions (Holmes & Pillo, 2000). Clinicians can begin by reading the book and discussing the main character's experience witnessing a terrible event, then shift the focus to a Creative Minecraft world where the client can express their terrible event through building or other game mechanics.

Acknowledging Changes

Similar to directive interventions used with sand trays, clients can use Minecraft to express, demonstrate, and process changes after experiencing traumatic events. In the vignette at the start of the chapter, a client is inspired to rebuild the room of a house that was lost in a fire. As the work with the client progresses, they may be prompted to build a replica of their new room. The "before" and "after" build process can assist the client in processing the grief of the traumatic experience, while also staying in the present and looking toward the future with their new circumstances.

Topics clinicians can ask about include: did everyone in the family experience the same changes? Do others understand what the changes have meant to them? Have they told their friends about the changes, and if so, who do they tell and why? Last, clinicians can acknowledge that, even amid significant changes, many things may have stayed the same.

Helping Children Cope

Children's reactions to a traumatic event can vary significantly depending on their development and emotional well-being. Directive interventions in Minecraft can help children navigate the aftermath of trauma by reminding them of strategies that were useful in the past while also exploring new ways to seek comfort and soothing. The Child Mind Institute (2025) suggests universal strategies for children and adolescents, including fostering a sense of safety through physical affection, maintaining consistent routines, and encouraging enjoyable activities. The creative opportunities in Minecraft can help clients move toward experiences of positive affects by exploring a happy place and five coping categories that can be referenced in times of distress.

The Five Coping Categories

Clinicians can use the game to explore and prompt awareness of diverse coping skills. This can be similar to a character's "skill tree" in role-playing video games. These five categories can be used in different ways depending on the situations and needs.

Physical

When clients engage with the digital world in the game, clinicians can begin to prompt awareness and discussions about the physical actions their character may perform on the screen. Running, jumping, swimming, and moving heavy objects are physical coping skills that can be applied to how a child copes outside the game as well. Playful conversations about the wish to fly and have elytra (a type of torso armor that enables soaring) in real life can lead to celebrating coping skills not found in Minecraft, such as riding a bike.

Cognitive

The act of playing Minecraft is a cognitive coping skill in itself, as it provides the child a way to think through setting goals, problem-solving, and bringing their imagination to life in the game. Other cognitive coping skills outside the game include puzzles, board games, cooking, reading, and any other activity in which the child consciously engages in thought-based activities to help them cope with distress.

Social

Social coping skills serve as a reminder that family, friends, and being around other people can be helpful coping tools when the other categories may not be effective. For some clients, this may involve intentionally setting aside time from individual play to connect in person or online with other players. Older clients can be reminded to reach out to their peers and have reminders to call or text friends when they are feeling alone or isolated. If being around other people is too stimulating or activating, listening to a podcast or audiobook can be a good alternative, as hearing another person's voice activates the ventral vagal nerve of the autonomic nervous system (Porges, 2011).

Soothing

Soothing coping skills can include anything that feels good and that the client does just for themselves. The five-senses mindfulness and grounding activity can be revisited here to find soothing practices and items related to the five senses. Again, this can be integrated with Minecraft and also used as a standalone practice. For example, the music in Minecraft can be soothing for many players while they play. Recognizing this could help strategically use the game's music to help fall asleep or destress in moments of dysregulation. Acknowledging the powerful, soothing benefits of music can also lead clients to consider which other music or sounds elicit similar positive responses.

Spiritual

For families with spiritual practices, coping skills that reflect one's sense of purpose and connection to the world, and discussions around shared family values can be integrated as sources of strength and comfort. This can influence how a client relations to building a "Safe Space" at home, engages with the End Poem during the final credits of the game, and how they perceive communal interactions in villages.

Clinical Vignette 1

It is the first session, and verbal communication has been minimal. The child keeps focus on the game as interactions with me are on an as-needed basis. It is an encouraging sign that they are even playing at all and have agreed to show up. Their comfort with the mechanics and the game is evident in how efficiently they move throughout the digital world. Observing their non-verbal cues, I notice their body tension relax and soften with big exhalations, and a softness emerges in their voice when they mention some of the "cute" animals in the game, as well as the noises they make.

"I wonder what it would feel like to be standing in that biome right now?"

"It looks really sandy. I bet the sand would stick to my shoes." They are on a coastline; the blue water stretches out before them.

"What would it be like to really dig your heels in the sand? Could you imagine taking a couple of big breaths and sinking into that spot?"

The child smiles, "I bet the sand would feel good through my toes!"

"It would be very different than where you are sitting while playing the game right now."

The child nods, and their character moves on.

As they walk along the ocean, I begin to prompt a mindfulness exercise, "What are all the things you see in this biome? What can you touch?"

The child opens up a bit more, and we talk about the other senses, including what they might hear and smell. When I ask what they imagine they could taste, they respond, "seafood!" and we both laugh together.

As the session progresses, I ask if they would like to build a safe space in the game. A place that is special and personal just for them. They ask for my help selecting and placing blocks. The child builds quickly, and we move on to another build.

"I know that sometimes kids can have really big worries, and it can feel like there's no place they can go. We can build a Worry Box in this world that can hold all of your worries, so you can keep them in there every time we meet. When you're at home, you can imagine this worry box in your mind and practice putting all of your thoughts, emotions, and yucky feelings in your body, into this box."

"I would need to build it so that it's REALLY strong."

"Yes, that's important to me too - that it's really strong."

"I want it to be made of Bedrock so that nothing can destroy it either." The child sits upright and focuses on the menu of his inventory as he selects Bedrock blocks. He drops them in front of me, and we begin to build his worry box together as he tells me some of the things that he thinks about before going to sleep at night.

Family-Level Processing

A child's trauma inevitably reverberates through the entire family system, especially in instances when the whole system is impacted by an event such as a natural disaster. While the family-level Minecraft sessions described in Chapter 8 build connection, here their function intensifies: they become a structured yet flexible platform for processing the trauma itself. The goal shifts from building general safety to creating a relational container secure enough to hold the child's most painful experiences.

The clinician facilitates this by adapting familiar interventions for trauma work. The child's guided tour of their world is no longer just about empowerment; it becomes a contained form of processing and narrative reconstruction. As the child leads their caregivers through a "before-and-after" replica of a lost home, or other changes following a significant loss, they are not merely sharing an interest; they are initiating the co-creation of a new, shared narrative. The parent's role, coached in real-time by the clinician, is to provide a regulated, witnessing presence that validates the child's experience without becoming overwhelmed themselves. This practice fosters mutual recognition of each member's experience, which is a vital part of family healing (NCTSN, 2010).

Similarly, a joint build, such as a "Worry Box," moves beyond the initial narrative exploration into a combined activity for the family. The act of collaboratively designing and constructing a structure to hold worries in the game and at home allows the family to physically enact the process of containment and mastery over otherwise dysregulating emotions. The clinician's focus is on using the principles of coregulation (Principle 4) to help the family stay within their WOT while engaging with this charged material.

The following vignette illustrates how these adapted interventions function in practice. It demonstrates the real-time process of a guided tour as both narrative reconstruction and a joint activity, serving as a family-level intervention, and shows how the clinician supports this work to embody Principles 6 and 7 simultaneously.

Clinical Vignette 2

The first vignette demonstrated grounding and mindfulness skills, concluding with the construction of a worry box. As referenced in the chapter's introduction, the following sessions evolved into the child building a before-and-after build to process the changes following a devastating fire. As the child processed experiences in the previous home and the current home, asking for my help along the way, it became time to bring the parents into the session for family-level processing:

With the parents watching in the Minecraft world, their child begins to show them a replica of the home that was engulfed in flames. Flying around the 3d structure, tears start to rise as the parents marvel at the level of detail that has been replicated. To help support their connection with their child, I offer a gentle prompt to begin the therapeutic dialogue. "This was something that your child built from the ground up, with no guidance or instruction. What is it like for you to see this right now?"

One of the parents wipes their eyes. "It's incredible. I know you were working on this for a couple of weeks, and I'm amazed at all the detail and thought you put into this."

"They even included the special chair that we used to have in the corner when they were younger." The parent says that while looking at me, so I redirect them to repeat it, but this time, looking at their child and connecting with them directly about that observation.

"I'm surprised you remember that chair ..."

The child's face brightens, "I remember how we used to move that to put the Christmas tree there too."

Tears well up once again, and the parents lean over to hug the child. "I see you getting quiet as you show us your old room. It's okay to feel sad. We get sad when we think of our old room, too. We're right here with you and we can get through this together."

After more memories are shared, both from the child and the parents, they move to take a tour of a build of the new house. This initiates conversations about what is missed about the old home, as well as what they truly enjoy about the new one. I acknowledge that there is enough space in this process for both sets of feelings.

"I like my room in the new house better because now that I'm older, I can design it more how I like it - it's like a fresh start." The child turns to their parents as they say this.

"I never knew that. I was so worried that you hated your new room because it was smaller." Again, the parent leans in for a hug.

I hear a worry being named and use that as an opportunity to prompt a way for them to work with their worries while also finding a bridge between the game and their interactions with the new home. However, as the child has already created a "Worry Box," I suggest that they use the book and quill to write down worries they might have. Together, they find a space in the house to put a chest and keep it there.

We take a break from the game and discuss how they can keep a notebook at home to write their worries in at night when they get too overwhelming. The parents suggest complementing that with a gratitude jar that can also be used and revisited every week to remind them what they are grateful for.

Before ending the session, one of the parents mentions that they would like to paint a couple of the rooms and asks if he can show the child in the game so they can all see what it might look like. The child agrees and the parents take the controller, replacing the original blocks with light green cement blocks.

"Whoa, that looks really cool!"

"I'm glad you like it! We can try different options too and see what we all like best."

This vignette illustrates how theoretical concepts come to life, highlighting the crucial shift from clinician-led to parent-led coregulation. The guided tour of the "before and after" build acted as a structured narrative reconstruction, enabling the child to control the pace of sharing traumatic memories. The clinician's initial prompt exemplified Principle 6, but the key moment was the parent's unprompted, attuned response: "I see you getting quiet ... It's okay to feel sad. We get sad too ... We can get through this together." This statement encapsulates the essence of the parent stepping into their role as the primary coregulator, as they independently recognize the child's emotional state, validate the emotion, and frame the family as a resilient unit. This fostered the mutual recognition essential for family healing.

The shift to the "Book and Quill" was a direct application of Principle 7, transforming an in-game mechanic into a tangible coregulation ritual for the home. The family was not just discussing worries; they were collaboratively designing a system to manage them. The parents' initiative to paint the rooms in-game met with the child's enthusiastic approval and cemented this new relational template. This progression from verbal coregulation to joint problem-solving demonstrates the secure, coregulated foundation established in Chapter 8 being actively built and internalized by the family.

Looking Ahead

From the initial grounding exercises to the complex narrative of rebuilding a lost bedroom, Minecraft offers a unique and powerful space for the multifaceted work of trauma processing. Its digital environment provides a controlled, predictable setting where the main symptoms of trauma, such as dysregulation, helplessness, and a fractured sense of safety, can be actively addressed. By intentionally applying the Seven Guiding Principles, clinicians can use this platform to help children and adolescents restore a sense of agency, practice essential regulatory skills, and gradually shape their internal experiences through the power of play.

The clinical applications in this chapter, from creating Safe Spaces and Worry Boxes to processing changes and developing coping skills, show the modality's adaptability. These strategies meet the child where they are, respecting both their developmental level and their therapeutic needs without requiring verbal expression before they're ready. Ultimately, this work doesn't have to be limited to the child-therapist relationship. As demonstrated, it can be effectively expanded to include the family system, utilizing the child's expertise to promote mutual understanding, shared healing, and a renewed sense of safety within the child's primary relationships.

By combining a thorough understanding of trauma, a solid foundation in trauma-informed care, and the structured flexibility of Minecraft, play therapists gain a new and highly effective tool to help children not only process their past but also to build a more resilient and hopeful future.

Helpful Tips

- **Rebuilding Agency and Control:** Minecraft addresses core trauma symptoms by providing a safe digital world and a ventral vagal anchor. Its fixed boundaries and user-controlled mechanics allow children to gain a sense of agency and control through structured and client-led experiences.
- **Customizing the Therapeutic Container:** Safety is established by intentionally modifying game features such as day-night cycles, weather, or character mortality (Peaceful Mode) to fit the child's unique triggers and WOT. This is essential for preventing re-traumatization and maximizing security.
- **Grounding and Dual Awareness:** Grounding and mindfulness are used as directive, stabilizing interventions. Clinicians use the game's sensory prompts (e.g., imagining the character standing on grass or sand) to help the child connect with their body and the present moment, creating a dual awareness to manage dysregulation.

- **Resource and Containment Builds:** Trauma symptoms are addressed using directive builds that adapt EMDR principles. Interventions like building a Safe Space, Happy Place, or Fortress provide resources for visualizing internal strength, while the Worry Box or Book and Quill help children externalize and contain distressing thoughts.
- **Family Trauma Narrative:** Minecraft serves as a platform for family-level trauma processing by facilitating structured narrative reconstruction, such as guided tours of "before-and-after" builds. This empowers the child to lead the process while caregivers provide a regulated, witnessing presence and engage in mutual recognition essential for healing.

Reflection Question

1 When preparing for a trauma session, what specific game setting (e.g., enabling Peaceful Mode, locking the time to daytime) would be my most powerful tool for proactively establishing safety and for which client would this be most critical?

References

Alvis, L., Zhang, N., Sandler, I. N., & Kaplow, J. B. (2022). Developmental manifestations of grief in children and adolescents: Caregivers as key grief facilitators. *Journal of Child & Adolescent Trauma*, *16*(2), 447–457. https://doi.org/10.1007/s40653-021-00435-0

Bartlett, J. D., & Steber, K. (2019). *How to implement trauma-informed care to build resilience to childhood trauma*. Child Trends. https://www.childtrends.org/publications/how-to-implement-trauma-informed-care-to-build-resilience-to-childhood-trauma

Browne, A. (2006). *Silly billy*. Walker Books.

Child Mind Institute. (2025). *Helping children cope after a traumatic event: A recovery guide for parents, teachers, and community leaders*. https://childmind.org/guide/helping-children-cope-after-a-traumatic-event/

Finch, E. (2021a). *How does counselling using Minecraft work?* Counselling-Directory.org.uk; Counselling Directory. https://www.counselling-directory.org.uk/articles/how-does-counselling-using-minecraft-work

Finch, E. (2021b). Therapeutic adventures in Minecraft. Playmode Academy; *BACP Children, Young People & Families*. https://playmodeacademy.org/resources-and-publications/featured-article-in-bacp-journal

Finch, E. (2022). *Thinking of using video games therapeutically?* Association for Counseling and Therapy Online. https://playmodeacademy.org/resources-and-publications/thinking-of-using-video-games-therapeutically

Finch, E. (2024). Game changer. *The New Psychotherapist*, *87*. https://www.psychotherapy.org.uk/media/dz3fbkfv/87_new-psychotherapist-autumn-2024_web.pdf

Gomez, A. M. (2013). *EMDR therapy and adjunct approaches with children: Complex trauma, attachment, and dissociation*. Springer Pub.

Holmes, M. M., & Pillo, C. (2000). *A terrible thing happened: A story for children who have witnessed violence or trauma*. Dalmation Press.

Kessler, R. C., Aguilar-Gaxiola, S., Alonso, J., Benjet, C., Bromet, E. J., Cardoso, G., & Koenen, K. C. (2017). Trauma and PTSD in the WHO world mental health surveys. *World Psychiatry*, *16*(2), 283–296.

Maiberger, B. (2009). *EMDR essentials: A guide for clients and therapists*. W. W. Norton & Co.

National Child Traumatic Stress Network. (2010). *Age-related reaction to a traumatic event*. https://www.nctsn.org/resources/age-related-reactions-traumatic-event

National Child Traumatic Stress Network. (2023). *About child trauma*. https://www.nctsn.org/what-is-child-trauma/about-child-trauma

Perry, B. D., & Szalavitz, M. (2008). *The boy who was raised as a dog and other stories from a child psychiatrist's notebook: What traumatized children can teach us about loss, love, and healing*. Basic Books.

Porges, S. W. (2011). *The polyvagal theory: Neurophysiological foundations of emotions, attachment, communication, and self-regulation*. W. W. Norton & Company.

Schwartz, A., & Maiberger, B. (2018). *EMDR therapy and somatic psychology: Interventions to enhance embodiment in trauma treatment*. W. W. Norton & Company.

Siegel, D. J. (1999). *The developing mind: How relationships and the brain interact to shape who we are*. Guilford Press.

Siegel, D. J. (2014). *Brainstorm: The power and purpose of the teenage brain*. Jeremy P. Tarcher/Penguin, a Member of Penguin Group.

Sukhorukov, O. (2025a). *Wonderworld: Minecraft & offline quest for Ukrainian refugee children*. HealGame Ukraine. https://healgameukraine.click/en/wonderworld-minecraft-offline-quest-for-ukrainian-refugee-children/

Sukhorukov, O. (2025b). *Luke Blackwood: The game has a hidden power*. HealGame Ukraine. https://healgameukraine.click/en/luke-blackwood-the-game-has-a-hidden-power/

United Nations High Commissioner for Refugees. (2025). *Global trends: Forced displacement in 2024*. United Nations High Commissioner for Refugees.

United Nations International Children's Emergency Fund. (2023). *The climate-changed child: A children's climate risk index supplement*. UNICEF.

van der Kolk, B. (2014). *The body keeps the score: Brain, mind, and body in the healing of trauma*. Penguin Books.

Winnicott, D. W. (1953). Transitional objects and transitional phenomena: A study of the first not-me possession. *The International Journal of Psychoanalysis*, *34*, 89–97.

Wonders, L. L. (2025). *Mindfulness-based play therapy: A transtheoretical and neurobiological approach to psychotherapy with children and families*. Taylor & Francis.

World Health Organization. (2022). *World mental health report: Transforming mental health for all*. World Health Organization.

Chapter 14

Engaging Neurodivergent Clients

Judy Singer (2017) is often credited with first introducing the term "neurodiversity" in 1998, when she wrote about the importance of reframing conditions like autism and attention deficit hyperactivity disorder (ADHD) as natural variations in the human brain. However, the concept and theory have deeper, collective roots. Recent archival findings show that the core idea of "neurological diversity" was in use years earlier (Botha et al., 2024), indicating that neurodiversity as a theory was collectively developed by neurodivergent people, with Singer playing a crucial role in naming and popularizing it (Botha et al., 2024). Her groundbreaking work emphasizes that these are not disorders to be cured or behaviors to be extinguished, but natural representations of the diversity found in human expression. Singer's advocacy, and the broader neurodiversity movement it fueled, has led to a growing need for neurodivergent children to have support that affirms this reality. The paradigm for providing care has thus shifted dramatically from Applied Behavioral Analysis (ABA) or Cognitive Behavioral Therapy (CBT) approaches to more affirming therapeutic frameworks (Delahooke, 2019; Grant, 2023; Price, 2022). The previous focus of traditional ABA and CBT was to change children's behaviors to meet the expectations of their neurotypical peers and cultural standards, sending the message that a neurodivergent child's way of being in the world is wrong and not preferred (Price, 2022). This shift has been heavily influenced by autistic adults, who now have a more influential voice in advocating for the type of support the next generation of neurodiverse children receives (Grandin, 2006; Price, 2022; Silberman, 2015).

Providing a neurodiverse affirming play therapy space means clinicians give room for the child's entire being to be witnessed without the conflict of judgment or desire to change. The importance of a neurodivergent child feeling safe, proud, and inspired to be themselves provides the opportunity for authentic expression and relationship with others (Delahooke, 2019; Grandin, 2006; Grant, 2023; Price, 2022; Silberman, 2015). Ultimately, neurodiversity encompasses a spectrum of needs and expressions. It is the

DOI: 10.4324/9781003614784-17

clinician's responsibility to learn about these needs for their clients and how to meet them in a safe, curious, and collaborative environment, all of which can be accomplished in Minecraft.

This paradigm shift to affirmative therapy encompasses support for all the mental health needs that neurotypical clients would typically seek, while prioritizing therapeutic approaches that support a child's natural and comfortable expressions of self, such as the neurodiversity-affirming framework of AutPlay (Grant, 2023, 2025). Additionally, clients can benefit from Polyvagal-informed interventions, which focus on understanding and helping a child's physiological states rather than their behavior (Delahooke, 2019). These approaches require the therapist to consider the entirety of the child in front of them, molding and adapting interventions to meet their unique needs. This further requires clinicians to be curious about a child's sensory needs and aversions, using that understanding to adjust the therapeutic environment and their own approach based on principles of sensory integration and sensory processing challenges (Delahooke, 2019; Grant, 2023).

This chapter provides information for working with neurodivergent clients, with a focus on supporting the needs of autistic children and ADHDers in the playroom. The Seven Guiding Principles can be applied to the skills and interventions that neurodiverse-affirming clinicians are already using to support neurodivergent children in their clinical practice. Drawing on the concepts presented in the principles, play therapists can utilize Minecraft as an intervention that complements the existing theories and models that underpin their work. Interventions and research from clinicians within the therapeutic Minecraft community are also discussed. As referenced in Chapter 6, it is also imperative for the therapist to examine their own thoughts and feelings, not only in relation to the client but also in relation to the role of neurodiversity in a neurotypical culture, as unconscious judgments can arise during the therapeutic process (Grant, 2023).

Emerging Evidence for Using Minecraft with Neurodivergent Children

The use of Minecraft in therapy, particularly for autistic children, is a growing and innovative practice. A small but compelling body of research and clinical observations is beginning to validate its effectiveness. The existing literature, which focuses on individual, family, and group applications, is still emerging, given the growing exposure the application of Minecraft is receiving as an intervention. Special key areas of benefit will be highlighted in this chapter, while Chapter 15 focuses specifically on group applications.

Initial advocacy and studies have demonstrated the effectiveness of using Minecraft in play therapy, supporting social-emotional learning and communication for autistic children (Madigan, 2020; Zolyomi & Schmalz, 2017). Further pilot work with children and their parents suggests Minecraft can be a valuable tool with children who previously struggled to engage in traditional therapy for exploring emotional recognition and regulation (Blackwood, 2025). A case study by Gerhardt and Smith (2020) with an autistic child processing trauma demonstrated improvements in relieving symptoms of depression and a reduction in perseveration about the trauma itself. Anecdotal reports from within the community powerfully highlight the game's role in fostering creative expression, self-advocacy, and a sense of voice (Stuart, 2015, 2024).

This chapter will build upon this foundational evidence by providing clinicians with a practical framework for applying these principles in their work with a diverse range of neurodivergent children.

Understanding Neurodivergence: Deepening Awareness and Accommodation

While the neurodiversity paradigm encompasses a wide range of neurotypes, this chapter will focus specifically on children who identify as autistic or as an ADHDer and uses identity-first, identity-affirming language to avoid a deficit-based terminology which could be considered stigmatizing. These neurotypes are frequently encountered in clinical practice and share commonalities in seeking support to address emotional regulation, sensory processing, executive functioning, and social communication that are highly relevant to the use of Minecraft in play therapy. Play therapists may find that the children they work with could have a formal diagnosis of autism or ADHD, or they may be self-identified. A formal diagnosis is not required for a child to identify as neurodivergent; however, it can be a helpful tool for receiving accommodations, self-validation, and understanding (Grant, 2023; Price, 2022).

Clinicians can support an affirming stance through their communication with the child, the adults in their life, and the systems to which they belong, such as schools and other educational programs. Grant (2023) informs clinicians that neurodivergent children come to therapy for the same reasons other children do: for a wide variety of mental health needs. This includes the topics presented in the previous chapters, such as working with emotional distress and dysregulation, negative self-talk and building self-esteem, grief and bereavement, processing the impact of trauma, and the need for social connection through group work. He further advocates that being neurodivergent-affirming means that clinicians are embracing all aspects of their clients' identities to adapt their play therapy approaches to meet the clients' interests and preferences. This can make Minecraft a critical intervention to reach neurodivergent youth who may not feel connected to other types of therapy.

Autism in the Play Therapy Space

Autistic children often require flexibility in communication styles, which can pose a challenge if clinicians are too rigid in their approach. A key strength of using Minecraft in person and online through telehealth is the variety of ways the child and the play therapist can communicate with each other. For children who may prefer precise, literal language and rules, the structure and logical cause-and-effect relationship of Minecraft can offer predictability through a rules-based understanding that resonates with children of that neurotype. Alternatively, children who are nonverbal can explore emotional expression through in-game or on-screen chat, use emotes and emoticons, and employ other engaging ways to express themselves, such as relying on different-colored blocks, preferences for biomes or weather cycles, and the type of engagement in the game.

Whether play therapists are working in person or online, it is vital to consider the sensory processing differences of their clients, including visual, tactile, and auditory stimulation, as well as anything that could lead to potential overwhelm. Children playing in the therapist's office may have requests for adjusting the room lighting, using objects as a fidget while playing, and preferences for the direct sound of the game, as well as ways to isolate noises, such as through the use of headphones. Online therapists can prompt caregivers and parents to consider these accommodations when meeting with clients online. Reminding the client at the start of the session to prepare their meeting space comfortably, find fidgets, and make their preferred audio adjustments can be helpful and affirming. This is also a key piece of the Second Guiding Principle, which is that the therapy begins even before the game is played.

When considering gameplay, it is also essential to recognize how clients may choose to engage with open-ended abstract questions or specific, directive requests. Understanding the child's preference can help inform decisions about whether non-directive interventions, which focus on free play, are the best fit or if the child might prefer directive interventions that provide structure and are more specifically oriented toward the linear approach of Survival mode or task-oriented gameplay. As the First and Third Guiding Principles state, the therapist does not have to be a good player, and the therapist is not playing for their own enjoyment. Prioritizing the safe and trusting relationship that the child has with the game and in the session can be a validating and reparative experience for autistic children who have not had those affirming experiences.

ADHD in the Play Therapy Space

Neurodivergent children who present with ADHD may have a need for novelty and high engagement, which can be supported by engaging the client's strengths and interests (Silberman, 2015). The need for prioritizing an individualized approach is crucial to further support autonomic nervous system activation (dysregulation in the form of hyperactivity), rejection sensitive dysphoria (RSD), and hyperfocus as areas of interest that clinicians need to take into consideration. Furthermore, there can also be challenges with working memory and following multi-step verbal instructions, which may be relevant to initial game set-up and engaging with task-based directive interventions.

Directive interventions can prioritize top-down approaches that engage the prefrontal cortex, providing clients with the structure and stimulation they need for direct focus on a specific area of engagement (Mate, 2019). This may be preferred by children who report feeling overwhelmed with free play and find the structure of following instructions soothing and regulating. The Fourth and Seventh Guiding Principles provide structure for clinicians orienting to their clients during non-directive play, as clients can benefit from coregulation skills that can also be taught to parents and caregivers and applied at home and away from the game.

ADHDers may also find that transitioning out of their sessions takes a lot of mental energy, as it is easy to get engrossed in a task (Price, 2022). The Fifth Guiding Principle serves as a reminder that intentional endings, no matter how challenging they may be, are an essential part of the work. It is not uncommon for clients to become deeply engaged in the game, making the transition from ending the session to returning to life outside the play therapy space even more challenging. This can also present as a secondary challenge for the play therapist if they also identify as an ADHDer or with neurotypes that can become easily immersed in the game play. Chapter 6 references the dynamics of countertransference that can arise when working with clients, and there is also a benefit to cultivating self-compassion and understanding of one's own neurodiverse traits.

AuDHD in the Play Therapy Space

Many adolescents and young adults who have found community through various social media platforms have connected over experiences that affirm neurotypes found in both autistic and ADHD traits. Embracing the identity-first language of the neurodivergent community, the self-proclaimed AuDHDers discover unique and distinct overlaps in their experiences that are validated as different identities, rather than just a comorbidity. This can include executive functioning challenges, sensory preferences and aversions, a mix of bottom-up or top-down processing, challenges with interoception and the ability to describe emotions (alexithymia), and the overall difficulty of asking for help and getting one's needs met. Understanding this profile allows the therapist to move beyond general conceptualizations and tailor the Minecraft experience to the individual's unique sensory, cognitive, and emotional needs.

Minecraft as a Neurodivergent-Affirmative Intervention

Minecraft is neurodivergent affirming in that it can adapt to the unique abilities, identities, and expressions of each child (and the adults playing with them). Offering Minecraft to clients removes barriers to further exploration of a client's interests and passions. Joining a child's excitement about the game communicates the message that the play therapist is open to all of the child's unique interests. This could begin with other topics being integrated into the gameplay, such as building dinosaurs, creating train systems using rollercoasters, and exploring the nuances of programming and engineering with Redstone.

Adjacent interests, such as LEGO, can be directly integrated into the sessions by exploring the similarities and differences with Minecraft, helping to build rapport and interest in the therapeutic relationship. This process of integration can function as a transitional intervention, using the client's passion for Minecraft to build bridges to other toys and means of play within the therapy room. A child who feels safe with the play therapist can have a sense of pride about who they are and how they experience the world.

The gameplay mechanics in Minecraft build on this sense of safety due to the level of control they offer. As mentioned in Chapter 13, the world in Minecraft can be utilized as a grounding and mindfulness intervention by bringing the client's awareness to the dual experience of both being in session and the imagined experience of being in the game environment. Due to the potential impact of this intervention, it may be overstimulating for clients who have sensory preferences or aversions. To remedy this, the therapist and client can collaborate on creating sensory-friendly worlds that place the client in a non-triggering biome, along with other visual and auditory elements that feel more comfortable and safe.

The use of Creative mode supports this type of client-focused intervention and can be further utilized for its open-world, sandbox-style strengths, which include player-led engagement. Clients who struggle with the rigidity of requests (perhaps identified with pathological demand avoidance) may be drawn to the open expression provided through the game mechanics. If play becomes more collaborative, it may naturally transition from working together on creative tasks to later moving into Survival mode as a way to explore working together under the external perceived pressure of the threat that comes at night.

The Clinician's Role: Understanding and Empowerment

When I speak to parents and caregivers about the possibility of using Minecraft in play therapy sessions with their neurodivergent child, I assess whether the child is interested in digital games, if there is a preference to being in person or online, if there is interest in group game play, and if there might be any limitations to playing the game together. Often, these considerations are known and addressed upfront. Parents and caregivers will typically seek out digital play, knowing specifically that their child is drawn to that type of play. Others may be curious because other play-based interventions had not been effective, and the idea of an alternative play model might resonate with the child's neurodivergent strengths and interests. This aligns with findings from Blackwood (2025), who observed that the therapeutic implementation of Minecraft led to positive changes in emotional regulation skills among children, in part due to their engagement and interest in the game.

The same can be said for the desire to be online or in person. Neurodivergent children who struggle with eye contact or social stimulation after a long school day might benefit from the safety of a screen when interacting and feel more grounded being in their home or familiar space. Being online also provides the safety of having control over whether the child wants to be seen with the screen on or if they prefer only to be seen in the game. The power to turn the screen on and off provides an element of control that can fulfill the magical wish of being invisible at school or in social situations. Conversely, others may find their home environment too stimulating, with family members and other distractions, so having a special place, such as a play therapy office or other designated meeting place, might be preferred.

Structuring the Session

To determine the best path forward, it is essential to inquire about preferences for meeting once a week for 45–50 minutes sessions or twice a week for 30 minutes. Longer weekly sessions can provide more focused time for clients to settle into the session and complete self-identified objectives or follow more complex directive prompts. Shorter, more frequent sessions can reduce cognitive load, make therapy feel less demanding, and provide more opportunities to practice intentional endings (see also Chapter 7).

Inquiries can also be made about what time of day the child feels most engaged and active. Other considerations include whether morning or mid-day appointments might be a better fit than an afternoon or early evening meeting. While this is susceptible to the scheduling availability of both the client and the clinician, it can be essential to discuss the child's individual processing styles: an ADHDer may have no cognitive resources left after school. At the same time, an autistic child may be overstimulated.

For clients who benefit from structure in sessions, clinicians can create a pre-built world that utilizes signs as reminders for time-related transitions and choices for directive interventions. If this approach is helpful, it can also be adapted by parents and used at home with printed out graphics from the game (Grant, 2023). If the in-game daylight cycles are being used, clinicians can draw attention to the passage of time (10 minutes for each) and explicitly state what that means in relation to the session structure. As mentioned in Chapter 7, routines associated with starting and ending each session can also be helpful and provide a collaborative relational experience by creating a greeting and/or closing interaction.

Communication Accommodations

It is also discussed during the initial intake whether the child has needs for nonverbal methods of expression that could be accommodated within the gameplay. This demonstrates the affirming and flexible nature of Minecraft as a play intervention by educating parents and caregivers on the various ways clinicians can communicate with the child during the session. When meeting online, the on-screen chat function and emoji feature can be used to express a wide range of emotions. Players can also use the in-game chat feature to communicate; however, for privacy concerns, it is recommended that they refrain from discussing clinical content (see Chapter 18). While it is easy to talk and play at the same time with attention divided between both tasks, clients would momentarily be pulled away from the gameplay to type and process the communication at their own separate pace. The in-game emote feature can also be used for nonverbal emotional expressions. All of these options are affirming to the child and also offer the added value of providing intentional breaks for expression and connection.

Incorporating Movement and Regulation

Rhythmic and vestibular input (such as jumping) can help regulate the autonomic nervous system by downregulating a fight-or-flight response or energizing a shutdown state, thereby prompting a child to engage in higher-level cognitive or emotional work (Delahooke, 2019) (see also Chapters 6 and 8). This principle can be seamlessly integrated into a play therapy session in several ways, both while playing the game and during breaks from it. Clinicians might keep a small trampoline in their play therapy space for the child to use at any time during the session while playing the game to provide active stimulation. While it might be challenging to do both, clients can easily step on and off when there are natural transitions or breaks in the game, like sleeping through the night. For children who play at home, it could be prearranged for them to have access if needed while they are on the call. The clinician can also coregulate with the child by jumping along with them in person or on the screen (see Chapter 6). Other movement ideas include shaking out one's arms and legs, intentional segments of standing up and sitting down, and having dance party breaks.

The game itself provides built-in rhythmic, regulating actions that can bring awareness to the child's body and the world around them. The general movement required to navigate the world and the repetitive motions of mining can help bridge the child's experience in the game to their interactions offline. Clinicians can draw attention to how the characters move in the game, including their jumping, swimming, crouching, and carrying of heavy objects. The in-game activity of mining can be acknowledged as a rhythmic, repetitive action that is soothing and even serves as a type of digital fidget, bridging the on-screen activity with the off-screen action of what the client's hands are doing. Further discussions can be prompted by reflecting on what blocks might require more energy, strength, and resources to destroy, and which ones feel most satisfying. This can lead to discussions about fidgets or items that the child has in real life that help with regulation. The goal is not to see the game and the body as separate, but to use the child's engagement with Minecraft as an opportunity to practice and integrate mind-body regulation.

Sensory Accommodations

The sensory stimulation that can arise in Minecraft gameplay can also be powerfully regulated with physical proprioceptive tools, soothing the body through external input. As Delahooke (2019) explains, tools such as weighted blankets or stuffed animals provide input that directly affects the autonomic nervous system, promoting a physiological state of safety and calm. Clients can use a weighted blanket while playing to receive crucial sensory input that helps their brain and body regulate, allowing them to engage more fully in the therapeutic process and the digital world. For children who feel too restricted by weighted blankets, lap pads can be a more comfortable alternative, especially when sitting with a controller or at the keyboard.

Auditory information can also provide sensory input that may need to be supported throughout the sessions. Grant (2023) writes about the paradoxical experience of ADHDers, who may be distracted by noise while also needing noise to focus. Clients with sensitivity to sounds can use headphones when meeting online to manage the mix of game audio and the therapist's voice, while reducing external environmental noise. This strategy can also be adapted during in-person sessions if the client and therapist are sitting close enough to hear conversational dialogue while reducing the noise that might be overheard from other rooms or hallways. In-game sounds can also be muted entirely and supplemented with different music or none at all, depending on the client's preferences.

Clinicians can also be mindful of using adjustable lighting during in-person sessions to minimize screen glare, avoid fluorescent lights, or consider any other accommodations that could be helpful. Similarly, clinicians can work with caregivers to ensure that online sessions are comfortable, taking into account any adjustments made to contrast with screen lighting and the overall ambiance of the client's space.

Clinical Vignette: Using the Health and Hunger Bar for Mind/Body Awareness

To help a child overwhelmed by sensory overload, I leveraged the Minecraft Health and Hunger Bars to build on our work with interoception and expand their Window of Tolerance. I began by drawing their attention to how they monitored these mechanics in-game.

"I noticed you have kept a lot of food items in your chest. It seems important that you're character doesn't get too hungry."

They nod in acknowledgment and mention the impact their Hunger bar has on their health; they need to monitor that as well to be at full capacity. We discuss how a variety of interactions in their Survival world cause their Health bar to deplete.

"I'm okay if I have, like, half of my hearts left, but if I'm only down to one or two hearts, then I don't want to go into a cave or be caught out at night because I'll die right away." As they say this, the child is describing the observation of their character's window of tolerance in the game.

I recognize this awareness and respond with the intention of bringing together multiple pieces of our work, "That's kind of like how we do our check-in at the beginning and ending of our meetings. Just like we have a scale of 0-10, your character does too!"

"Yeah, I guess so..." I hear some hesitation in their voice as it can be hard to talk about their 'real life stuff' when playing

the game. "Have you noticed that there are some days when you come home from school and you might feel exhausted and don't want to do anything, while other days you might feel better?"

"Yeah ..."

"And sometimes going to the doctor's office can feel like a HUGE deal, while going to the store isn't?"

"I HATE when I have to go to the doctor's office! All I want to do is sleep when I get home."

"That makes a lot of sense. It's like you had a full health bar and by going there, you used almost all of your hearts. It doesn't mean it's a bad thing, it just means that you might need more rest after, and you don't have enough hearts left to do something else."

"You're right! That is what's it's like. But sometimes my mom will have snacks ready for me and if I'm able to eat right after, I don't need to rest as much."

"Exactly! Just as your hunger bar helps your energy in the game, noticing that in real life can help your ability to take on bigger challenges."

"That's so cool. I wish I had a golden apple in real life."

"Me too! But maybe we can find something similar. Is it okay if we talk to your mom about this so she can have a better understanding of how some activities and some days may take away more hearts than others? Then we can all make a plan together to figure out what items you need in your real life 'hot bar' to keep in your backpack - does that sound good?"

"Sure!"

This in-game conversation provided a concrete metaphor for the client to assess their own capacity. This intervention operationalizes a concept akin to "Spoon Theory" (Miserandino, 2003, as cited in Miserandino, 2020), which articulates the finite energy reserves of chronic illness and has been widely adopted by the neurodivergent community to describe mental capacity. This collaborative, system-wide understanding is essential, transforming an in-game metaphor into a shared family language for managing energy and sustaining regulation.

Looking Ahead: From Individual to Group Work

In advocating for an antidote to isolation, Price (2022) suggests that the initial step in self-discovery is embracing your true self and then exploring others with similar experiences. Silberman (2015) writes about the empowering experience of autistic people finding affirming group spaces that allow interaction at their own pace and in their own language, providing potential corrective opportunities for experiences they may not have had previously. More significantly, a vast majority of the current research and literature about the use of Minecraft in play therapy focuses on autistic children and group work. The natural tendency for neurodivergent youth to form affirming communities around shared interests, including in digital spaces like the AutCraft Community (Ringland, 2019a, 2019b; Ringland et al., 2016), provides a ready-made foundation for therapeutic group work that counteracts isolation (see also Stuart Duncan in Chapter 20).

Minecraft play therapy groups can be an affirming antidote to isolation and social avoidance, while embracing the interest of digital play and engagement. The principles of affirmation and accommodation described throughout this chapter seamlessly transition into supporting neurodivergent youth in groups. Utilizing the child's established interest in Minecraft and the positive therapeutic relationship built upon the individual sessions, authentic social engagement can be encouraged and explored. As individual therapy using Minecraft can help autistic children, ADHDers, and AuDHDers accept who they are, offering the opportunity for social connection in a group can help share the message that they are not alone.

Helpful Tips

- **Embrace the Affirming Paradigm:** Minecraft supports the neurodiversity-affirming paradigm, which reframes conditions like autism and ADHD as natural variations rather than disorders to be cured. Clinicians must provide a space free of judgment to encourage the child's authentic expression.
- **Integrate Specialized Frameworks:** The shift away from traditional ABA/CBT requires adopting affirming approaches like AutPlay and Polyvagal-informed interventions that prioritize the child's physiological states. The Seven Guiding Principles can be applied to support these specialized approaches.
- **Customization for Accommodation:** Minecraft is highly adaptable, allowing clinicians to tailor the environment to the client's sensory and cognitive needs, including flexible communication methods (nonverbal chat/emotes), adjustments for sensory processing differences (audio, lighting, fidgets), and accommodating needs for either directive structure or open-world free play.
- **Leverage Regulation and Movement:** The game supports autonomic nervous system regulation through intentional use of rhythmic movement (like jumping or mining) and physical proprioceptive tools (weighted blankets or lap pads). This integration helps children connect with their body and manage dysregulation.

- **Translate Mechanics for Interoception:** Clinicians can use core game mechanics, like the Health and Hunger Bars, as a concrete metaphor to build interoception (awareness of internal physical and emotional sensations). This reframing creates a shared family language for managing energy and capacity (akin to "Spoon Theory").

Reflection Question

1 Think of a neurodivergent client you work with. How could the metaphor of the Minecraft "Hunger Bar" or "Health Bar" provide a more concrete way for them to understand and communicate their needs for energy, rest, or sensory regulation?

References

Blackwood, L. (2025). Legend land: An evaluation of a telehealth videogame for the emotional regulation of autistic children. *Good Autism Practice*, *26*(1), 35–44. https://www.ingentaconnect.com/contentone/bild/gap/2025/00000026/00000001/art00007

Botha, M., Chapman, R., Onaiwu, M. G., Kapp, S. K., Ashley, A. S., & Walker, N. (2024). The neurodiversity concept was developed collectively: An overdue correction on the origins of neurodiversity theory. *Autism*, *28*(6). https://doi.org/10.1177/13623613241237871

Delahooke, M. (2019). *Beyond behaviours: Using brain science and compassion to understand and solve children's behavioural challenges*. John Murray.

Gerhardt, L., & Smith, J. (2020). The use of Minecraft in the treatment of trauma for a child with autism spectrum disorder. *Journal of Family Therapy*, *42*, 365–384. https://doi.org/10.1111/1467-6427.12297

Grandin, T. (2006). *Thinking in pictures: And other reports from my life with autism* (Expanded ed.). Vintage Books.

Grant, R. J. (2023). *The AutPlay therapy handbook*. Routledge.

Grant, R. J. (in collaboration with the AutPlay Therapy Advisory Board). (2025). Neurodiversity affirming care in child and play therapy. AutPlay Therapy. https://autplaytherapy.com/neurodiversity-affirming-care-in-child-and-play-therapy/

Madigan, N. (2020, February 24). Breakthrough therapy uses Minecraft to empower children with ASD. *Health Times*. https://healthtimes.com.au/hub/autism-spectrum/63/practice/nm/breakthrough-therapy-uses-minecraft-to-empower-children-with-asd/4723/

Mate, G. (2019). *Scattered minds: A new look at the origins and healing of attention deficit disorder*. Vermillion.

Miserandino, C. (2020). The spoon theory. In *Lymphoma Action*. https://lymphoma-action.org.uk/sites/default/files/media/documents/2020-05/Spoon%20theory%20by%20Christine%20Miserandino.pdf

Price, D. (2022). *Unmasking autism: Discovering the new faces of neurodiversity*. Harmony Books.

Ringland, K. E. (2019a). A place to play: The (dis)abled embodied experience for autistic children in online spaces. *Proceedings of the SIGCHI Conference on Human Factors in Computing Systems (CHI '19)*. https://doi.org/10.1145/3290605.3300518

Ringland, K. E. (2019b). "Autsome": Fostering an autistic identity in an online Minecraft community for youth with autism. *Information in Contemporary Society, 11420*, 132–143. https://doi.org/10.1007/978-3-030-15742-5_12

Ringland, K. E., Wolf, C. T., Faucett, H., Dombrowski, L., & Hayes, G. R. (2016). "Will I always be not social?": Re-Conceptualizing sociality in the context of a Minecraft community for Autism. *Proceedings of the 2016 CHI Conference on Human Factors in Computing Systems—CHI '16*. https://doi.org/10.1145/2858036.2858038

Silberman, S. (2015). *NeuroTribes: The legacy of autism and the future of neurodiversity*. Penguin Random House.

Singer, J. (2017). *Neurodiversity: The birth of an idea*. Amazon.

Stuart, K. (2015, March 4). *Minecraft's creator will always be a hero to me, he gave my autistic son a voice*. The Guardian. https://www.theguardian.com/technology/2015/mar/04/minecraft-creator-notch-will-always-be-a-hero-to-me-he-gave-my-autistic-son-a-voice

Stuart, K. (2024, May 30). *A place that made sense: Minecraft is 15 years old and still changing lives*. The Guardian. https://www.theguardian.com/games/article/2024/may/30/a-place-that-made-sense-minecraft-is-15-years-old-and-still-changing-lives

Zolyomi, A., & Schmalz, M. (2017). Mining for social skills: Minecraft in home and therapy for neurodiverse youth. Scholarspace.manoa.hawaii.edu. https://doi.org/10.24251/HICSS.2017.411

Chapter 15

Group Applications

Group therapy is a well-established, evidence-based intervention for supporting children's mental health and well-being. Building on the foundation of the Seven Guiding Principles, using Minecraft in groups can be particularly effective, as it adapts various therapy models through a medium that is intrinsically engaging for children. This chapter examines the integration of Minecraft in play therapy groups, providing information that play therapists and clinicians need to implement it in their practice effectively. Minecraft as a group intervention is especially relevant for providing neurodiverse-affirming care, as the game's predictable, interest-based, and low-demand environment offers an ideal setting for neurodivergent children to practice social skills that are often challenging in unstructured contexts. Furthermore, Minecraft groups extend the benefits of individual play therapy by introducing crucial peer-to-peer interactions. Skills such as collaboration and self-expression, often first practiced one-on-one with a therapist, become the foundation for navigating peer relationships and building social connections within the structured, supportive context of the group.

It is essential to distinguish this clinical application from educational uses of the game. While classroom activities might focus on academic collaboration, therapy groups are facilitated by a trained mental health professional who guides members to understand their thoughts, feelings, and behaviors in real-time, directly addressing clinical needs and reducing feelings of isolation (Sheppard & Thieneman, 2023). As a tool, Minecraft offers significant practical advantages, serving as a versatile and cost-effective alternative to traditional play-based group interventions, such as using art, LEGO, and sand trays. It eliminates the need for physical supplies and cleanup while providing an unlimited digital inventory.

However, a primary disadvantage is the absence of the rich tactile and sensory feedback that traditional play items can provide. These can be grounding for some children and crucial for personal expression and regulation. As referenced in Chapter 14, group members who seek

DOI: 10.4324/9781003614784-18

more proprioceptive feedback can utilize fidgets and other items, such as weighted blankets or lap pads, while playing. Additionally, while Minecraft's digital item library is vast, it may lack the specificity of physical miniatures or magazine clippings that are necessary for a child to fully represent their unique world. Clinicians can get creative in this area and consider other ways to bridge the theme and universe of Minecraft beyond the actual gameplay, if group members want an outlet to explore different creative expressions.

This chapter will explore the implementation of Minecraft in play therapy groups, positioning its use in groups as a vital component of comprehensive clinical mental health practice. The group structure will be explored, along with how play therapists can shift their focus to become effective group facilitators. The benefits of directive and non-directive interventions are studied as a reference to taking Minecraft groups to the next level. Two clinical vignettes are presented to illustrate the different group dynamics that may occur with a middle-aged group, as referenced in Chapter 6, and an adolescent group comprising four members.

Applying Minecraft to Group Therapy

When applying Minecraft to group therapy, a robust foundation is critical for success. In their method article, *"Therapeutically Applied Minecraft Groups with Neurodivergent Youth,"* Kilmer et al. (2023) provide an essential, evidence-based protocol outlining the session structure and group composition, based on a 90-minute, three-part structure that includes check-in, active gameplay, and check-out. This chapter integrates their structural model with the theoretical framework of the Seven Guiding Principles, reoriented toward the unique benefits that groups derive from using Minecraft. Riordan and Scarf (2017) attribute Minecraft's highly social and collaborative nature to what makes the game such a powerful tool for fostering social connectedness, collaboration, and community building. These benefits are incredibly helpful when paired with community connection. They can carry greater potential when utilized in therapeutic groups for a variety of mental health concerns, such as emotional regulation, working with negative self-talk, grief and bereavement, trauma, and overall social connection.

To translate theory into practice, this chapter will explore the application of play therapy techniques, drawing from both structured, directive interventions (Beckett & Finch, 2024; Kilmer et al., 2023; Lane, 2024) and non-directive interventions, which are informed by the Seven Guiding Principles and the chapters in Section 2. Furthermore, the chapter will emphasize that the therapeutic frame in a digital space is paramount, exploring how to establish and maintain group agreements and a culture of psychological safety, as demonstrated in community-based implementations (Hembree, 2025). The intentional focus on a proven structure, theoretical foundation, practical interventions, and a strong clinical framework will equip clinicians to harness the unique potential of Minecraft in a way that matches their own unique clinical identity and style, ultimately fostering connection and facilitating healing within a group context.

The Foundation: A Clinically-Informed Structure

The foundation of any effective therapeutic group is a consistent and predictable structure, which Kilmer et al. (2023) detailed through their three-part format: check-in, in-game activities, and check-out. Intentional structure in groups can actively foster group cohesion and culture, as the group's container creates a sense of safety through a dependable format. The check-in and check-out periods, in particular, serve as core routines that offer predictable ways for members to engage one another. Similar to individual sessions, the check-out routine can help integrate the experience of the game while also practicing the experience of positive endings in a more socialized setting than just with the play therapist (see Chapter 7 and Principle 5).

When considering the three-part structure, I often advise clinicians to flex the timing of the check-in and check-out based on the group's energy and needs. A group engaged in a compelling collaborative project may benefit from a shorter check-in to preserve momentum. At the same time, an earlier check-out might be beneficial if interpersonal group dynamics arise that require additional time to process. Similar to the individual process explored in Chapter 4, the check-in routine can be more introductory during the beginning stages of the group as members share and discuss their characters. As group cohesion builds, members may choose new ways of checking in and checking out. Those higher-level processing conversations often occur at the start of groups and illustrate the Second Guiding Principle: that therapeutic work can happen even before the game begins.

The start of the group can also include discussions around the choices of naming a new world, what biome or seed is chosen, and what elements of gameplay mechanics are enabled (such as weather cycles, friendly fire, and mobs spawning). These conversations, particularly when used with new groups, can serve as therapeutic data on how members engage and further set the tone for group culture.

Directive Interventions as In-Game Activities

The central in-game activity segment can be adapted through both directive and non-directive play, depending on the style and preferences of the group facilitator. Many facilitators use directive group interventions to provide a structured framework for the in-game playing time. In writing a guest blog for Minecraft Education, Lane (2024) provides a model for scaffolding social demands through progressively collaborative tasks, such as using the in-game library and maps with *Blockbeard's Gold Race*, and *Capture the Flag*. Kilmer et al. (2023) use a mix of Creative mode interventions (building team-based maze challenges or "Habitat in a Box" which prompts members to build a home for a specific animal) with Survival mode prompts, such as the facilitator providing group-level challenges for members to interact with one another by finding particular items significant for the other players. Another creative intervention they share is a school anxiety processing activity in which group participants, anticipating the return to school after summer vacation, were given a pre-made model of a school within Minecraft and asked to select a classroom and modify it to make it resemble the one at their school. While this relies on access to a school template, either in Minecraft Education or through pre-made mods, the intervention can easily be adapted to prompt group members to build their own representation of their classroom and what it feels like to be inside, using the game's items for emotional expression.

Beckett and Finch (2024) provide a robust framework for integrating specific individual therapeutic activities, such as creating "safe places" or facing challenges like battling the Ender Dragon, into group-level interventions. In their documentary video *Bridging the ChASM: Creating Accessible Services using Minecraft – A Guide,* Beckett and Finch (2024) brilliantly demonstrate how an individual intervention, such as building a safe place (see also Chapter 13), can be adapted into group when the members are invited to create ways to connect their safe places (such as tracks for a train or rollercoaster.) As group members transition to the challenge of battling the Ender Dragon they are exposed to different perspectives of the challenge which are uniquely different than if the client was playing alone or with the therapist individually.

The Play Therapist as Group Facilitator

Within this structured environment, the play therapist's role evolves from focusing on the experience of an individual client to an even more nuanced process of attuning to the needs of a small group. Sheppard and Thieneman (2023) acknowledge the dual space that clinicians may occupy, as they can take on the roles of facilitator or leader. A facilitator role may be needed when helping the group navigate decisions and interactions. In contrast, a leadership role may be more appropriate when critical decisions need to be made and the group is required to stay within the context of the agreements, such as adhering to start and end times. An example of this is at the start of a new group, when there may be a need for the clinician to take on a group leadership role and make a decision about the parameters of creating a new world, versus facilitating discussions about the different options. The ages of the group also play a role in this choice, as younger groups will benefit from group leadership, while adolescent groups may benefit from the facilitation process. *Author's note: The terms group leader and group facilitator are used interchangeably throughout the chapter for readability and general role identification; however, it will be made specific when the term "leader" or "facilitator" relates to the particular function of that role in the group.*

This is a complex role in which the therapist must navigate the container of the group's culture, as they are also responsible for establishing and upholding group agreements. I prefer to use the word "agreement" over "rules" as it emphasizes the collaborative nature of the group, as opposed to the potentially punitive and authoritarian notion of "rules." This subtle shift in language highlights that when members agree to specific guidelines, there is the recognition that one's choices have an impact on other members. Examples include the agreements against "griefing" (destroying others' builds) and respecting in-game items of other players as one would in real life. These agreements proactively foster a culture of empathy and safety within the group's community.

Additional agreements will be modified as needed, depending on the group's developmental level and the requests of its members. A middle-aged group may request agreements around respecting boundaries of personal builds – asking the group if items, structures, or objects belong to others before claiming them for their own. Groups may be divided on whether they choose to play player-versus-player (PVP), and agreements could be made about not engaging players who choose to spectate or play in an unrelated manner. Adolescent groups may initiate conversations around more developmentally advanced topics, such as the nuances of honoring confidentiality (especially if they are within the same social or community circle), respecting identities and social locations, and creating space for vulnerability outside of game-related contexts.

Some facilitators may hold firm boundaries around certain aspects of the gameplay and can be supported within the customizable nature of the game. Clinicians who are opposed to any PVP or aggressive engagement against any representation of humans in the game, such as non-playable characters (NPCs) may disable player-vs-player combat and frame boundaries as a foundation for clinical conversations about how people connect and relate (Hembree, 2025).

Next, the therapist's focus shifts to consciously facilitating the relationships among group members as they interact individually with the game and socially with one another. This is adapted from the Third and Fourth Guiding Principles: that drawing from the concept of the "setup" group members will show the facilitator what it is like to be themselves, while the group facilitator can help the members and the group coregulate (see Chapters 5 and 6). From this framework, the relationship between individual members and the group, facilitated by the therapist, serves as the agent of change. The therapist intentionally utilizes opportunities for connection, perspective-taking, and authentic relationship-building that define therapeutic social connection (Riordan & Scarf, 2017).

If this sounds like an intense focus, it can be. Clinicians are encouraged to form their groups with the number of members that makes the most sense for their own Window of Tolerance. In their method article, Kilmer et al. (2023) describe their Minecraft groups with between three to five members and one facilitator. However, another approach can utilize two facilitators, even for a group of three, where one facilitator plays a character in the game and the other serves as an outside observer, supporting individual members and reflecting on the group process (Beckett & Finch, 2024). This approach also provides a practical application of how both the in-game process and the interpersonal process in the room are rich in emotional material to be mindful of.

Clinical Vignettes: Working with Non-Directive Game Play

1. Avoiding Scapegoating: Revisiting the Attack of the Iron Golems from Chapter 6

The case vignette in Chapter 6 was used to illustrate the Fourth Guiding Principle, which is that the play therapist can model how to work with the stimulation in the game to help the child learn more about themselves while playing. In the vignette, I describe my experience in the group, as my brain begins to feel fuzzy, my body becomes tense, and I struggle to understand what is actually happening. By naming my internal experiences, I brought attention to the practice of interoception for the group members and coregulated with the group by stepping away from the game and shaking off my emotions. This then led to the group collaborating on the idea of refreshing the world as a broader coping strategy, involving resetting and starting over. The "setup" in that group could be further recognized as "Is the World Okay?" (see Chapter 5). That example is revisited here as it provides a deeper study into group dynamics and possible facilitation choices.

While the example does not explicitly demonstrate the challenge of "griefing" in groups, it is suggested that a group member was intentionally doing something that was disrupting the group. Given the themes of the setup, it could be a therapeutic moment for the member and group to process the intensity of uncertainty and chaos in their lives. However, due to the level of disruption it caused, it also presents potential challenges to group dynamics, such as being mindful of scapegoating and how to work with conflict resolution. By not focusing on finding the member who may have been initiating the massive spawning, the group leader prevents singling out a member out of fear that the group will turn on them. Instead, the facilitator acknowledges the impact of the conflict and uses it as an opportunity for deeper individual exploration. This becomes a leadership role that is being taken on, as the choice is not to facilitate an exploration of "Who is doing this?" but to intentionally direct focus toward how to acknowledge the impact and resolve the challenge.

Engaging in this way supports the group with what Sheppard and Thieneman (2023) refer to as observational learning, while further citing Miller's concept of vicarious reinforcement, that new behaviors and norms can be adapted from what is reinforced. Those two concepts illustrate that group members can observe the actions of the group without singling out members, while reinforcing that regulating and navigating the impact of the disruptive behavior is the focus of attention. Last, this can lead to a group-as-a-whole intervention (Sheppard & Thieneman, 2023) if the leader chooses to revisit the chain of events during the checkout process. This instance may require ending the in-game time a few minutes earlier to process the dynamic.

2. When the Facilitator Steps Out of the Way: A Teen Group Takes Over

As adolescents reach the emotional developmental stage of "Who Am I?", their search for identity can lead them to balance the need for adult support with the desire for understanding from their peers (see Chapter 5). I have observed this dynamic in many teenage groups, where members find security in the presence of the adult facilitator and the group's established agreements, allowing them to explore the complex dynamics of being a teenager with their peers (this is similar to the roller coaster safety bar analogy from Chapter 9). Consider the following vignette, which illustrates how this can unfold within the structure of check-in, in-game play, and check-out.

This is the fifth meeting of an online adolescent group. There are four members, plus myself as the facilitator. The previous meetings have included the group collaborating on different builds and themes that they want to work on. At the start of the group, a member checks in as a "3 out of 10," which indicates a low mood. Other group members express empathy, and one acknowledges they've had a hard week as well. The first group member follows up, saying that they really want to focus on building a mini-game during the group.

As the group progresses to the in-game stage, I fly around the world helping members when invited. The first group member has been quiet, and I gently check in, letting them know that I see them but not being imposing: "It looks like you've been making progress on your mini-game. Let me know if I can help in any way."

"No thanks," they reply. "I can do it myself."

Moments later, they ask the group if someone could help them stack blocks to build a large structure. I refrain from replying, recognizing that they did not ask me directly and had declined my initial offer.

The second group member, who also acknowledged having a hard week during check-in, unmuted their screen and responded.

"Hey, yeah, I can help, I'm pretty much done with what I'm working on." The second member flies over and the two begin working together.

As they begin talking about different blocks, the mechanics of Redstone, and the hypothetical weight of wearing diamond armor versus gold, another member un-mutes and expresses excitement, "You guys, that looks really cool! Can I play it when it's finished?"

The fourth member also expresses excitement and says that they want to play it too.

During these interactions, I hang back – both in the game, hovering away in the distance – and over the telehealth screen as the members are actively engaged in the primary healing force of group: connection with one another.

The content of the conversations shifts from Minecraft to an upcoming school event, where teachers are trying to ban cell phones from the classroom, and complaints about parents and their expectations for weekend homework. I hate to intervene with their socialization, but I jump in to let them know there are five minutes left to group, and we have our check-out agreement.

The group member who checked in at a three, enthusiastically checks out first. "I'm definitely a ten right now. That was awesome. Thanks, everyone, for helping to build the mini-game."

"I'm at a ten, too. That was super cool."

"I'm at a nine because I'm still upset about all the homework I have this weekend, but yeah, that was fun."

"I'm at a nine point nine five. That final hundredth of a point is deducted because we couldn't play longer."

This vignette demonstrates the power of community when members feel the support and safety needed to roam and express themselves freely, both in Minecraft and emotionally with their peers. It also demonstrates the power of non-directive group play and trusting the process that unfolds within the group's container, which is established by the structure and agreements in place. When these are established, sometimes the best intervention for adolescents in a group is to step out of the way and let them take over.

Looking Ahead

When navigating the challenges that play therapists may face in implementing Minecraft groups into their practice, the integrated framework discussed provides the necessary clinical tools to begin using Minecraft in ways that promote connection while having fun. A strong, co-created group culture (Hembree, 2025; Riordan & Scarf, 2017) serves as the primary buffer against social-emotional risks, while a fluency in directive interventions (Beckett & Finch, 2024; Lane, 2024) allows the clinician to transform challenges into therapeutic moments.

Referencing Principles 3 and 4 of the Seven Guiding Principles provides group facilitators with a framework for non-directive interventions that allow the group to naturally evolve to where the wisdom of the healing is needed. As with the other topics in this book, Minecraft-informed group therapy is not defined by the game itself, but by the clinician's ability to weave a structured protocol (Kilmer et al., 2023) with a theoretical understanding of group dynamics (Sheppard & Thieneman, 2023) and practiced clinical artistry. By doing so, therapists can begin confidently building accessible, effective, and transformative digital group spaces for the clients who need them most.

As recognized with the First Guiding Principle and the second case vignette, the success of a Minecraft group depends less on your gaming prowess and more on your unique, authentic presence as a clinician and your commitment to the therapeutic process. The game is just the medium; the healing still happens in the relationships.

Helpful Tips

- **Targeted Population & Benefits:** Minecraft groups are an evidence-based intervention, particularly relevant for providing neurodiverse-affirming care, as the low-demand, predictable environment is ideal for neurodivergent children to practice social skills and engage in peer-to-peer interactions.
- **Structured Format Is Key:** Success relies on establishing a consistent and predictable three-part structure (check-in, active gameplay, check-out),

where the check-out routine helps members integrate the experience and practice positive endings in a socialized setting.

- **Establish a Culture of Safety:** Clinicians must establish a strong therapeutic container by using collaborative "agreements" (e.g., respecting boundaries and prohibiting "griefing") instead of "rules," which proactively fosters a culture of empathy and psychological safety.
- **Adopt Dual Intervention Styles:** Facilitators must leverage both directive interventions (structured, collaborative tasks and builds) and non-directive interventions (trusting the group process and stepping back) to address various clinical needs and dynamics.
- **Focus on the Therapeutic Relationship:** The play therapist's role evolves into a nuanced facilitator or leader who attunes to the group dynamics. The healing is driven by the relationships and authentic presence of the clinician, not by gaming prowess, as the game is simply the medium.

Reflection Question

1 How does my primary responsibility change when I shift from being a one-on-one play therapist to a group facilitator, and what part of that new role feels most challenging?

References

Beckett, M., & Finch, E. (2024). *Bridging the ChASM: Creating accessible services using Minecraft—A guide* [Video recording]. University of Cambridge. https://www.educ.cam.ac.uk/research/programmes/chasm/

Hembree, D. (2025, September 10). *Minecraft therapy opens powerful world for children and teens.* MindSite News. https://mindsitenews.org/2025/09/10/minecraft-for-child-and-teen-therapy/

Kilmer, E., Spangler, J., & Kilmer, J. (2023). Therapeutically applied Minecraft groups with neurodivergent youth. *F1000Research*, *12*, 216. https://doi.org/10.12688/f1000research.129090.1

Lane, J. (2024). *Autism group therapy.* Education.minecraft.net. https://education.minecraft.net/fr-fr/blog/autism-group-therapy

Riordan, B. C., & Scarf, D. (2017). Crafting minds and communities with Minecraft. *F1000Research*, *5*, 2339. https://doi.org/10.12688/f1000research.9625.2

Sheppard, T. L., & Thieneman, Z. J. (2023). *Group psychotherapy with children.* Taylor & Francis.

Section IV

Clinical Practice Considerations

Chapter 16

Case Conceptualization and Treatment Planning (Bringing It All Together)

Creating a treatment plan for using Minecraft in play therapy can be like navigating the road between two seemingly conflicting needs: an administrative task that must be completed for compliance with licensing and reimbursement purposes, while also serving as a clinical map to guide you through the uncharted world of the child's play. Additionally, case formulation requires the language and understanding necessary to undertake the administrative tasks of the clinical work while honoring the moment-to-moment possibilities that arise in a session. This chapter provides a guide for framing treatment plans and conceptualizing the play that align with the Seven Guiding Principles, bringing together the topics presented in the previous chapters in a manner accessible to all clinicians, regardless of their modality or documentation style.

The power of this work lies in play therapists' clinical validation of their use of Minecraft in sessions, as well as their ability to effectively communicate the therapeutic benefits to colleagues, parents, caregivers, and other relevant professionals in the child's life. The structure and considerations described below will help make the creative, unpredictable, and perhaps even chaotic world of Minecraft safe enough for "surviving" the demands of case formulation and clinical record keeping.

Starting at the Beginning

The Consultation

As demonstrated in the short vignettes at the beginning of many chapters, the initial outreach by caregivers serves as a crucial point of contact to determine whether there is interest in using Minecraft. In cases where the approach is new and unexpected, the initial consultation may focus on addressing the questions raised throughout this book such as: "How is it different than 'just' playing video games together" (Chapter 1), "What if they become more distressed when playing video games?" (Chapter 10),

DOI: 10.4324/9781003614784-20

"How can we have a better relationship with it as a family?" (Chapter 8), and "Will it be too much screen time?" (Chapter 9), among many others. Clinicians may choose to recommend this text directly to adults who are interested in this approach or share Appendix D as a reference point to inform their decision. Some families may be familiar with the modality, and the clinician can proceed directly to inquire about the specific therapeutic needs for which they are seeking help. This relates to the First Guiding Principle that the play therapist does not have to be a good player to use Minecraft in play therapy; offering the game as an intervention can be an inclusive approach for those seeking the dynamic support it can provide.

The Initial Intake

Play therapists reading this likely have their own style for engaging with initial consultations, intakes, and assessments. Clinicians have different approaches regarding whether they meet with the parents and child together first, individually, or a combination of both. Drawing from a relational approach to the intake process, adopted from the Synergetic Play Therapy (SPT) model, I prefer to meet with the caregivers first, to begin to attune to and support their nervous system activation using the same relational principles I would apply with a child (Dion & Norman, 2024). This provides the opportunity for coregulation to be modeled for the caregivers right at the start of our work together while also leaving space to hear more specific details about their current concerns and hopes for the therapeutic process.

One's current theoretical approach can serve as the foundation for one's practice and clinical orientation, which remain at the center of this work; however, there are specific nuances that are essential to consider to implement the use of the game in sessions effectively. Dion and Norman (2024) acknowledge the benefit of providing adults with an expectation of how the intake time will be spent to help establish a grounded experience to track the information discussed. For example, clinicians will need parents or caregivers to sign a digital consent form acknowledging the risks associated with playing the game with the child (see Chapter 18). There will also need to be a discussion about which console or platform the child will be using (or if your practice or agency supplies a device), whether they have access to online play, and what additional subscriptions or services are required to ensure the first session is as smooth as possible. Last, clinicians will need the client's gamer tag if they are using their own account and playing online. Additional considerations for protecting privacy and ensuring everyone's safety in a digital world are outlined in Chapter 18.

Depending on the child's and family's needs, time may be spent during the initial intake discussing the family's perspective on gaming and how Minecraft is played and experienced at home. Readers can refer to Chapter 8 for questions to ask parents about their personal gaming history and any judgments they may have that could be a barrier to implementing the game in session. Play therapists can use their clinical judgment to determine if an additional session with parents or caregivers would be beneficial in helping them understand and appreciate the benefits of using the game. That time could also be used to discuss ways the family can play together at home while setting the expectation for future conversations on how to implement some of the coping skill strategies that can be applied offline (see also Appendix B). Last, the intake can be used to discuss preferences for scheduling and the length of sessions (see Chapter 14), as well as whether group work is recommended or could be an option in the future.

The Intake with the Child

Along with the session with the adults, there will also be the first meeting with the child. Principle 2 reminds us that clinical work begins even before the first session of playing the game occurs; in this case, it is about how one connects with the client during the intake process. Before introducing avatars and entering the digital world together, it is essential to understand the child's relationship with Minecraft and their potential playing preferences and style, which could influence their engagement with the sessions. For example, Luke Blackwood, creator of *Legend Land*—a Minecraft server specifically designed to help children and adolescents with emotional regulation and social connection—trains his staff to explore with the child four distinct play styles that a client may exhibit in the game:

- **Mining** – Prefers repetitive tasks and collecting resources.
- **Exploring** – Enjoys discovering new areas and interacting with non-playable characters (NPCs).
- **Combat** – Likes action-based play, battling mobs, and using strategy.
- **Building** – Loves constructing structures and expressing creativity (Sukhorukov, 2025).

Exploring these styles together during intake helps the clinician understand how the child might approach the game and how the therapist can best engage in ways that resonate most directly.

The intake can also be used to set expectations for the sessions and discuss specific approaches the clinician may take that may differ from how the child plays at home or with friends. Ellie Finch, with PlayMode Academy (see foreword and Chapter 20), has a conversation with clients informing them that the play will be different from how they might play on their own and that they will join a specific world created for them (Sukhorukov, 2024). This could be an island with natural water boundaries or a flat world pre-arranged with walls designed to establish a sense of containment and provide stronger security and boundaries, reducing the potential of overwhelm due to the game's open-world feel (Finch, 2022; Sukhorukov, 2024).

Discussing whether the child prefers a guided experience (directive) or free-to-roam (non-directive) play style can also be helpful. As mentioned in Chapter 14, children have different preferences, and part of the intake process can help understand how they might need to play to express themselves. Gathering this information, along with other relevant clinical details, helps build the therapeutic alliance and supports the initial stages of gameplay, such as the identity exploration discussed in Chapter 4.

Gameplay as Case Formulation and Assessment

The transition from intake to ongoing therapy is where Principles 3 and 4 become the guiding forces behind case formulation. Described in Chapters 5 and 6, these principles help clinicians develop their assessment of the child's individual, unique needs, including their strengths, limitations, and personal goals (which may differ from those of the caregivers). Naturally, younger children may not have specific goals that they state; however, their relationship to the clinician and the gameplay could provide details that the caregivers are unaware of or have not fully understood. Adolescents may likely have a more nuanced understanding of what they would like support with and could be more expressive about their needs. In both instances, by being in the experience of the game (Principle 3) and working within the child's Window of Tolerance (WOT) (Principle 4), clinicians can draw on concepts of the setup, emotional developmental tasks, and play styles to start forming an idea of how the child may need to be supported while also working toward the clinical goals established during intake.

Clinicians can also evaluate the child's experience by observing how the child's autonomic nervous system responds during play: is the child dysregulated before they start? If so, the initial treatment plan may need to focus on creating a safe, regulated experience from the beginning of the session (however that may be for the client), as described in Chapter 10. This approach also involves assessing the child's WOT and their response to coregulation. It further adopts a developmental perspective, emphasizing safety through regulation first, then relational connection, and finally problem-solving (Perry & Szalavitz, 2008).

While clinicians will always consider issues outside the playroom, including family history and developmental concerns, the most effective assessments often result from observing the child in real-time. This approach allows the clinician not only to integrate Minecraft in ways that might be most helpful to the client but also provides an opportunity to gain a deeper understanding of the child's response across all interventions.

Treatment Planning

Collaborative Approach to Setting Goals

Goals and objectives are the heart of a treatment plan and also follow the arc of how the client's journey in therapy may unfold. The client's goals will likely be identified by the parent or caregivers who bring the child, and they are also something that clinicians keep in mind as a developmental destination, related to the child's emotional and chronological age, as well as their play style (see Chapter 5). For example, a goal for a ten-year-old coming to play therapy for anxiety at school could be to "reduce symptoms of anxiety when overwhelmed." When using Minecraft as an intervention, the clinician may also track a goal of helping the child transition from the emotional developmental task of "Is the World Okay?" to the task of "How Well Can I Do It?", which would be congruent with their chronological age.

From this framework, the objectives become the specific, observable, and measurable interactions that indicate progress toward the goal. This can also be thought of as the "how" of reaching the goal. An objective for the primary goal could be: "Within 10 sessions, the client will increase their ability to identify and name emotions, recognize body symptoms of anxiety, and identify coping skills to soothe and regulate." The secondary objective related to emotional developmental tasks could be "increase the client's sense of safety and support exploration into creative and expressive play."

While goals often focus on what is addressed during the session, Principles 5, 6, and 7 help the clinician develop goals that connect the session activities to skills that can be supported at home, resulting in a more comprehensive and integrated plan. These principles form the basis for additional goals that play therapists can include in their sessions after discussing them with caregivers during the intake process. Principle 5 emphasizes the importance of intentionally ending the game during the session, serving two key purposes: establishing a predictable framework for play therapy and providing clients who need it with practice in transitions. For some clients, being mindful of ending the game and transitioning smoothly is simply part of their routine, while for others, it may be a specific goal within their treatment plan. For example, the goal of "increasing ability to manage transitions from the game to dinner" can be supported by objectives such as "Within 5 sessions, the client will practice intentional endings through routines; set individual goals for each session's game, and identify goals for the next session," among others.

Other clients, such as those grieving or working through traumatic experiences, may benefit from extra focus on this principle as a key part of their treatment plan. A specific goal for grief could be to: "Increase the client's capacity to recognize and process the impact of their grief within the safety of the game world." The corresponding objective would be: "The client will engage in a metaphorical processing task, such as building a grief cave or memorial, and practice identifying when they may encounter memories in 3 out of 5 consecutive sessions." The conceptual goal is to support the client in expressing their inner narrative of grief and identifying grief waves through directive play therapy interventions, while also allowing space to play openly and freely, honoring moments when they may not want to engage directly with those emotions.

Following Principle 6, clinicians and families can work together to incorporate game play at home by adding goals that suit the frequency needs of each family. For example, an objective that supports collaborative engaged play at home could be: "Once a week, parents will engage in co-play at home to help the client identify and name emotions, recognize body symptoms of anxiety, and practice coregulation." The secondary objective could be, "Parents practice curiosity-driven questions and enlist the support of the client as an expert in gameplay."

Last, Principle 7 helps clinicians translate a child's skills from the game into creative coping strategies that can be used offline. For example, for a child who struggles with transitions, a goal such as "increasing the variety of coping skills to use when going to new places" can be supported by an objective like "identifying items at home that the client can bring to help feel confident in new situations." A secondary objective might be:

> The client will identify and utilize an object from home (a favorite keychain, a smooth stone) that shares a symbolic quality with a protective or comforting item from Minecraft (the durability of a Diamond Sword, the safety of a Shield) to use during real-world transitions.

Framing Interventions

A common question among clinicians is how to integrate Minecraft interventions as a key part of a client's treatment plan. Specific Minecraft-based interventions can be incorporated into the client's treatment plan objectives, as they may be one of several interventions used to achieve the overarching therapy goal. The chapters in Section 3 examine the use of both directive and non-directive interventions; however, the focus here shifts to how one conceptualizes the interventions used. When considering the relational approach of being engaged in the game together, it is helpful to remember that interventions often occur spontaneously, depending on what happens during play and the evolving nature of the relationship. This can help resolve the tension many therapists feel when caught between adhering to a structured plan and following in-the-moment attunement. This can be remembered by considering how one differentiates the action from the clinical description.

For example, a treatment plan may outline the goal of "reducing symptoms of anxiety when overwhelmed," with specific interventions focused on distress tolerance, such as identifying emotions and practicing coping skills. In session, this could be demonstrated by noticing that a client who responds well to non-directive play becomes overwhelmed by the in-game nightfall in Survival mode or is upset that their building remains unfinished at the end of a session. The therapist's authentic and attentive response in this moment is the intervention:

> *Oh no! This is becoming so overwhelming, and it can be really frustrating. I know a lot of players would feel that way. I can feel my hands buzzing. I'm going to take a big breath, shake it out, and then respawn.*

While spontaneous, this response directly supports the treatment plan through a clinical approach of "working to identify and name emotions, recognize body symptoms of anxiety, and identify coping skills to soothe and regulate."

Clinical Vignette: Bringing It All Together

This case vignette follows the journey of a fictional client assembled from various chapters, while providing a new therapeutic arc. Starting with the initial consultation, intake, assessment, and treatment planning, the vignette follows a child who is being brought to play therapy following a traumatic experience. The intentional familiarity of some pieces of the vignette may provide a comforting reminder for the reader to connect different elements of the principles and related chapters that have been previously represented.

The Consultation

I answer the phone and begin talking with a parent interested in play therapy for their child. The parent asks about my approach and background. After I explain my training, clinical orientation, and how I conceptualize cases (assessing play through the relationship), I mention that I use Minecraft as a powerful, play-based intervention. The parent is hesitant but also quite curious, saying that their child has just started playing Minecraft and has been reluctant to attend sessions to work through a traumatic experience. They express hope that this could be an appealing option for them.

I briefly outline the steps we take to maintain privacy and confidentiality, and inform the parent that during the initial intake, we will discuss any additional concerns about playing the game during sessions and at home. After our intake together, I inform them that I will then meet with the child.

The Intake with Parent and Child

I meet with the parent first to hear more about their concerns, the family history, and any other information that would be helpful for me to know without the child present. I also inform the parent of the time-limited structure of this first meeting and the need to cover the technology-related pieces related to beginning the Minecraft sessions. The parent shares a brief story about a traumatic event and explains how the child has been experiencing increased anxiety and worries about going to school and visiting new places. The parent also mentions that they welcome the child's interest in video games and often play with them when they have time. I use this as an opportunity to celebrate that meaningful connection they share and suggest that there might be ways to strengthen the work done in session by playing together at home. They appear appreciative of having guidance on how to bridge what is happening in the session to how they can support their child at home.

Speaking with the child individually, they immediately tell me how they like to "chill out" playing the game. I note this as the "exploring and building" styles mentioned earlier in this chapter. They also say that they find the music very relaxing, and they might even turn on a YouTube video of the game music to help them sleep. When asked if they had ever been in a situation that they thought they or someone they loved might have been hurt or in danger, they briefly nodded and said they didn't want to talk about it.

We discuss different options for how we might play Minecraft together during our session. I also ask if they would be interested in exploring other ways to use Minecraft at home beyond just playing, and their face lights up with a nod. To keep the therapeutic gameplay of Minecraft separate from their fun, casual gaming, we decided to build in a world that I keep private on my account and only play when we meet.

Gameplay as Assessment

Knowing that the client preferred to "chill out" during gameplay, I adopted a non-directive approach by inviting them to play openly and freely. They introduced their character to me and described a new skin they had just started using. I asked how they wanted me to join, and they said they preferred to build by themselves. I clarified if they wanted me to help, watch, or build on my own. They responded that I could go somewhere else and build independently.

What started peacefully began to change.

Where I was once relaxed and loosely engaged, blocks started exploding all around me. We are in Creative mode, so I didn't die, but I would notice quick flashes indicating an impending explosion, and then parts of what I was building would be destroyed.

This was so unexpected and unsettling.

I couldn't quite see what was causing it, and I would tense up and become cautious, wary of something suddenly happening again.

I named the tension and hypervigilence I was experiencing:

> There are so many scary things happening around me. My body feels so tense and I am noticing I'm holding my breath. I want to be able to relax but I can't - I keep thinking something is going to happen again. Is this happening where you are too?

"Wow, that's strange, no I'm just working on my base."

When I hear that response, the part of me that is in the experience of the game with the child feels alone and isolated. It feels like I am the only one this is happening to and I am scared. There is also the part of me that knows the client is making themselves invisible and coming over to where I am building and blowing up things around me to send a message about how they want me to understand and experience what the world is like for them. My heart aches as I touch into both my fear and my awareness of what they want to show me.

Conceptualizing the play of this session, I think of the setup and the emotional developmental tasks (Chapter 5.) My experience was that I suddenly felt like I was the only one exposed to this fear and left to ask the question, "Is the world okay?" For a brief moment, there was a quality of being unsure about what I had actually experienced, leaving me to question whether it was even really happening. While I could feel the experience within my body, the client was distant from it and denied even being aware that something was different. I wondered if this might be an indicator of their body having a limited Window of Tolerance to handle the distress, but more sessions would be needed to assess further.

Therapeutic Goals, Objectives, and Interventions

Reflecting on information provided by the parent in the intake and in a brief follow-up after the session, they reported that the client had experienced an unexpected weather-related disaster while on vacation. They were together as a family, but no one else was around. Upon returning home, they reported that the child's friends did not believe them and often made fun of them for making up what was thought of as a lie. This led the client to have nightmares, avoid talking about what happened, and not want to go to new places. Considering this information and the experiences from the first play session with the client, therapeutic goals, objectives, and interventions in this situation would take a trauma-informed approach that honors the themes that arise in the play while also providing support for the family at home.

Author's note: The following is a reference to further illustrate the concepts presented above and is adapted from Beckley-Forest and Johnson (2024); *clinicians are reminded to work within their level of training and competence.*

- **Goal #1:** Establish emotional safety in play.

  Objective 1: In the first two sessions, the child will identify a safe space within the game and identify two or three items that help them feel powerful.

  Intervention: Directive and non-directive play therapy, including prompt to build a safe space.

- **Goal #2:** Integrate safety in session into safety at home.

  Objective 2: Child and family will practice imagining the safe place at night before going to bed.

  Intervention: Parents will ask curiosity-led questions about child's safe space in the game, while listening to Minecraft-themed music.

- **Goal #3:** Process impact of traumatic event.

  Objective 3: Within 12 sessions child will process personal narrative of traumatic event.

  Intervention: Using trauma-informed modalities including narrative story-telling, client will explore beginning, middle, and end of traumatic experience.

- **Goal #4:** Support the client in sharing their experience with family members.

  Objective 4: At the end of 12 sessions, client and family explore Minecraft world together to increase communication about the client's experience of the event.
  Intervention: Collaborative gameplay within the session and prompts of playing together at home for general relationship building.

- **Additional considerations:** Group support to reduce feelings of social isolation.

In this example, the four goals track the topics discussed in the initial intake as they work with the immediate and long-term symptoms of the child's presenting problem of experiencing a traumatic event. The objectives and interventions draw upon the child's strengths and interests in Minecraft while also empowering the family to support the child at home in various ways. A specific, family-level goal is provided at the end to build on the work of the previous goals. Last, the additional consideration of a group intervention can serve as a helpful reminder for the clinician to be aware of other children in their practice who may have experienced traumatic events or to be mindful of specific offerings within the community. While the objectives and interventions may change, the goals serve as guiding posts along the way.

Looking Ahead: Weaving the Clinical Narrative in Documentation

The process of consultation, assessment, and treatment planning established in this chapter creates a cohesive clinical narrative for the work. The final, crucial step is documentation, where this narrative comes to life. In the next chapter, the focus is on how to translate the child's in-game experiences into progress notes that demonstrate the clear connection to their therapeutic goals, while also understanding the distinct purpose of the private psychotherapy note.

Helpful Tips

- **Dual Purpose of Treatment Planning:** Treatment planning serves two essential functions – it acts as the necessary administrative task for compliance (licensing/reimbursement) and operates as the clinical map that guides the therapist through the unpredictable, creative world of the child's play.

- **Essential Intake Preparation:** The intake process must proactively address common caregiver questions (e.g., "How is this different than 'just' playing?") and secure essential technological details (digital consent, console, online access, gamer tag) to ensure a grounded and smooth start to the first session.
- **Assessing Play Preferences:** During the intake (Principle 2), clinicians explore the child's distinct play styles (Mining, Exploring, Combat, Building) and discuss preferences for containment, such as playing in a specific world with boundaries (like walls or an island), to manage the open-world feel and reduce overwhelm.
- **Gameplay as Real-Time Assessment:** Case formulation is driven by real-time observation (Principles 3 and 4), where the clinician continually assesses the child's autonomic nervous system response and WOT during gameplay. The therapist's spontaneous, authentic response in moments of distress constitutes the key intervention that directly supports documented goals.
- **Integrate Home/Transition Goals:** Treatment plans should utilize Principles 5, 6, and 7 to bridge session work to home life, establishing goals for practicing intentional endings/transitions (Principle 5), supporting collaborative family play (Principle 6), and translating coping skills from in-game items to real-world objects (Principle 7).

Reflection Question

1 Using the Seven Guiding Principles as a checklist, what is one therapeutic goal I could draft for a current client that successfully integrates a session-based objective (e.g., coregulation), a family-system objective (e.g., curious engagement), and a home-translation objective (e.g., skill adaptation)?

References

Beckley-Forest, A., & Johnson, R. (2024). Therapy planning with EMDR® and play therapy. In L. L. Wonders & M. L. Afee (Eds.), *Play therapy treatment planning with children and families: A guide for mental health professionals* (pp. 187–190). Routledge. https://doi.org/10.4324/9781003334231

Dion, L., & Norman, J. (2024). A synergetic play therapy approach to treatment planning. In L. L. Wonders & M. L. Afee (Eds.), *Play therapy treatment planning with children and families: A guide for mental health professionals* (pp. 161–168). Routledge. https://doi.org/10.4324/9781003334231

Finch, E. (2022). *Thinking of using video games therapeutically?* Associaton for Counseling and Therapy Online. https://playmodeacademy.org/resources-and-publications/thinking-of-using-video-games-therapeutically

Perry, B. D., & Szalavitz, M. (2008). *The boy who was raised as a dog and other stories from a child psychiatrist's notebook: What traumatized children can teach us about loss, love, and healing*. Basic Books.

Sukhorukov, O. (2024). *Ellie Finch: "Children are having real meaningful relationships in these games."* HealGame Ukraine. https://healgameukraine.click/en/ellie-finch-children-are-having-real-meaningful-relationships-in-these-games/

Sukhorukov, O. (2025). *Luke Blackwood: The game has a hidden power*. HealGame Ukraine. https://healgameukraine.click/en/luke-blackwood-the-game-has-a-hidden-power/

Chapter 17

Interpreting Game Play into Clinical Language

The treatment plan provides the map, and the session is the journey. Now, clinicians face the important task of documenting the terrain covered: translating the lively, often chaotic experience of shared play into clear, clinical language for the progress note. This chapter guides you in finding the words to describe what occurs during Minecraft play and how to interpret and communicate a child's digital play into a narrative of growth and healing that validates your work and charts the path forward. Central to this task is understanding the different purposes of two types of notes: the progress note, a formal part of the legal record meant to convey your clinical reasoning to others, and the psychotherapy note, a private space for your raw impressions and hypotheses. Knowing what belongs where is the first step in turning Minecraft play into clinical language that communicates the deep therapeutic work being done in session.

In practice, writing a progress note can be a complex task that requires the play therapist to consider what happened during the session and how it aligns with treatment goals necessary for reimbursement by third-party payers. Anecdotally, I have found that it is not uncommon for many clinicians to feel pressure when completing progress notes, as they are usually expected to be finished right after a session or at the end of the day. This can add unnecessary stress to clinicians who are quickly moving into their next session or trying to complete tasks for multiple clients at the end of a busy day.

Psychotherapy notes are different because they are not intended to be shared with other entities or providers, providing a more flexible format for clinicians. While these notes follow the same ethical standards for record-keeping and privacy as an individual's practice, they must be kept separate from the formal record to preserve their protected status (American Psychological Association, 2007). Also known as "process notes," these documents may include clinicians' working theories about the setup, observations of emotional developmental tasks, and considerations of specific countertransference experiences that might be unique to that particular client.

DOI: 10.4324/9781003614784-21

"Do I Mention Minecraft in the Note?"

The question of whether to specifically mention "Minecraft" in a progress note often comes up during my presentations and workshops at conferences. It is clearly a matter that involves best practices, ethical documentation, and third-party reimbursement.

Pros of Mentioning "Minecraft" in the Progress Note

- **Demonstrates Deliberate Practice:** Naming the modality shows you are using a deliberate, consented-to intervention. It answers the implicit question, "What did you actually do in the session?" This is aligned with ethical practice, proving you are not just "playing video games" but employing a planned therapeutic tool.
- **Strengthens the Clinical Narrative:** Using the specific language of the intervention (Minecraft) strengthens the clinical narrative. It directly connects the treatment plan (which should mention Minecraft as the modality) to the progress note, creating a clear, coherent story for anyone reviewing the record.
- **Validates the Clinical Work for Professionals and Families:** For professionals, it provides crucial context for the child's experience and the therapist's methods. For parents or others reading the note (in specific circumstances), it validates that their investment in this novel approach is being utilized and that there is therapeutic specificity.
- **Positions You as a Forward-Thinking Clinician:** As the use of Minecraft in play therapy becomes more common, being transparent about the modality positions your work as forward-thinking and defensible. Furthermore, hiding it could be perceived as a lack of confidence in the modality itself.

Cons of Mentioning "Minecraft" in the Progress Note

- **Risk of Misinterpretation by Non-Clinical Readers:** This is the single biggest risk. An insurance reviewer, judge, or parent with preconceived biases may see "Minecraft" and dismiss the session as "recreational," regardless of the clinical language surrounding it. They may not understand the therapeutic power of play and may see it only as a casual game.
- **Potential for Rejection by Third-Party Payers:** Despite its clinical validity, some outdated insurance policies or uninformed reviewers might deny claims for "video game therapy." While this is often appealable, it creates an immediate administrative hurdle.
- **Diverts Focus from the Clinical Process:** The core of a progress note should be the *client's process and the therapeutic interaction*, not the

tool itself. Over-emphasizing the tool ("we built a castle in Minecraft") can accidentally obscure the clinical meaning ("the client practiced sustained focus and collaborative problem-solving to create a symbol of safety").

An Established Guideline

As a documentation reference for clinicians, *Play Therapy Treatment Planning with Children and Families* (Affee & Wonders, 2024) does not contain a specific rule dictating whether or not to name the toy or tool used in play. However, the book's overarching documentation principles and templates offer clear guidance. The sample session notes demonstrate that therapists frequently do name specific tools, such as "pastels," a "ball maze," or a "dollhouse," but they always do so within a broader clinical context. The text's guidelines structure the primary focus of a session note around the therapeutic process, the child's play themes, and the clinical goals.

Therefore, the specific tool used is secondary to the therapeutic action and its overall meaning. Following the precedent set by the various play therapy modalities in the text, a therapist would not primarily write a list of toys used (e.g., "The client used the bop bag"). Instead, they would embed the toy's use within a clinical description of the child's behavior, identifying specific play themes like "Aggressive" or "Mastery/Competence," noting the interventions used to help the child process their feelings, and evaluating the child's progress toward their targeted symptom and growth objectives. Ultimately, if mentioning a specific toy enhances this clinical description and clarifies the child's therapeutic progress, it is highly appropriate to include it. While these examples draw from traditional play therapy modalities, the same documentation principles apply when Minecraft serves as the therapeutic tool. The focus remains on the child's process, themes, and goals, not the specific game mechanics.

A Practical Guide: Moving from Tool-Focused to Clinically-Focused

The following guide outlines how to strike a balance between progress note transparency and clinical purpose, ensuring the latter remains unmistakable. In the treatment plan, clinicians can be explicit and clearly state "Minecraft-Based Play Therapy" or "Therapeutic Minecraft Interventions" as one of their modalities. This sets the stage and justifies its use from the beginning. In the progress note, clinicians can lead with the clinical information, and follow with the contextual. The note can begin by outlining the clinical process and goals, with Minecraft mentioned as the context, but with a clear connection to the therapy.

Instead of This (Tool-Focused)	*Use This (Clinically-Focused)*
"The client built a house in Minecraft."	"The client engaged in a sustained, goal-directed project to practice finding safety, demonstrating improved Window of Tolerance response when designs did not initially work."
"The client and I fought zombies in Minecraft."	"Engaged in non-directive, collaborative Minecraft gameplay; the client practiced coregulation and problem solving, to achieve a self-identified goal."
"The client's character hid in a cave for the entire session."	"The client appeared to isolate throughout the game (as evidenced by withdrawing to a secluded cave); client demonstrated skills of setting boundaries when requesting therapist does not try to find them. Further inquiry needed to assess feelings of overwhelm with game or clinician."

A clinician's psychotherapy or process notes may look quite different as the clinically focused content develops into deeper considerations that are not relevant for quick and concise progress notes. However, the reflections provided here can be essential for case conceptualization during later stages of therapy, if there is a break in appointments, or if the clinician is feeling stuck and discusses the case in supervision. The reader will notice that some psychotherapy notes include questions, as that can indicate ongoing assessment or considerations to track for more information.

Progress Note (Clinically-Focused)	*Psychotherapy Note (Personal Reference)*
"The client engaged in a sustained, goal-directed project to practice finding safety, demonstrating improved Window of Tolerance response when designs did not initially work."	Developmental Task of "How well can I do it?" setup of working hard to get it right when focusing on my own build. Noticed myself getting sleepy suddenly halfway through session.
"Engaged in non-directive, collaborative Minecraft gameplay; the client practiced coregulation and problem solving, to achieve a self-identified goal."	Intense gameplay! Felt a little underskilled when playing in Survival. Setup or something personal? Do I also consider directive prompts to help with problem solving?
"The client appeared to isolate throughout the game (as evidenced by withdrawing to a secluded cave); client demonstrated skills of setting boundaries when requesting therapist does not try to find them. Further inquiry needed to assess feelings of overwhelm with game or clinician."	Lots of feelings of sadness. But I didn't explicitly name them in the session. In fact, I didn't notice it until writing this now. What is that? Consider checking-in with parent prior to next session to see if any other info would be helpful.

Looking Ahead

Translating the meaningful work of play therapy sessions is the essential final step that links the use of Minecraft in the playroom to the permanent record. This documentation ensures the client's journey is recognized not just as playing a game, but as a recorded story of therapeutic growth, as described throughout the Seven Guiding Principles. The framework in this chapter offers a straightforward approach to writing progress notes with confidence, ensuring they are clinically thorough and defensible. At the same time, this process also respects the role of the psychotherapy note as a private space where the play therapist, as a feeling, thinking, and active participant, can process the raw impressions that influence the clinical work. Ultimately, this dual practice does more than fulfill administrative requirements; it honors the depth of the client's experience and the therapeutic relationship, creating a meaningful narrative for all involved to see the measurable steps toward healing.

Helpful Tips

- **Differentiate Note Types:** Clinicians must understand the distinct purposes of two note types: the Progress Note (a formal, legal record for external communication and reimbursement) and the Psychotherapy Note (a private space for raw impressions, hypotheses, and countertransference).
- **Focus on Clinical Process Over Tool:** The primary focus of a Progress Note must be the therapeutic process, the child's themes, and clinical goals. The tool itself (Minecraft) is secondary to the therapeutic action and its meaning; avoid simply stating "The client built a house in Minecraft" and instead focus on the resulting growth or skill practiced (e.g., finding safety or sustained focus).
- **Use Minecraft Explicitly and Defensibly:** Mentioning "Minecraft" in the Progress Note demonstrates a deliberate, consented-to intervention and strengthens the clinical narrative, positioning the therapist as forward-thinking. However, be mindful that non-clinical readers may misinterpret it as "recreational" or dismiss claims, requiring careful, clinically focused wording.
- **Psychotherapy Notes for Deeper Processing:** Psychotherapy notes are essential for processing the clinician's internal experience, including observations of the emotional developmental tasks, raw impressions, and considerations of countertransference (e.g., feelings of being underskilled or sleepy), which are crucial for case conceptualization but should be kept separate from the formal record.
- **Document Narrative of Growth:** The final documentation step links the play to the permanent record, ensuring the client's journey is recognized

as a recorded story of therapeutic growth. The goal is to translate the experience into a straightforward narrative of healing that is both clinically thorough and defensible.

Reflection Question

1 What is a common, mundane in-game action (e.g., "the client mined for iron for ten minutes") that could be easily dismissed, and what are two different clinical descriptions I could provide, demonstrating clinical thinking and documentation?

References

American Psychological Association. (2007). Record keeping guidelines. *American Psychological Association*. https://www.apa.org/practice/guidelines/record-keeping

Affee, M. L., & Wonders, L. L. (2024). *Play therapy treatment planning with children and families*. Routledge.

Chapter 18

Protecting Privacy

Using Minecraft in play therapy extends the clinician's ethical duty of care into the digital world. Protecting client privacy and ensuring a secure online environment are just as essential as maintaining confidentiality in a physical office. This involves specific knowledge and protocols to safeguard client confidentiality and prevent violations of laws like the Health Insurance Portability and Accountability Act (HIPAA) or the European Union's General Data Protection Regulation (GDPR), along with other relevant regulatory agencies that promote best practices for managing client medical information during online therapy sessions involving Minecraft. This chapter provides a clear protocol for creating and maintaining a safe, contained digital space for using Minecraft in therapy, addressing both technical and emotional safety concerns. Clinicians can also better protect themselves and their clients by using the Digital Consent Form provided in Handout 1.

Account, Device, and Network Security

The first point of consideration is securing the accounts and devices used when online. This includes both Minecraft use and the telehealth platforms being used if meeting online. Enabling two-factor authentication (2FA) is a non-negotiable ethical standard; it dramatically reduces the risk of unauthorized access and ensures that devices and apps are safe (TherapyNotes, LLC, 2017). Online sessions should be conducted only over a private, password-protected Wi-Fi network, as public Wi-Fi is highly vulnerable to data interception (TherapyNotes, LLC, 2017). As a baseline, ensure your computer has automatic updates and reputable antivirus software enabled (TherapyNotes, LLC, 2017). An additional consideration is using a virtual private network (VPN) to provide further protection and anonymity.

DOI: 10.4324/9781003614784-22

Creating the Secure Therapeutic World

The foundation of safe practice lies in the digital environment itself. A private, invite-only Realm, world, or server created by the clinician provides the most secure setting for therapy, functioning like a digital playroom with a locked door (Fitzgerald, 2017; TherapyNotes, LLC, 2017). This structure prevents interactions with strangers, eliminating concerns about unknown players joining the session, friending the client, or engaging in any disruptive behavior that breaches confidentiality. All three options have advantages and disadvantages depending on access, technical skills, and personal preference.

Realms are invite-only worlds, allowing the clinician to control who joins. This creates a safe and secure environment for the player, allowing them to access it even when the clinician is offline. This can be a therapeutic benefit for some clients who want to revisit therapeutic builds created during a session, such as a safe space, worry box, or memorial garden (see Chapters 12 and 13). However, clinicians seeking to maintain control over what is accessed after a session may choose to unfriend the client at the end of each session or remove their access to the Realm.

Worlds created by the play therapist can be accessed only when the clinician is in that world, and if the player is linked as a friend. This provides more containment during sessions but can also present the risk of other clients joining unexpectedly, which could compromise confidentiality and disrupt therapy. Similar to the Realms, a solution is to unfriend each client at the end of their session so that no other clients are connected to one's account when not in session. Additionally, some clients may choose to play in their own world, serving as the host and inviting the therapist in during each session. This can be helpful if therapeutic activities (such as safe space, etc.) are recommended for use and practice outside of sessions; however, there is a risk that the client's friends and connections could see them online and join during the therapy appointment. While this can happen, agreements can be made when reviewing and signing the Digital Consent Form that state that such instances will require the friend to be removed from the world. To prevent this from happening again and to soothe any hurt feelings, caregivers can be informed and encouraged to speak with the other player's caregivers.

I have encountered situations where this has happened before, both when a non-scheduled client joins a game uninvited and when a client's friend unexpectedly joins their world. Although undesirable, both instances have led to meaningful therapeutic discussions.

In the first case, the client who joined unexpectedly was removed from the world. After the session, I contacted their caregiver to discuss what occurred. In the next session with that client, we reviewed the importance of confidentiality and emphasized how these sessions are valuable for each individual at that time. They stated that they understood and were looking forward to their next session to continue their work.

On the other side of the situation, the scheduled client expressed excitement that another child knew me, had also met with me, and had joined. The interaction helped normalize the experience of receiving mental health support and raised the awareness that other children do this work as well. When the client expressed disappointment about not being able to play with this unknown visitor, it sparked an engaging discussion about the possibilities and interest in joining a group.

When playing in a client's world and one of their friends joined, it was an opportunity to explore the special time that play therapy was for the individual client and how important it was to have time to themselves. In one instance, a client who shared attention with many siblings appreciated this, demonstrating that it is a helpful intervention to boost self-worth and value, especially within the therapeutic relationship.

In another case, the client was disappointed that they could not also spend the time playing with their friend. This led to a vulnerable conversation about how they were experiencing the play therapy sessions and whether it was the right fit for them. After discussing this incident with their caregiver, it was decided that the client was primarily interested in playing for fun overall and that therapeutic Minecraft play was not the most suitable intervention (see Chapter 19). These examples demonstrate the need for digital boundaries to be discussed and established before working together. Missteps can certainly happen along the way, and, as shown above, they can even enrich the therapeutic relationship. The ethical obligations of the work require proactive steps to minimize risk.

A Framework for Clinical and Emotional Digital Safety

When establishing digital boundaries with clients, clinicians can recommend that clients create and use a gamertag in games that does not include any identifying information, rather than their real name. They should also avoid creating profiles or signs that disclose personal details, such as their home address or school (Finch, 2022a). Similarly, the play therapist can create a neutral gamertag that does not reveal their role as a clinician or associate with a specific practice. Additionally, these considerations can be applied when naming worlds or Realms used during sessions. This helps clinicians take extra steps to maintain confidentiality. Recognizing digital boundaries can also be part of the joint intervention during the intake process, providing an additional benefit of the Second Guiding Principle. Officially documenting these practices helps reinforce the therapeutic agreement and sets a clear framework for safe online engagement (see Digital Safety Contract, Handout 1).

Managing Communication and Data

To maintain a confidential therapeutic space while playing, clinicians need to inform clients about communication risks posed by in-game features. To ensure that all therapeutic conversations remain private, it is advised that clinical content not be shared through the in-game chat or displayed in the world (Finch, 2022a). Instead, if playing online, clients can utilize a separate video platform (such as Zoom, Google Meet, or a specific electronic telehealth app) to ensure confidential and secure communication, preventing the sharing of personal information. This ensures that all communication is covered by a Business Associate Agreement (BAA) offered by companies such as Zoom and Google. It is also advised to spend time understanding the in-game player permissions to help control interaction levels, thereby supporting and maintaining therapeutic boundaries and safety, as different platforms have different considerations (Fitzgerald, 2017). For example, play therapists using Xbox Live can adjust communication settings through the Xbox Live privacy panel, paying close attention to the "Others can communicate with voice, text, or invites" setting (Fitzgerald, 2017; Geere, 2023).

Considerations for Working with Minors

For parents and caregivers setting up Microsoft online accounts for their child (under age 13, or 16 in the European Union (EU)), they will need to use a "Child Account." It is important to note that these accounts have multiplayer and communication features disabled by default (Fitzgerald, 2017; Geere, 2023). It is not necessarily the clinician's role to guide the parent through enabling these features for therapeutic purposes; however, they must be aware of this during the consultation or intake. The caregiver will be required to log into their associated Microsoft account and adjust the settings. For detailed, step-by-step guides on configuring these safety settings for both Bedrock and Java editions, clinicians can direct parents to the resources from PlayMode Academy (Finch, 2025a, 2025b).

For clients who are already playing online with family or friends, this may already be taken care of; however, for new players and account holders, this process could be too time-consuming to complete during a session. This process can also be discussed when presenting the Digital Consent Form and further ensures informed parental consent is obtained and documented. Furthermore, be aware that your own profile and activity (friends list, online status) can be visible; therefore, adjust your privacy settings accordingly to maintain professional boundaries (Finch, 2022a). When available, clinicians may also choose to use separate devices or profiles to maintain a clear boundary between clinical and personal use.

Minecraft Education as a Safe Alternative

For therapists seeking the highest level of built-in safety, Minecraft: Education is a highly recommended option (Finch, 2022a, 2022b). Designed for classroom use, it is inherently more secure and does not include access to a complex social network. It is free for clients, as the clinician purchases and has access to the individual licensing agreements, and can significantly simplify privacy settings for the clinician.

The Digital Consent Form

The protocols outlined in this chapter are the foundation of your ethical contract with the client and their family. To implement them effectively, a comprehensive Digital Consent Form is essential. This contract serves as formal informed consent for the use of Minecraft in therapy.

The handout template provided in Section 6, is designed to be adapted for your practice with consideration to legal and ethical guidelines for clinicians holding different licenses worldwide. The handout provides clear language to secure consent for the specific safety measures we have discussed, including:

- The use of a private server and non-identifying gamer tags.
- A protocol for using a separate, secure video platform for communication.
- The acknowledgment of inherent data risks, including applications that may lack a BAA.

Using this contract ensures transparency, manages risk, and formally establishes the interactions that occur in the Minecraft world as a secure digital space of a professional therapeutic environment.

Looking Ahead: Informed Consent and Contract

The core of your informed consent process for using Minecraft can be the Digital Consent Form (Handout 1), which covers platform limitations, data risks, and agreements to online safety rules. Before beginning, secure explicit informed consent that covers the use of Minecraft. Clinicians, group practices, and agencies may be drawn to creating their own informed consent and digital safety contract. Items to include are: the potential benefits and challenges, what a session will look like, communication boundaries, and a clear explanation of the data protection risks and the steps you take to mitigate them, such as storing world files on an encrypted, password-protected device (Finch, 2022a; TherapyNotes, LLC, 2017).

Crucially, your informed consent must explicitly acknowledge that while some enterprise services from Microsoft may offer BAAs, along with Minecraft Education, the consumer gaming platforms used for Minecraft (Bedrock, Java Edition, Xbox Live network …) do not. A BAA is a HIPAA-required contract that legally binds a vendor to protect patient data. While services like Zoom for Healthcare offer this, Microsoft's consumer gaming services do not. Therefore, while clinicians can implement every technical and contractual safeguard possible, the platform itself operates outside the specific protections of HIPAA. Documenting this understanding with the client and/or their guardian is an essential step in managing risk and maintaining ethical transparency.

References

Finch, E. (2022a). *Thinking of using video games therapeutically?* Association for Counseling and Therapy Online. https://playmodeacademy.org/resources-and-publications/thinking-of-using-video-games-therapeutically

Finch, E. (2022b). *Minecraft Education Edition: An engaging therapeutic tool.* Education.minecraft.net. https://education.minecraft.net/en-us/blog/therapeutictool

Finch, E. (2025a). *Essential steps for keeping your child safe when they are playing Minecraft (Bedrock Edition).* Playmode Academy. https://playmodeacademy.org/resources-and-publications/essential-steps-for-keeping-your-child-safe-when-they-are-playing-minecraft-bedrock-edition

Finch, E. (2025b). *Essential steps for keeping your child safe when they are playing Minecraft (Java Edition).* Playmode Academy. https://playmodeacademy.org/resources-and-publications/essential-steps-for-keeping-your-child-safe-when-they-are-playing-minecraft-java-edition

Fitzgerald, M. (2017). *How to stay safe online.* Minecraft.net; Minecraft. https://www.minecraft.net/en-us/article/minecraft-multiplayer-server-safety

Geere, D. (2023). *Parental controls in Minecraft.* Minecraft.net; Minecraft. https://www.minecraft.net/en-us/article/parental-controls

TherapyNotes, LLC. (2017). *5 ways to boost the security of your EMR.* TherapyNotes. https://blog.therapynotes.com/5-ways-to-boost-the-security-of-your-emr

Chapter 19

Disadvantages and When the Game Might Not Be a Good Fit

The integration of Minecraft into the play therapy space represents a significant and promising evolution in clinical practice. The benefits of the Seven Guiding Principles and how the game's open-world, sandbox nature can enliven the clinical process have been well documented in preceding chapters. However, it would be unrealistic to assume this would be the best fit for all clients and families. The enthusiasm for this intervention must also be held alongside a critical evaluation of its limitations, disadvantages, and potential for clinical misapplication. Furthermore, this evaluation must extend beyond the client and their family to include a sincere assessment of the clinician's own comfort and theoretical alignment with the modality. An ethical and practical clinician will not merely ask, "How can I use this?" but must also inquire, "When shouldn't I use this?" and "For whom might this cause harm or prove ineffective?"

This chapter provides a necessary counterbalance, drawing from clinical experience, including my own mistakes and learning. Only highlighting the successes of using Minecraft in play therapy would be a disservice to the field, risking an uncritical, inconsistent adoption of the modality. This chapter will go beyond its therapeutic potential and explore practical, systemic, and clinical contraindications. Tangible barriers, such as poor internet connections and differing family values, will be discussed, including how these can make the intervention impractical. More importantly, client-specific factors and clinical situations where Minecraft might be a poor fit will be examined, with consideration of how they may cause resistance or hinder progress. These challenges will be addressed, not to discourage clinicians from using this powerful tool but to help them develop the judgment needed for its careful and effective use. The aim is not to avoid failure altogether but to learn from mistakes and ultimately deliver more competent, client-centered care.

DOI: 10.4324/9781003614784-23

When Resources and Systems Pose a Barrier

Access and Resource Equity

Before a clinician can consider the therapeutic process within the game, they must first navigate a series of real-world obstacles. These pragmatic concerns are not mere inconveniences; they are fundamental ethical and clinical considerations that can determine the feasibility of the entire intervention. The first and most immediate barrier is access. Minecraft is a commercial product that requires specific hardware and software. The clinician must not assume that clients have instant access to necessary resources. Not every family owns a computer, gaming console, or tablet capable of running the game. Even if the hardware exists, the cost of buying the game, which varies by device type, can be a major obstacle for many. This raises an immediate equity concern: are we offering an advanced therapeutic modality only to those with the socioeconomic means to access it?

In a clinical setting, the burden often rests on the practice to provide the necessary technology. Chapter 1 described the benefits of using Minecraft in place of the many costs associated with curating a playroom, and it would be amiss to ignore the costs of this modality on the clinician or agency. Implementing Minecraft in one's practice requires an initial investment in purchasing devices and licenses, along with ongoing costs for maintenance, updates, and eventual replacement. For publicly funded or nonprofit agencies working with tight budgets, these costs can be prohibitive, effectively excluding their clients from this type of intervention. The clinician is thus faced with a difficult choice: invest heavily in this single modality or risk creating a two-tiered system of care within their practice. This digital divide highlights that technological advancements in therapy do not automatically improve access.

Technical Disruptions

The therapeutic frame relies on consistency, predictability, and safety. Technical failures pose a direct threat to this frame, interrupting the process of the client's play (Young, 2025). A play therapy appointment honors an agreement that the clinician is available and dependable during the scheduled time; when 15 of those minutes are consumed by updating an operating system, troubleshooting a Wi-Fi connection, or resolving a digital conflict, the clinical process is severely compromised.

Poor internet connection, in particular, is a common and frustrating disruptor. In online therapy, delays between a player's action and its appearance in the game can break the sense of shared presence, making collaborative play discouraging and unproductive. In an in-person session, even local network issues can cause similar disruptions if playing with a small group. In these cases, the clinician suddenly shifts from therapist to IT support, a role for which they are likely untrained and that directly conflicts with their therapeutic presence.

These obstacles can be minimized by troubleshooting before sessions and by being aware of the tools used. For clinicians playing individually in person, internet connection is less significant than in online play. Those playing online likely already have those aspects resolved as a part of their telehealth practice and can navigate glitches as they arise. However, the potential for technology-related challenges can serve as a counterargument to the First Guiding Principle: while the play therapist does not need to be a skilled Minecraft player, a working understanding of the technology required to play is essential to creating a smooth therapeutic experience. Clinicians who are new to playing with others and/or playing online can schedule times to practice with their colleagues, peers, or family to build confidence in initiating sessions and managing potential disruptions (see Chapter 3).

Navigating Confidentiality, Privacy, and Security

As described in the previous chapter, Minecraft was not originally designed to be a therapeutic platform compliant with the Health Insurance Portability and Accountability Act (HIPAA). Using a public server or Minecraft world that is shared with the general public is not advised as it exposes clients to potential interactions with others and risks compromising confidentiality and emotional safety. Even when players are in different areas, it can prevent unwanted crossover of in-game processing and content. Using individual worlds or servers with strict therapist-client boundaries is essential to ensure each client has a private, separate environment (see Chapter 18). The clinician must also have clear protocols for managing those worlds, ensuring each client's virtual space remains confidential and that worlds are archived or deleted in accordance with agreements (see Section 6, Appendix F). A workaround to these concerns would be to use Minecraft Education, as it includes built-in security features most commonly used to protect students during classroom use.

Considering if Using Minecraft Is the Best Fit

The Imperative of Caregiver and Child Buy-In

The clinician must consider the values and beliefs of the child's family and support system. For some parents and caregivers, the idea of using digital games in play therapy seems like a strong contradiction. They may view games such as Minecraft as conflicting with what therapy can provide, potentially leading to increased behavioral challenges, or as directly opposing their family's beliefs about screen time and recreational activities. These topics are explored in Section 2 and addressed within the framework of the Seven Guiding Principles. However, in some cases, it might simply not be the best fit.

Trying to enforce a game-based approach despite opposition can lead to misalignment and a disruption in the therapeutic alliance with both the family and the child. Some parents express a valid concern that Minecraft could reinforce a sedentary, "active couch potato" lifestyle (Lepp et al., 2023), especially if their child already struggles with physical activity. The clinician's first goal in these cases is not to persuade but to understand and collaborate. This includes psychoeducation about the Seven Guiding Principles and aligning the intervention with the parents' goals for their child. For example, I may say something along the lines of:

> *I understand your concern about bringing a digital game into the play therapy space, and you are absolutely right to question it; I'm glad you feel comfortable enough with me to raise your concern. In play therapy, we are using the game not as entertainment or a distraction, but as a tool to help your child learn more about how to identify, name, and regulate their emotions (among many other things), which you mentioned were concerns. Are there specific concerns you have that we could talk through together?*

It is my duty to advocate for the modality in this way, especially if it is of strong interest to the child; however, I will not push it further if it is clear there is no interest.

In some cases, a trial period can be an effective compromise, with agreements to follow up at a pre-determined time. This can include identifying and assessing the family's concerns about the use of the game in session, and whether any of those concerns have been observed. Other times, the clinician must honestly recognize when it's not a good fit and revert to traditional play therapy methods such as harnessing the therapeutic goals of the game through non-digital means, as detailed later in this chapter.

The Child's Relationship with the Game

Assuming the pragmatic barriers can be overcome, the clinician must then conduct a nuanced assessment of whether *Minecraft* is suitable for the specific individual present (see Chapter 16). Its open-ended, nondirective nature benefits many, but can be a significant drawback for others. Introducing Minecraft to a child or adolescent who has no interest in video games or dislikes them altogether may send the message that the clinician is not fully affirming the child's needs in the playroom. The child might see it as the therapist's agenda, leading to misattunement that prevents how they may want to be seen when engaging in the therapeutic process. Any insistence on using the game ignores the client's voice and risks making the therapy feel coercive rather than collaborative. In such cases, the game can become a barrier to building rapport. The therapist must be willing to adapt, let go of their plan, and follow the client's lead to an intervention that feels comfortable and of their choosing.

Conversely, some clients can become seemingly obsessive and overdependent on the game, using it as a crutch and a maladaptive coping strategy. Price (2022) writes that some neurodivergent and autistic players may find themselves immersed in the isolation and detachment of video games, making it an obstacle to using it in the intended therapeutic ways. Clinicians are always advised to use their clinical judgement to help clients and families determine the impact the game has on each child and their circumstances. This risk also highlights the powerful antidote of intentional clinical use, such as practicing endings and encouraging socialization through groups, which can help reframe the relationship with the game (see Chapters 7 and 15).

When the Game Fuels Clinical Resistance to Engagement

Some clients may use the modality and intervention of the digital game as a barrier and defense to vulnerability or as a nonverbal demonstration that they do not want to engage any further in therapy. This can occur when clients view the opportunity to play the game as an extension of their personal play objectives. For example, when meeting with clients online, some may have been playing for an extended period before the session and plan to continue immediately after it ends. In these situations, clients may ignore directive prompts, disregard non-directive prompts, and demonstrate minimal response to the clinician's engagement. During in-person sessions, this could present as a resistant fixation on their own objectives that ignores any acknowledgement of the therapist in the room. These are undoubtedly challenging and complex dynamics.

There are instances when this could be part of the setup and emotional developmental tasks (see Chapter 5). The therapist could have thoughts such as "Do I exist?", "Do I matter?", and "What is the point of this?" These experiences could all be part of the setup that the client may be communicating to the clinician, thus representing a much younger emotional age than they are chronologically.

In working with the setup in this scenario, I may say things such as:

> *I'm feeling so ignored. It hurts and it's also really sad. This is a special time for us to be together and it seems like there is no way for me to be involved. I really wish there could be a way for me to play too.*

If it is part of the setup, then the emotional communication of identifying "hurt" and "sadness," along with the relational acknowledgment of feeling "ignored," can be a powerful way for the client to be seen if that is an experience they are having. Anecdotally, I have witnessed powerful shifts happen in those instances.

Other times, that behavior could be the client simply implying, "I don't want to be here." In my experience, when the behavior is very explicitly ignoring and resisting any connection with the therapist, it has been the client expressing disinterest in therapy rather than a deep emotional process. In those cases, I have an honest conversation with the caregiver and the client. There are circumstances in which the caregiver may believe their child needs therapy when the child is really having difficulty communicating that they are "okay." Having referrals for parent coaches or therapists who work with adults individually can be helpful if the adult feels stuck in their own process with the child. It takes time, patience, and trust in the process to work through such complex dynamics, and clinicians are always advised to refer back to the training, clinical judgement, and consultation.

Another form of resistance arises not from opposition to therapy itself, but from a desire to protect a valued activity. Some children who love playing Minecraft may have an aversion to using the game when it feels too important to mix with therapeutic material and process. As discussed throughout this book, Minecraft is an incredible outlet for coping on so many levels. Some children may love playing Minecraft but have an aversion to playing it in session out of valid concern that it could change their relationship to casual game play. As with all client interests and preferences, clinicians can honor that preference and reflect the power of awareness in a client's ability to recognize what is best for them.

When the Medium Itself Is a Limitation

The Somatosensory Deficit

As a digital modality, Minecraft is inherently limited in its ability to engage the full sensory spectrum directly. Aside from the controller, keyboard, or mouse, the game provides no direct tactile sensory stimulation and offers no reliable channel for addressing proprioceptive needs, which can be so impactful for regulation and grounding (Delahooke, 2019). For children who present with sensory processing challenges or who require kinesthetic, hands-on input for emotional regulation, the digital interaction with the game can be a significant barrier. There are ways to modify and add interventions during gameplay; however, traditional play therapy interventions like sand trays, kinetic sand, finger paints, *Play-Doh*, or building with physical blocks may be far more effective. The virtual blocks of Minecraft lack the weight, texture, and physical resistance that can be crucial for grounding and somatic feedback in the play therapy room.

The Clinician's Aversion: Theoretical and Countertransference Hurdles

While much of the focus is rightly on the client's relationship to the game, the clinician's own aversion can be the most significant obstacle of all. This resistance can come from several sources. A clinician grounded in a particular theory (e.g., strict psychodynamic, Jungian, or cognitive-behavioral) may see the game as a distraction that interferes with pure symbolic expression or the verbal therapeutic process. This is a valid philosophical stance, not a failure. The clinician may also have personal negative beliefs about video games, influenced by their own family and social values. This can show up as subtle disapproval or a lack of genuine engagement in the Minecraft world, which the client will inevitably notice.

Ultimately, as explored in Chapter 6, a significant disadvantage can arise not from the game itself, but from the therapist's subjective countertransference. A therapist's conscious or unconscious biases against video games (Young, 2025) can become a significant barrier to effective implementation. If these factors are not addressed through self-reflection, training, or consultation, they can compromise the therapeutic relationship and are a clear indicator that the modality may not be a good fit for that particular clinician at that time.

Clinicians unfamiliar with gaming may feel anxious or incompetent, as a fear of losing control of the gameplay in the Minecraft worlds can be a significant barrier to authentically engaging with the client. Ignoring this discomfort is a clinical misstep. The ethical path is to first engage in supervision or consultation to understand the root of the aversion. If it stems from a fundamental theoretical disagreement, it is perfectly valid to conclude that the modality is not a fit for one's practice. If the aversion is based in bias or anxiety, the clinician must decide if they are willing to engage in a learning process. The First Guiding Principle aims to ease this distress, but, like some clients, it might not be the best fit for you. If readers have made it this far and do not have any interest in using the game themselves, that is okay. In fact, it's a great sign of dedication to the field of therapy to seek more knowledge even when the framework or intervention is not a perfect match. Simply being informed about Minecraft can strengthen one's relationship and understanding of a child for whom it is essential.

Ethical Considerations: Navigating Virtual Worlds and Values

Beyond clinical fit, the use of Minecraft invites ethical reflection on the values embedded in its gameplay. A salient criticism is that the core mechanic and assumed superiority of resource gathering and land alteration can unintentionally promote a colonialist mindset (Dooghan, 2016). The player is encouraged to explore uncharted territories, extract resources without consent from a virtual ecosystem, and claim land for their own purposes. When working with clients from cultural backgrounds with deep ties to the land or histories of colonization, this dynamic may be problematic. The ethical clinician must be aware of this subtext and, if using the game, be prepared to name and process these themes, potentially reframing the interaction as one of stewardship and co-creation with the environment rather than domination and extraction.

Additionally, clinicians must be consciously aware of the impact of screen-based interventions on the child's overall well-being (see Chapter 9). In an era of increasing sedentary behavior, relying exclusively on a digital modality could inadvertently contribute to an "active couch potato" lifestyle (Lepp et al., 2023). The evolution of this modern dilemma is that a child can be physically active during the day through physical education classes and recreational sports, yet also accumulate 4–8 hours of sedentary time daily (Lepp et al., 2023). Approximately an hour a week using Minecraft in their therapy session may not be enough to change the impact of outside sedentary time. Still, it also raises awareness of the overarching contrast between active and passive engagement. Therapists can provide an antidote (albeit small) by being intentional about incorporating physical coping skills that combine movement and physical play into the overall treatment plan, ensuring that Minecraft is one tool among many in a holistic therapeutic approach (see also Physical Coping Skills in Appendix B).

Clinical Adaptations for When the Game Is Not a Fit

During times when clients are unable to play the game during the session due to access, values, or technical problems, clinicians can still find ways to tap into the client's interests and develop effective therapeutic interventions. This might be necessary if the game is inaccessible, there is no internet, or there is misalignment between family or clinician values. Clinicians can leverage their understanding of the game's themes to create interventions that better suit the client.

For example, physical and tactile items like *LEGO*, wooden blocks, and sand trays can help a child show how they might play if they were using the game. Expressive arts supplies can be used to draw Minecraft-themed characters, mobs, and resources that clinicians can reference when adding other interventions. Minecraft-branded items, such as tools, blocks, and characters, can also be used as traditional play therapy toys. For more specific ideas on how to include Minecraft concepts in offline activities—whether during a session or at home with family—please see the Coping Skills Glossary in Appendix B.

Looking Ahead

The journey of integrating Minecraft into clinical practice is one of continuous learning, requiring as much humility as expertise. This chapter has not sought to dissuade clinicians from this innovative path, but to equip them for its inevitable challenges and pitfalls. The pragmatic, systemic, and clinical disadvantages are real and significant. They demand from us a rigorous assessment of our resources, our technical capabilities, and, most importantly, the unique individual sitting with us.

The Seven Guiding Principles remain unchanged, as intentional, clinical focus on the child and adolescent seeking our support still applies even if the game is not the best fit. How one arrives at a decision can still be an authentic therapeutic relationship that maintains a commitment to the child's well-being.

While Minecraft is just a tool, it is not the therapy itself. The therapy happens in the relationship. When the game strengthens that relationship and creates space for self-exploration and mutual understanding, it is effective. When it distracts, disrupts, or harms it, it is our professional and ethical responsibility to set it aside. By understanding its limitations and contraindications as well as its potentials, we shift from being merely enthusiastic early adopters to becoming discerning, competent, and client-focused clinicians in a digital age.

Reflection Question

1 How will I move beyond my own enthusiasm to rigorously assess a client's fit for Minecraft, manage the ethical and practical drawbacks, and ensure I have a non-digital alternative ready when the game is not serving the therapeutic purpose?

References

Delahooke, M. (2019). *Beyond behaviours: Using brain science and compassion to understand and solve children's behavioural challenges*. John Murray.

Dooghan, D. (2016). Digital conquerors: Minecraft and the apologetics of neoliberalism. *Games and Culture*, *14*(1), 67–86. https://doi.org/10.1177/1555412016655678

Lepp, A., Dowdell, B., Yim, B., & Barkley, J. E. (2023). Esports gamers, recreational gamers, and the active couch potato lifestyle. *American Journal of Lifestyle Medicine*. https://doi.org/10.1177/15598276231184159

Price, D. (2022). *Unmasking autism: Discovering the new faces of neurodiversity*. Harmony Books.

Young, H. (2025). Exploring the potential of Minecraft to embody the therapeutic powers of play, acting as a core agent for change in the play therapy process. *British Journal of Play Therapy*, *19*(1), 47–59.

Section V

The Future of Minecraft Therapy

Chapter 20

Research, Funding, and Advancing the Application

At this stage in the book, I hope readers will feel inspired by the therapeutic potential of using Minecraft in play therapy. The previous sections and chapters provided the foundation for adapting clinical theory through practical non-directive and directive play therapy interventions rooted in Polyvagal Theory (Porges, 2011), interpersonal neurobiology (Siegel, 1999), non-directive and directive play therapy interventions, family systems work, trauma-informed care, and emotionally focused parenting. Utilizing the Seven Guiding Principles of using Minecraft in play therapy, clinicians can reference a clear framework for implementation, along with a vision for how this modality can transform child mental health care with the children they serve in their practices. Families, caregivers, and other helping adults can benefit from adapting Minecraft to enhance their playful interactions with the children and adolescents in their lives, drawing on information from the concepts of emotionally focused parenting and the simple yet powerful impact of play.

The clinical vignettes provided throughout the chapters illustrated how clinicians may work with skepticism and hesitation from caregivers inquiring about the use of Minecraft in play therapy for a variety of common clinical dynamics. The fictional narratives of children exploring their emotional world through gameplay in Minecraft further illustrate how the game's dynamic features become an open canvas for creative and therapeutic expression. Readers were introduced to the clinical benefits of creating characters, practicing mindfulness, "being" in the game with the child, coregulating through distress, encouraging a growth-oriented mindset, and helping families transfer the child's interest in the playable elements of the game to practical offscreen strategies for coping flexibility.

The journey does not end here, however; the true promise lies in expanding this orientation and skillset to all children worldwide, particularly those in underserved communities where traditional therapy is scarce. This final chapter looks ahead, exploring how the use of Minecraft in play therapy can evolve through ongoing research, funding, and the advancement

DOI: 10.4324/9781003614784-25

of its application in all the innovative ways that clinicians have already been utilizing the game to transform the lives of children everywhere. This book would not have been possible without the impact of the pioneers in this work, who have recognized the therapeutic benefits of the game in ways that have extended beyond the walls of a traditional playroom.

Research, Funding, and Advancing the Field

The future of using Minecraft in play therapy hinges on evidence-based validation and sustainable funding for the communities that need it most. While studies show its efficacy in working with neurodivergent and autistic youth (Blackwood, 2025; Kilmer et al., 2023; Ringland, 2019; Ringland et al., 2016; Zolyomi & Schmalz, 2017), more large-scale research is needed for the wide variety of mental health challenges and diagnoses that play therapists encounter in their practices. Key priorities could include longitudinal studies on outcomes for many of the clinical presentations referenced in the previous chapters, such as supporting LGBTQIA+ youth, racial identity within systems of oppression, grief, trauma, neurodivergence, and working with groups.

To support the on-going study and development of evolving modalities and applications, clinicians and researchers could collaborate with grant funders in the United States such as the National Institutes of Health (NIH), the National Science Foundation (NSF), global nonprofits worldwide such as the United Nations Children's Fund (UNICEF), and the independent, non-governmental organization Save the Children, to lessen the financial obstacles to provide the items needed for widespread outreach and study. Given the inherent digital nature of Minecraft, clinicians and researchers could also partner with technical representatives and organizations that would also benefit from further research and visibility. This could include gaming companies that are moving into the mental health and wellness genre, leveraging the popularity of Minecraft and utilizing modern applications such as app-based support, virtual reality, and artificial intelligence, as potential future avenues for play-based engagement.

Further areas of focus could include randomized controlled trials comparing the efficacy of Minecraft therapy when compared with interventions found in traditional play therapy outcomes for presenting issues such as anxiety, depression, trauma, and PTSD. Functional magnetic resonance imaging (fMRI), which studies brain activity related to specific tasks, can be used to investigate how Minecraft play affects different regions and functions of the brain when individuals play it alone or in groups. Global efforts could focus on formal research on the work already being done to support the children and adolescents impacted by natural disasters, wartime traumas, and refugee status, human trafficking, and other critical needs (see voices from the field below).

Reaching Children Where They Are

Using Minecraft in play therapy enables clinicians to extend their reach beyond the play therapy room, as it can be adapted for use in schools, hospitals, and disaster-response settings. As described in Chapter 2, schools worldwide already utilize Minecraft Education for social-emotional learning; integrating the therapeutic use of the game into school counseling programs could bridge gaps in mental health support by providing access to a familiar, engaging entry point for students who might otherwise avoid services. Children's hospitals and pediatric treatment centers can utilize Minecraft to reduce stress, anxiety, and the potential effects of loneliness due to isolation from peers (Hollett & Ehret, 2014; see Gamers Outreach Foundation, n.d.). Disaster clinics worldwide could deploy quick, game-based interventions for traumatized children in the field as a supplement to mental health first aid, as well as short-term group therapy. The goal is to meet children in their world, both in the game and in their hearts, wherever the element of human connection may intersect with them.

Voices from the Field

To illustrate this momentum, first-person testimonials from a series of global pioneers are presented to highlight the real-world impact and the unique, groundbreaking work being done. Their voices are italicized to draw attention to their distinctive phrasing and perspective on this work.

Luke Blackwood (Australia)

Luke Blackwood, clinical psychologist and director of Full Potential Psychology, created Legend Land, a Minecraft-based therapy world (Legend Land Server—Full Potential Psychology, 2024; Madigan, 2020). Utilizing story-driven quests facilitated by his team of trained clinicians, Legend Land supports children in emotional learning through an intentionally curated and designed world focused on directive interventions. Some of the quests offered by Luke and his team include multiplayer experiences that teach players about the relationship between brain functions and emotional regulation, as well as a "Time Traveler Quest" to explore and observe the relationship between anxiety and survival responses (Sukhorukov, 2025b).

Now in its sixth version, it delivers telehealth sessions through both semi-structured gamified quests and flexible sandbox play, providing children with a safe, engaging therapy experience. Quests incorporate Cognitive

Behaviour Therapy (CBT) and Acceptance & Commitment Therapy (ACT) treatment plans, focusing on emotional regulation, cognitive interventions, acceptance, and values-based action.

Sessions are delivered by a registered psychologist via telehealth, with integrated video and audio allowing the client and psychologist to see and speak with each other while their characters interact in the digital therapy world.

A pilot study on Legend Land as a telehealth intervention with autistic children (aged 9–10) found reduced emotional and conduct difficulties, fewer peer problems and meltdowns, and improved coping strategies (Blackwood, 2025). While further research is needed, a multiplayer version is now available to clinic clients, with plans for wider access.

Rachel Conlisk (United Kingdom)

Rachel Conlisk is the founder and director of Creative Active Lives CIC, where she has launched *MineMania*, a Minecraft server, to support the self-confidence and self-esteem of neurodiverse youth through peer relationships and skill-building (Mine Mania, 2023). This private and secure server offers a variety of gameplay modes, including Survival multiplayer, mini-games, build challenges, and even a calm world to support ventral vagal states.

At Creative Active Lives CIC, we use Minecraft to support the whole child – from playing with friends, to mentoring when needed, through work experience, post-16 opportunities, and beyond.

I set up MineMania, a secure community Minecraft server for neurodiverse children and young people. For many of those we work with, school or mainstream clubs are not accessible or comfortable, and social isolation is a daily reality. MineMania gives them a safe and supportive space to meet others like them, build friendships, and develop skills. We run Survival multiplayer, mini games, build challenges, and a calm world designed to help young people regulate. Children can join build teams, contribute to community projects, and even step into responsible roles such as Server Admin if they want to.

As the server has grown, so have the opportunities. We now offer in-person work experience placements, career talks with professional artists and Minecraft builders, and courses in coding and game design. Alongside MineMania, we run carefully designed holiday clubs and family events, using our Minecraft LAN gaming outreach bank of laptops. Our aim is to "get children off their screens and onto ours" in a safe, structured way. This has been especially effective in encouraging isolated children to leave the house, come to our events, and meet their online friends in real life. At these sessions, children play together on and off screen, building confidence and friendships, while parents connect with one another for peer support.

By using Minecraft to bridge online and real-life relationships, we not only help young people grow in confidence and self-esteem, but also reduce isolation for whole families and strengthen community ties.

Stuart Duncan (Canada)

Stuart Duncan was a web developer and creator of *AutCraft,* the first Minecraft server specifically offered to support children diagnosed with autism (Duncan, n.d.). Recently celebrating their 12th anniversary, the server boasts over 18,000 approved player names. To ensure that the server provides a safe and inclusive experience for all players, Autcraft requires players to agree to rules governing gameplay and the use of the chat function, along with an understanding of potential warnings and consequences.

When I started my Minecraft server for autistic people and their families, I had no idea what I was getting myself in for. My only intention was to keep people safe, and to give people a place to play their favorite game without fear of people being toxic. What I've witnessed since, though, is nothing short of amazing.

Children are learning how to read and write, to make friends and how to be a friend, to work well in teams and even to be leaders. Some non-verbal children have even found their voice. And it's not something we're doing, it's just happening. Something profound happens when a child is having fun and not afraid.

The progress was even greater when parents would join their children. There's an expression in the autism community that goes "Your child is not ignoring you, they're simply waiting for you to join them in their world." and I can think of no more literal interpretation of this than Minecraft. Parents who take the plunge and join their children create bonding experiences that they just can't get any other way. Instead of complaining that their children won't stop talking about Minecraft, now they're talking together, and planning projects, making friends, setting play dates, fighting monsters, building a second home together exactly the way they want it, and so much more.

This is all anecdotal, of course, just my observations over the last twelve and a half years but I've witnessed this happen over, and over, and over again, and it warms my heart each and every time. My greatest reward, as a Minecraft server owner, doing what I do, is hearing from parents and children alike that they've grown so much, they've created close new bonds, and that so much progress is made in their lives all by loading up a game together and playing together.

When a person is having fun and there is no fear to try new things, to take risks, to truly be themselves there is no limit to what a person can accomplish.

Ellie Finch (United Kingdom)

Ellie Finch, clinician and writer of the foreword to this book, is a social worker, clinical supervisor, and counselor who has brought the experience of therapeutic Minecraft to professionals worldwide in her training programs, and virtual *Sandtray Therapy Minecraft World* (Finch, 2024) – designed alongside Dan Noble (see below).

Ellie is also the founder and director of PlayMode Academy, a nonprofit social venture dedicated to widening access to therapy and support services. The organization equips professionals with the confidence, knowledge, and practical skills to utilize creative digital tools – such as Minecraft and digital Sandtrays – in ways that are meaningful, ethical, and engaging. Moving the world of Minecraft forward, Ellie is also bringing therapeutic Minecraft play to adults and couples (Stuart, 2025).

Last, Ellie is part of the University of Cambridge research team behind *Bridging the ChASM: Creating Accessible Services using Minecraft* (Beckett et al., 2024), a project funded by the Arts and Humanities Research Council (AHRC) that explores the therapeutic potential of video games and how they can be used to create more inclusive mental health support.

Dan Noble (United Kingdom)

Dan Noble is a Minecraft education consultant, content creator, and overall advocate for the endless possibilities for utilizing Minecraft in fun and educational ways. His blog *OutsidetheBlocks* is a trusted resource for users of Minecraft Education and a first-stop destination for clinicians interested in learning more about in-game features and commands to take their work with clients to the next level (Noble, 2022). Dan is also a co-designer of the *Sandtray Therapy Minecraft World* (Finch, 2024).

Minecraft changes lives for the better. We've seen the power of purposeful play aptly demonstrated in the education sector with Minecraft Education as an accessible product that teaches many subjects, and imparts much knowledge, but Minecraft has many empowering applications beyond that.

Minecraft as a therapeutic tool is equally powerful.

What parents, teachers, students, clients, and even casual players may not often be consciously aware of is that while they may be building things in Minecraft, they are also actively building themselves! I've witnessed players gaining new or improving existing skillsets with incredible speed, building: self-confidence, self-reliance, communications, leadership, empathy, cooperation, sharing, emotional awareness, deductive reasoning, creativity, and many more, all while overcoming their own perceived limitations.

Watching people thriving and becoming the best version of themselves through harnessing Minecraft is a magical thing to experience. The power of Minecraft for good is limitless.

Oleksii Sukhorukov (Ukraine/Germany)

Oleksii Sukhorukov is a Ukrainian psychologist and founder of HealGame Ukraine, a project for the study of video games and the development of a game-based project for emotional support of youth. In 2025, together with Ukrainian child psychologist Anna Shulha, who also uses Minecraft in her work with children, and with the technical support of Donetsk National Technical University, he started WonderWorld Quest for Ukrainian refugee children aged 11–13 in Germany, who lived with their families in the dormitories of Malteser Werke charity (Sukhorukov, 2025a). Wonderworld is a magical world that needs the help of children, and at the same time helps them discover their own strength, and also connects online and offline (between the gaming sessions, there are offline tasks that help the children progress in the game). In the moderated multiplayer world in Minecraft Education, children cooperate toward common goals, gather their positive emotions in personal Places of Power, and establish friendships with peers from other dormitories. Some of them were able to recreate things lost to them due to the Russian war, ranging from their homes to their peer relationships.

Recognizing the emotional and physical need for children to bridge their online experience with real-world experiences, Sukhorukov integrates offline activities that keep players not only engaged but connected to one another. (Stuart, 2025)

Unfortunately, as a Ukrainian who lost their home and became a forced refugee with a 13-year-old son, I have to speak about one of the darkest circumstances in which Minecraft may be used with children.

In his article "Children's Play in the Shadow of War," Daniel Feldman compares the underground games of children in Syria with the secret play of children during the Holocaust, showing how play becomes a means of survival and a way to make sense of reality during war. He writes: "Children's play typically becomes one of the first targets of armed conflict" (Feldman, 2019). Today, for children in war zones, under occupation, in refugee camps, or living in unfamiliar towns and countries that may feel hostile or unsafe, digital games can sometimes be their only way to play and connect with friends. This may be especially true for children with physical disabilities and neurodivergent kids. The main danger is that the vulnerable children who may not have enough support and attention from adults are the number one target for online extremists and predators. But at the same time, professionals also can use their favorite video games to talk about online threats as well as build a bridge to these new places in the physical world – excellent examples can be found in the book by Dr. Robert Rice Video Games in Psychotherapy (Rice, 2023). That is why I am developing quests bridging Minecraft and the physical world, which will allow refugee children to make friends with new people and places, as well as learn more about the new culture they are faced with.

It is also important that for refugee children the online space may be the only opportunity to receive psychological support and help in their native language. That is why I am passionate that as many Ukrainian professionals as possible learn about Minecraft. But Minecraft is something more for refugee children, something that is hard to imagine in peacetime. Let's Plays in Minecraft by Ukrainian children on YouTube, dedicated to war, occupation, Russian captivity and torture, are unique documents of the digital age and evidence of Russia's terrible crimes against Ukrainian children and humanity, which are yet to be studied. And at the same time, children do not lose hope. Together – refugee children, internally displaced, under shelling in Ukraine and in Russian occupation – they build their worlds together. I think they hope that adults will do the same with the physical world – despite everything.

These stories underscore the creativity that is driving the implementation of using Minecraft in play therapy forward, while also demonstrating the worldwide need and interest.

Looking Ahead: A Call to Action

The path ahead requires advocacy, collaboration, and innovation. Readers are encouraged to move the conversation forward by finding ways to contribute to research via publishing case studies and/or participating in future trials. Clinicians and advocates for this work can also consider ways to implement pilot programs in nontraditional play therapy settings such as libraries, community centers, faith organizations, and anywhere else children in need might go in a time of solace. Last, play therapists are encouraged to stay connected and involved in their mental health and wellness communities by seeking ways to raise funds for hardware and licenses on both the local and global levels. The true potential of this modality lies in its ability to transcend traditional clinical spaces, reaching children globally, wherever access to mental health care is needed or limited. By thinking beyond the play therapy room, the use of Minecraft in play therapy can become another way for children to have the opportunity to process complex emotions through the flexibility of Minecraft in the way that we know can change their lives.

Reflection Question

1 This book has laid the groundwork for Minecraft's capacity to help children. The next step is to build support systems through advocacy, research, and sustainable funding that can expand this work. As a clinician in this field, what will be my first act of advocacy or innovation to help advance this modality beyond my own practice and reach children worldwide who need it?

References

Beckett, M., Finch, E., McLellen, R., & Peacock, F. (2024). *Creating accessible services using Minecraft. Faculty of Education.* Cam.ac.uk. https://www.educ.cam.ac.uk/research/programmes/chasm/

Blackwood, L. (2025). Legend land: An evaluation of a telehealth videogame for the emotional regulation of autistic children. *Good Autism Practice*, *26*(1), 35–44. Ingenta Connect. https://www.ingentaconnect.com/contentone/bild/gap/2025/00000026/00000001/art00007

Duncan, S. (n.d.). *Autcraft: The first Minecraft server for children with autism and their families.* AutCraft. https://www.autcraft.com/

Feldman, D. (2019). Children's play in the shadow of war. *American Journal of Play*, *11*(3), 288–307. https://files.eric.ed.gov/fulltext/EJ1220280.pdf

Finch, E. (2024). *Sandtray therapy Minecraft world.* Play Mode Academy. https://playmodeacademy.org/visit-our-sandtray-world

Gamers Outreach Foundation. (n.d.). *Gamers outreach: Helping others level up. Video game charity for kids.* Gamers Outreach Foundation. https://gamersoutreach.org/

Hollett, T., & Ehret, C. (2014). "bean's world": (Mine) Crafting affective atmospheres of gameplay, learning, and care in a children's hospital. *New Media & Society*, *17*(11), 1849–1866. https://doi.org/10.1177/1461444814535192

Kilmer, E., Spangler, J., & Kilmer, J. (2023). Therapeutically applied Minecraft groups with neurodivergent youth. *F1000Research*, *12*, 216. https://doi.org/10.12688/f1000research.129090.1

Legend Land Server—Full Potential Psychology. (2024). *Legend Land: Unlock Your Magic—Official Server Trailer.* YouTube. https://www.youtube.com/watch?v=rnyQ7lsTftI

Madigan, N. (2020, February 24). Breakthrough therapy uses Minecraft to empower children with ASD. *Health Times.* https://healthtimes.com.au/hub/autism-spectrum/63/practice/nm/breakthrough-therapy-uses-minecraft-to-empower-children-with-asd/4723/

Mine Mania. (2023). *Mine Mania: A Minecraft server for neurodiverse children and young people.* Mine Mania. https://www.minemania.co/

Noble, D. (2022). *Outsidetheblocks.* Blogspot.com; Blogger. https://outsidetheblokz.blogspot.com/

Porges, S. W. (2011). *The polyvagal theory: Neurophysiological foundations of emotions, attachment, communication, and self-regulation.* W. W. Norton & Company.

Rice, R. (2023). *Video games in psychotherapy* (1st ed.). Routledge. https://doi.org/10.4324/9781003222132

Ringland, K. E. (2019). "Autsome": Fostering an autistic identity in an online Minecraft community for youth with autism. *Information in Contemporary Society, 11420*, 132–143. https://doi.org/10.1007/978-3-030-15742-5_12

Ringland, K. E., Wolf, C. T., Faucett, H., Dombrowski, L., & Hayes, G. R. (2016). *"Will I always be not social?": Re-conceptualizing sociality in the context of a Minecraft community for autism.* Proceedings of the 2016 CHI Conference on Human Factors in Computing Systems—CHI '16. https://doi.org/10.1145/2858036.2858038

Siegel, D. J. (1999). *The developing mind: How relationships and the brain interact to shape who we are.* Guilford Press.

Stuart, K. (2025, July 14). "The way a child plays is the way they live": How therapists are using video games to help vulnerable children. *The Guardian.* https://www.theguardian.com/games/2025/jul/14/the-way-a-child-plays-is-the-way-they-live-how-therapists-are-using-video-games-to-help-vulnerable-children

Sukhorukov, O. (2025a). *"Wonderworld": Minecraft & offline quest for Ukrainian refugee children.* HealGame Ukraine. https://healgameukraine.click/en/wonderworld-minecraft-offline-quest-for-ukrainian-refugee-children/

Sukhorukov, O. (2025b). *Luke Blackwood: The game has a hidden power. Healgameukraine.click.* https://healgameukraine.click/en/luke-blackwood-the-game-has-a-hidden-power/#a-lot-of-the-time-parents-don8217t-feel-confident-in-how-to-make-the-gaming-safe-for-their-child

Zolyomi, A., & Schmalz, M. (2017). *Mining for social skills: Minecraft in home and therapy for neurodiverse youth.* Scholarspace.manoa.hawaii.edu. https://doi.org/10.24251/HICSS.2017.411

Section VI

Appendices

Appendix A

The Seven Guiding Principles

A Therapeutic Framework for Using Minecraft in Play Therapy

Principle 1: The Play Therapist Does Not Need to Be a Skilled Player to Utilize Minecraft in Play Therapy

Play therapists who are new to the game can show up with the truth of their experience and still be the helping clinician they would be otherwise.

Principle 2: The Therapy Starts Even Before the Game Is Played

The initial tasks of designing characters, beginning new games, and even navigating the technology of playing together become therapeutic moments as opportunities for a variety of interventions can arise in those instances.

Principle 3: The Play Therapist Is Not Playing Minecraft for Their Own Enjoyment; They Are Playing to Be in the Experience of the Game with the Child

The intention and focus is always set on the experience of the child. This is done by noticing how the child's brain, body, and nervous system may be stimulated by certain aspects of game play, as well as how our own thoughts, feelings, and nervous systems respond while playing together.

Principle 4: The Play Therapist Can Model How to Work with the Stimulation in the Game to Help the Child Learn More About Themselves While Playing

Play therapists can use their experiences of being in the game to help model regulation, build interoception, and increase the child's Window of

Tolerance. Utilizing the benefits of coregulation, play therapists can help children regulate in real time while working through moments of distress that might occur while playing.

Principle 5: How the Game Ends in a Session Is Practice for Endings and Transitions Outside of the Play Therapy Space

Practicing intentional endings of the game during sessions provides the experience of working with endings and transitions away from the game.

Principle 6: Parents and Helping Adults Can Support Their Child in Having a Therapeutic Experience with Minecraft at Home by Being Curious and Learning About the Game Together

Bringing the child's interest in Minecraft into family discussions and activities can help reinforce positive attachments between the child and their parents or caregivers. Children have the opportunity to become experts, while adults become curious observers of the child's experience.

Principle 7: The Benefits of Playing the Game Reach Far Beyond the Play Therapy Space and the Digital World of Minecraft

Bringing intentional focus on the child's experience of the game builds awareness for how the child perceives and relates to their world outside of the game. This includes adapting game mechanics into practical coping skills for real life.

Table A.1 The Seven Guiding Principles for Using Minecraft in Play Therapy

Guiding principle	*Core therapeutic function*	*Theoretical and clinical influences*	*Foundational references*
Principle 1: Gaming Experience Not Necessary	Acknowledging strengths, building confidence, modeling adaptive behaviors	Non-Directive Play Therapy	Axline (1947); Finch (2021); Young (2024)
Principle 2: Starting at the Beginning	Validation of client interests and creation of early therapeutic moments	Child-Centered Play Therapy	Axline (1947); Landreth (2012)
Principle 3: Being in the Game with the Child	Maintaining therapeutic intention and focus, observational assessment of internal states	Synergetic Play Therapy, Interpersonal Neurobiology	Dion (2018); Siegel (1999)
Principle 4: Coregulation and Working with Stimulation	Modeling regulation, building interoception, increasing child's Window of Tolerance	Polyvagal Theory, Interpersonal Neurobiology, Synergetic Play Therapy	Porges (2011); Siegel (1999); Dion (2018)
Principle 5: Practicing Positive Endings	Acknowledging and working with transitions and endings	Play Therapy Rituals, Limit-Setting	Landreth (2012)
Principle 6: Playing Together at Home	Strengthening family bonds, reinforcing positive attachment, and increasing communication	Attachment-Based Family Therapy for Depressed Adolescents	Diamond et al. (2014)
Principle 7: Bridging Online Play to Offline Play	Translating problem-solving skills and applying game strategies to real life	Therapeutic Metaphor	Mills and Crowley (2014)

Appendix B

Coping Skills Glossary

Minecraft Themed Interventions

When Minecraft is unavailable due to access issues, value conflicts, or technical problems, the client's interest in the game can be effectively redirected through these adaptive coping skills. These can also be applied as family-level strategies or used at home when the game is not being played.

The Five Coping Categories

These five categories can be applied to explore and prompt awareness of various coping skills, depending on the situation and needs.

Physical

Coping skills that use the body to regulate the nervous system and release energy.

- **Mining IRL – Transitioning from the Game**

  Use this to: Help a child struggling to disengage from the game by transferring the first-person perspective to the real world.
  Try this: "*Let's go mining for cool things in the real world. Point your 'screen' (this phone) and tell me what 'blocks' you see.*"

- **Potion of Movement – Boosting Energy**

  Use this to: Introduce quick bursts of physical activity as a tool to shift low energy or a bad mood.
  Try this: "*You look like you need a 'Potion of Movement'! Let's do 10 jumping jacks to give our bodies a boost.*"

- **Rest & Respawn – The Reset Button**

  Use this to: Frame rest as essential and "failure" as a temporary state for learning, promoting a growth mindset.

Try this: *"Sometimes it helps to take a break and try again. How can we 'rest and respawn', starting over to try a new strategy?"*

- **Sunrise Timers – The Natural Day Cycle**

  Use this to: Help clients who struggle with waking up to start a new day.
  Try this: *"It can be really hard to get up in the mornings. 'Sunrise' alarm clocks can help mimic the morning of a Minecraft world as it gradually gets lighter when it's time to wake up."*

Cognitive

Coping skills that involve problem-solving, planning, and using conscious thought to manage distress.

- **Adventure Maps – Planning for New Places**

  Use this to: Help a child who struggles with anxiety about new situations or changes in routine by pre-planning and visualizing the steps.
  Try this: *"Let's make an 'adventure map' for [the new school, the doctor's visit]. What are the different places we'll see? What tools do we need to pack in our backpack to feel ready?"*

- **Crafting Table Problem-Solving – Combining Ideas**

  Use this to: Break down overwhelming problems by showing how smaller ideas can be combined to create a new solution.
  Try this: *"We're stuck. Let's use our 'crafting table' brains. What are three different ideas we have? Now, how can we combine them to make a whole new solution?"*

- **Window of Tolerance Chart – Tracking Your Nervous System**

  Use this to: Give a family a shared, nonverbal language to communicate their level of arousal and regulation throughout the day.
  Try this: *"This chart shows just how much we are feeling. Let's each move our magnet to show where we are right now. Towards the right we are in the 'overwhelmed' zone, or on the left we are in the 'shut down' zone. The middle is when we are at our best to take on anything!"*

Social

Coping skills that leverage connection with others to foster a sense of safety and belonging.

- **Ambient Social Connection – Soothing with Sound**

  Use this to: Provide a form of social nourishment for a child who finds direct social interaction overwhelming, by leveraging the calming effect of the human voice.
  Try this: *"If being with people feels like too much, you can still get some connection. Listening to a calm audiobook or podcast can help your nervous system feel like someone safe is nearby."*

- **The "Allay" Helper – Knowing When to Ask for Help**

  Use this to: Reframe asking for help as a strategic strength, not a weakness, and identify support people.
  Try this: *"Sometimes we need an 'Allay' to help us. Who is a safe person you could ask for help when you're feeling overwhelmed?"*

- **Multiplayer Team Projects – The Power of Collaboration**

  Use this to: Translate the experience of in-game collaboration into real-life family or peer connection through a shared, tangible goal.
  Try this: *"Remember how we built that castle together in the game? What's a project we could do as a family at home (like cooking a meal or building a fort) that would need that same teamwork?"*

- **Village Trading – The Reciprocity of Friendship**

  Use this to: Teach the give-and-take nature of healthy relationships in a concrete, non-threatening way.
  Try this: *"Friendship is like trading with a villager. What is something you can 'offer' a friend, and what do you hope to 'get' in return?"*

Soothing

Activities that calm the nervous system and promote a sense of safety and well-being.

- **Ambient Sounds – Creating a Soothing Soundscape**

  Use this to: Help the child identify and utilize auditory cues to regulate their nervous system, starting with a familiar in-game reference.
  Try this: *"The Minecraft music is so calming. Let's find other sounds that give you that same peaceful feeling, like rain or white noise, to help you relax or sleep."*

- **Backpack Inventory – Your Personal Toolkit**

  Use this to: Empower the child by creating a tangible, portable collection of soothing items they can use to self-regulate in moments of distress.

Try this: *"Just like your Minecraft character has an inventory, let's fill a real backpack with 9 things that help you feel safe and calm. What should we put in it?"*

- **Character Skins – Your Armor of Confidence**

  Use this to: Reframe daily routines as an act of self-empowerment and explore how we can "armor" ourselves for challenging situations.
  Try this: *"Getting dressed is like choosing your character's skin and armor. What clothes make you feel powerful? What 'armor' do you need to feel brave for [a specific event]?"*

- **Healing Potions – Nourishment as Self-Care**

  Use this to: Reframe healthy consumption (hydration, nutrition) as an active, empowering strategy for managing different emotional states.
  Try this: *"You look like you could use a 'Potion of Sleep' (warm milk) or a 'Potion of Strength' (a healthy snack). Which one would help you most right now?"*

- **Health & Food Bars – Tuning into Your Body**

  Use this to: Build interoception (awareness of internal body signals) by using the game's visual meters as a metaphor for energy and capacity.
  Try this: *"If your health bar is low, what kind of rest or potion do you need? If your real-life hunger bar is low, what's one thing you can eat to fill it up?"*

Spiritual

Skills that connect to meaning, values, and a sense of purpose, providing comfort and perspective.

- **Safe Space at Home**

  Use this to: Co-create a physical "respawn point" in the home where family members can go to self-regulate or where the family can come together to communicate needs safely.
  Try this: *"Just like we build a safe base in Minecraft, let's design a 'Safe Space' in our home. What are the rules for this space? What makes it feel safe for everyone?"*

- **The End Poem – A Connection to Something Larger**

  Use this to: Facilitate conversations about a child's sense of purpose, their connection to the world, and what gives their life meaning.

Try this: *"The End Poem in Minecraft talks about the universe and our place in it. What do you think your role is in our family's 'universe'? What makes you feel connected to the world?"*

- **Village Values – Translating Gameplay to Virtues**

Use this to: Use the cooperative and peaceful mechanics of the game (like trading, managing food supplies) as a concrete starting point for discussing core family values.

Try this: *"Trading with villagers is all about fair exchange and sharing. How can we practice 'village values' like sharing, fairness, and helping each other in our family and community?"*

Appendix C

Directive Minecraft Interventions

Clear, Consistent Routines

Clinical Goal: To establish predictability and safety, creating a secure therapeutic container. This practice also supports the work of Principle 5 (managing endings).

Preparation: A consistent opening and closing ritual. This could be a specific greeting, a check-in using a particular item, a number from zero to ten, or a shared gesture.

Directive/Prompt: *"Just like our sessions always have a clear beginning and end, let's start by placing a block that represents how you feel and end by naming one thing you were most proud of today."*

Clinical Note: The ritual itself is the intervention. Prompting the child to look inward at the start and end of the game.

Family Fortress: The Shared Defense

Clinical Goal: To practice collaborative problem-solving and coregulation as a family system by designing a shared defense against a common "threat."

Preparation: A Creative world or Survival mode world on "Easy" or "Peaceful" to manage the threat level (difficulty can increase to "test" the build.)

Directive/Prompt: *"Night is coming, and the mobs will come out. Let's work together to build one fortress that can keep you safe. What does the family need to feel protected? Who is good at gathering resources, and who is good at building? You have to communicate and problem-solve to survive the night together."*

Clinical Note: This is a live enactment of family dynamics. Observe roles: who leads, who follows, who struggles to collaborate? The therapist coaches the family in real-time on communication and coregulation, helping them practice new in-game patterns that can support other interactions.

The Five Senses Tour

Clinical Goal: To practice grounding and mindfulness within the game environment by intentionally directing attention to sensory details, building a bridge between digital immersion and present-moment, embodied awareness.

Preparation: Choose between Creative or Survival mode (you can also explore to discover interesting biomes).

Directive/Prompt: *"We're going on a special tour to notice what our character is experiencing with their five senses. Let's find:*

Sight: *'Your favorite thing you can see right now? What colors and shapes stand out?'*

Sound: *'What sounds can you hear? Is it the music, water, or animals?'*

Touch: *'What would it feel like to stand where you are? Is the ground soft grass, rough sand, or cold stone?'*

Smell: *'If you could smell this place, what would it smell like? Pine trees in a forest? Wet mud near a river?'*

Taste: *'What would the air taste like here? Clean and fresh? Salty from the ocean? Is there anything you would like to eat?'*

Let's travel to a new biome and see how the senses change."

Clinical Note: This intervention can be implemented with a new client or when introducing Minecraft into your sessions for the first time. This can also be shared with caregivers and completed offline in an imaginative way.

The Grief Cave

Clinical Goal: To externalize and contain feelings of grief, allowing the child to gain a sense of mastery and autonomy.

Preparation: A dedicated space in a Creative or Survival world with access to a variety of blocks and items, including torches, chests, and mob spawn eggs.

Directive/Prompt: *"Think of your grief as a dark cave. What does it look like inside? Which 'mobs' (feelings) live in there? What tools or 'torches' (supports) do you need to feel safe exploring it?"*

Clinical Note: The choice of mobs can be symbolic and individual (e.g., Creepers for explosions of anger, Skeletons for feelings of being startled by grief, Wardens for overwhelming emotions). The act of placing torches can also represent finding moments of insight and safety amidst the pain.

Grief Waves

Clinical Goal: To give form to the non-linear, unpredictable, and sometimes overwhelming nature of grief, and to collaboratively identify coping strategies for navigating it.

Preparation: An open, flat area or an ocean biome with access to water, lava, buckets, and other items.

Directive/Prompt: *"Grief can feel like waves. Sometimes they are calm, and sometimes they are huge and crashing. Use water and lava to build what these 'grief waves' look like. What do you need to help you ride them out? A boat? A wall? A lighthouse? What keeps you safe when a surprise wave hits?"*

Clinical Note: This intervention provides a powerful metaphor for reflecting on the impact of grief and prompting emotional regulation. The child can build structures to block the waves (containment), ride them (acceptance), or find safety above them (distraction), while also drawing inspiration from the five coping categories.

The Invisible String

Clinical Goal: To provide a visual and interactive representation of enduring bonds and connections to loved ones, even after a loss or separation. Can be used after reading the book *The Invisible String* (Karst, 2001).

Preparation: A Creative mode world. Gather blocks of different colors, redstone, levers, and buttons.

Directive/Prompt: *"The Invisible String is a connection of love that can't be broken. Let's use these colored blocks to build a path from you to everyone and everything you feel connected to. What does your string of connections look like?"*

Clinical Note: Clients are encouraged to observe the length, path, and stability of the connections they identified. This reveals their perceived network of support and can open conversations about feeling close to someone who is far away or gone. This can become a more advanced build if the child uses redstone.

Memorial Building

Clinical Goal: To create a tangible, enduring object to honor a loss, hold memories, and provide a dedicated space for ongoing connection.

Preparation: A dedicated area in a Creative mode world with a wide variety of items, including decorative items, and a Book and Quill.

Directive/Prompt: *"Let's build a special place dedicated to [person/thing lost]. What should it look like? What objects or symbols can you include that represent what was most important to you? We can write down the memories in the Book and Quill too."*

Clinical Note: The memorial serves as a stable, externalized container for their grief that can be revisited when needed. A child might practice in the clinician's world and recreate it at home in their world. They can also take a screenshot of the build if in the clinician's world.

Processing Changes: Before and After Builds

Clinical Goal: To externalize and process significant life transitions (e.g., move, divorce, loss) by visually representing the past and the new, often uncertain, present/future.

Preparation: A large, flat world in Creative mode or scouting the landscape.

Directive/Prompt: *"Let's build what life was like before the change in this half of the world. Now, let's build what it's like on the other side. What was important then? What's different or hard now? What might be good in this new place?"*

Clinical Note: This creates an opportunity for the child to observe their experience. Pay close attention to the details they include in the "before" build that are missing in the "after," as these can prompt further inquiry toward their grief.

Safe Space

Clinical Goal: To design and build an environment that represents and fosters a neuroception of safety, which can be used as a regulatory "anchor" during dysregulation.

Preparation: Creative mode. No hostile mobs. Considerations for weather triggers.

Directive/Prompt: *"Everyone needs a place where they feel completely safe. Let's build yours. What does it need to have in it? What are the rules for who can come in? What makes it feel protected?"*

Clinical Note: The features of the safe space (e.g., build qualities, specific items, sensory preferences) serve as information for the child's internal and external safety needs. This is a foundational intervention for trauma and can often be a great starting point for all new clients.

As I Grow Tree

Clinical Goal: To narrate a story of resilience, acknowledge strengths developed from past hardships, and identify hopes and goals for the future.

Preparation: A large, open area in a Creative mode world with a variety of wood, leaf, and decorative blocks. A pre-spawned tree in the world can also be used.

Directive/Prompt: *"Let's build a tree that tells the story of you. The roots are your past and what grounds you. The trunk shows the hard things you've grown through. The branches are who you are now, and the leaves are your hopes and dreams for the future."*

Clinical Note: This is a powerful, creative intervention, adapted from the Judi's House (Griese et al., 2018) *Pathfinders* curriculum that can encourage the child to explore the impact of the past, the challenges in the present, and the hope and aspirations for the future.

Visual Schedules

Clinical Goal: To reduce anxiety and support transitions by making the abstract flow of time in the session concrete, predictable, and interactive.

Preparation: Any world. Use signs, different colored blocks, or items to create a sequence that represents session goals or objectives.

Directive/Prompt: *"Let's build our schedule for today together. We'll use these signs to show what we're doing first, next, and last. You can check it anytime to see what's coming up."*

Clinical Note: This is especially crucial for neurodivergent clients. It builds executive functioning skills and transfers control to the child, decreasing power struggles and increasing a sense of safety. Clinicians can also prepare this prior to a session.

Worry Box

Clinical Goal: To provide a structured place and practice for externalizing, containing, and "putting away" anxious or intrusive thoughts.

Preparation: A Creative or Survival world. Build items, spawn eggs, anvil, and name tags.

Directive/Prompt: *"When worries pop up, they can take over. Let's build your official Worry Box. You can spawn scary mobs and name them with your worries and lock them in the box. You can decide if you want to destroy them later, or leave them here where they can't bother you."*

Clinical Note: The act of physically identifying the worry and placing it in the box is a practice of containment. This teaches children they can have a thought without being consumed by it. This can also be done offline, using a box or envelope to hold written worries.

Advanced Build

Breathing Glitter Jar

Clinical Goal: To provide a visual and interactive tool for practicing mindfulness and grounding. The structure helps illustrate the concept of intentional breathing while observing thoughts and feelings as they settle.

Preparation: A Creative world with the following materials:

For the Jar: Sculk blocks.

For the Glitter: Six soul sand blocks and six magma blocks.

For Ambiance (Optional): Three beacons, four pearlescent froglights, a Jukebox, and a calming music disc (like "Otherside" or "Cat").

Directive/Prompt: *"Sometimes our thoughts and feelings can feel scattered and overwhelming. Building a Minecraft glitter jar helps practice intentional breathing while settling those feelings. When we look at the jar from further away, watch how the bubbles seem to interact wildly. That's like our big feelings; they can feel like they're moving up and down at the same time. Now, let's take slow, big breaths together and watch how the bubbles can help. See how the bubbles on the left side slowly drift up? Let's focus on one bubble and breathe in as it rises. See how the bubbles on the right side slowly drift down? Now, let's focus on one bubble there and breathe out while it settles to the bottom. Our thoughts and bodies can settle like that, too, when we give them a moment of calm, quiet breathing."*

Building Instructions:

Build the Container: Create a three-sided "jar" with a front-facing viewing area. A square base that is seven blocks wide and five blocks deep is perfect. Build seven blocks high and fill in the top, back, and sides.

Place the Bubbles: On the ground, place the six soul sand blocks in a three-by-two pattern, then repeat on the other side with the magma blocks; place the three beacons in the middle for a glowing effect.

Create the Ambiance: Place pearlescent froglights on the top (three blocks in from each side and three blocks up from the back) and on the sides (one block down), creating a sparkle effect on the bubbles at the top.

Place the Jukebox: Find a spot where you can see the bubbles clearly, then place it with one of the music discs.

How to Use It (The Mindfulness Exercise):

The Observation: Prompt the client to rest in front of the jar while noticing the bubbles. These represent their thoughts and feelings.

Setting the Tone: Place a jukebox and play music to set an intentional resting place as the bubbles rise and fall.

Breathe: As the bubbles rise, prompt the practice of intentional breathing –

> *Breathe IN slowly through your nose as the bubbles swirl high in the jar. You can pick one to focus on. HOLD your breath for a moment as the bubble hangs at the top. Breathe OUT slowly, focusing on the feeling of the breath on your upper lip as the bubble falls to the bottom.*

Repeat: "*You can repeat this practice for as long as you need. You're welcome to come back to this spot as often as you wish.*"

Clinical Note: This intervention links the client's internal experience to the visual metaphor and felt practice of deep breathing. The rise and fall of the bubbles provide a concrete focal point for mindfulness. The client learns that they can observe their internal state without being controlled by it, and that they can be in charge of their focused breathing. The intentional viewing area and calming music help create a designated safe space, facilitating a transition from coregulation to self-regulation. Focusing on the feeling of the breath on the upper lip further activates the parasympathetic nervous system (Hanson & Mendius, 2009).

References

Hanson, R., & Mendius, R. (2009). *Buddha's brain: The practical neuroscience of happiness, love & wisdom*. New Harbinger Publications.

Griese, B., Burns, M., & Farro, S. (2018). Pathfinders: Promoting healthy adjustment in bereaved children and families. *Death Studies*, *42*(3), 134–142.

Karst, P. (2001). *The invisible string*. DeVorss Publications.

Appendix D

Common Questions and Quick Reference for Clinicians and Parents

This appendix compiles the most frequent and critical questions from clinicians worldwide, gathered through years of workshops and training on using Minecraft in therapy. It serves as a quick-reference guide for both new and experienced practitioners.

Getting Started

What Are the Top Three Most Important Things I Should Do Before the First Session?

1 Complete the Digital Consent Form with the parent.
2 Confirm the technology platform and online subscriptions.
3 Exchange gamer tags. Failure to do this will derail the first session.

What Technology and Hardware Do I Need to Play?

- **Platforms:** PC/Mac, Tablets (iOS/Android), Gaming Consoles (Nintendo Switch, Xbox, PlayStation).
- **Key Consideration:** Platform determines if you can play together online. Consoles/Tablets (Bedrock Edition) can cross-play, whereas PC/Mac (Java Edition) generally cannot cross-play. Minecraft Education is paid for and hosted by the clinician.
- **Essential for Online Therapy:** A paid subscription for the platform's online service (e.g., Nintendo Switch Online, Xbox Live) and dependable wi-fi connection.

Top Five Basic Game Skills that Would Be Helpful for Me to Know:

1 **Movement and Perspective:** How to walk, jump, and look around (1st person vs. 3rd person view). *Next Step:* How to teleport and navigate with coordinates.

2 **The Heads-Up Display (HUD):** Understand what the health, hunger, and hot bars represent. *Next Step:* Experience points in Survival; becoming familiar with inventory screens.
3 **Basic Interaction:** How to break/place blocks and use your inventory. *Next Step:* Begin crafting in Survival mode.
4 **Game Modes:** Know the core difference between Creative (unlimited resources, no death) and Survival (gather resources, manage health). *Next Step:* Joining with another player.
5 **The Day/Night Cycle:** Understand that night brings hostile mobs in Survival mode. *Next Step:* Exploring commands with in-game elements (changing time, weather, etc.).

Addressing Core Concerns

Should I Be Concerned About the Additional Impact of Children Being on Screens?

Yes, concerns about children being on screens are valid and frequently raised by parents and clinicians, often stemming from worries about excessive usage, problematic media use, and potential erosion of social skills. However, the sources advocate for shifting the focus from the quantity of screen time to the quality, context, and content of the engagement, utilizing frameworks like "digital nutrition" to ensure that the therapeutic use of Minecraft is a nourishing experience rather than just consuming empty content. This paradigm shift supports the intentional, therapeutic use of Minecraft in session, as not all screen time can be judged equally. Remember: this is not passive consumption; it is active, relational, and therapeutic coregulation facilitated through the video game.

I Like This Idea, but It's Just Not for Me – I Do Not Want to Use Video Games in My Therapy Sessions. Is There Still a Way to Incorporate Minecraft?

Absolutely. Use Minecraft as a conversational bridge to build rapport. Leverage its concepts metaphorically without ever logging in: use the "Health Bar" to discuss energy levels, or "character skins" to explore identity. A child can draw their "Safe Space" instead of building it. See Appendix B for additional ideas.

How Do I Protect Privacy While Using the Game in Session?

Protecting privacy requires maintaining the therapeutic Minecraft world on the clinician's account, and recommending that players refrain from discussing clinical content in the in-game chat feature. Additionally, the clinician must address logistical concerns about privacy and safety during the initial consultation, emphasizing the importance of making caregivers aware that a child's specific therapeutic builds must be kept private from other players at home to prevent accidental alteration.

Clinical Challenges in the Moment

What Do I Do if the Client Just Ignores What I'm Asking and Goes off and Does Their Own Thing in the Game?

This can be conceptualized as the "setup" that nonverbally communicates their internal world, as well as providing information about the Developmental Tasks they are working through and how that corresponds to their play style (see Chapter 5). The clinician can reference Principle 3 by prioritizing being fully immersed in the experience of being ignored, abandoned, and left confused. Principle 4 would then suggest modeling regulation and building the client's interoception by naming their own internal experiences, such as the weight of sadness or hurt of feeling ignored or left alone, thereby providing a coregulatory experience for the child.

How Do I Handle a Child Who Becomes Extremely Dysregulated or Has a Meltdown When It's Time to Stop Playing?

This is not a reason to avoid the game, but the core therapeutic work (Principle 5). Clinicians can leverage coregulation to stay connected with the client and manage the intensity of the situation. Shaking out the energy or sitting in the frustration with the child while naming the discomfort of ending can be powerful ways to integrate the experience of distress. This supports emotional regulation in real-time before moving to a forward-looking resolution, such as: "We need to save the game, and I know it's frustrating. What do you want to do when we start next time?"

Integration for Clinical Practice

How Do I Approach Treatment Planning When Incorporating the Game?

Treatment planning serves as a clinical map that draws on Guiding Principles 3 and 4, using the client's "setup," play styles, and emotional developmental tasks as a case conceptualization framework to identify individualized needs and appropriate developmental goals. Objectives must then be specific, measurable interactions that translate in-game progress into clinically focused narratives, integrating Principles 5, 6, and 7 to ensure skills learned in session – such as managing transitions, utilizing resources, and exploring coping strategies – are collaboratively applied at home.

How Do I Incorporate Game Play into Clinical Language?

This involves differentiating the formal progress note, which must align the modality with therapeutic goals and observable progress, from the psychotherapy note, a private space for tracking raw clinical impressions, client "setups," and countertransference. This translation is achieved by consciously shifting documentation from game-focused descriptions (e.g., "the client built a house in Minecraft") to clinically-focused narratives that prioritize the therapeutic action (e.g., demonstrating sustained focus, increasing the Window of Tolerance, or exploring safety through a goal-directed project).

What if I Am Going to Use This with a Client I Have Already Been Working with?

Treat the game as another therapeutic tool, applying one's existing clinical background and decision-making skills to adapt the client's interest in the game to support their established treatment plans and goals. This can begin by discussing the client's existing relationship with Minecraft, including their playing preferences and character choices, as well as their hopes for what kind of play experience they would like. It is also essential to discuss with caregivers and have them complete the Digital Consent Form for practice compliance.

Appendix E

Glossary of Minecraft Terms

The following glossary comprises terms intrinsic to the game *Minecraft*. These definitions are based on the common understanding and usage within the game's community and are provided to assist readers who are unfamiliar with the platform.

The definitions in this glossary were adapted from the Minecraft Wiki; for the most current information, please visit https://minecraft.wiki/w/Minecraft

Achievements: Challenges players can work toward to receive trophies and acknowledgments (differs between editions and consoles.)
Baby Zombie: Smaller, faster version of zombie (typically more challenging).
Bedrock: Final foundation block at the bottom of the world. Indestructible.
Biome: Geographical representation in the world, with unique elemental features.
Book (and Quill): Item for writing information.
Building Challenge: A competitive task with a set objective.
Crafting: Forming new blocks that serve as useful resources, such as wood to build structures, and minerals to form weapons and other items.
Creative Mode: Offers players endless choices and options, with immediate access to an inventory of items that can be used like a well-stocked LEGO shelf or a drawer full of expressive art supplies.
Creeper: A mob that follows a player and can blow up if provoked, causing damage to the player and surrounding blocks.
Coordinates: In game tracking numbers typically used to locate a player and/or area.
Day Cycle: Ten minutes of daytime game play experience. Generally, not as hostile as the night cycle when playing in Survival mode.
Days Played: A feature that tracks the number of in-game days played within that world. Can be disabled.
Elytra: A type of torso armor that can enable flight and the ability to soar.
Emotes: Character expressions for nonverbal communication. Must be set as a command. Free and for-purchase options available.

The End: Final stage of the game if playing for a narrative completion. Home to the Ender Dragon.

Ender Dragon: Final boss feature of the game, this objective is considered the final challenge and serves as a focus for players who seek a feeling of completion.

Ender Chest: A specific type of chest that is exclusive to the player who owns it. A valuable resource in groups for members who wish to keep a private inventory (or items private from the clinician in 1:1 sessions).

The End Poem: A narrative text included in the final credits.

Spider: Mob that attacks when provoked or in dark environments.

Glitchy: Slang for when the internet connection or the game's processing speed is slow. See also *laggy*.

Glow Stone: A type of luminous block that can be popular for expressive builds.

Griefing: When a player damages or destroys something made by another player.

Heart Health Bar: Ten heart icons represent the amount of the player's health in Survival mode.

Hotbar: Nine onscreen slots that show what items are immediately accessible.

HUD: An acronym for "heads-up display," referencing the crucial gameplay elements the player views on their screen.

Hunger Bar: Ten meat-style drumstick icons that represent the amount of energy used as a depleting resource in Survival mode.

Iron Golem: Utilized as protectors of villages, can be hostile to players if provoked.

Inventory: The place to hold your items (27 primary slots and 9 hotbar slots).

Keep Inventory Mode: Allows players to hold access to all items when defeated in Survival mode. Can be used to lessen the impact of defeat.

Laggy: Slang for when the internet connection or the processing speed of the game is slow. See also *glitchy*.

Lantern: Item found in inventory or crafted in Survival mode.

Lava: Mimics the real-world element.

Mobs: Short for mobiles and references threatening or harmless characters that can be engaged by players.

Mining: The act of breaking blocks for resources.

Open World: Entirety of the games landscape and mechanics are playable from the beginning.

Nether: Dark and threatening dimension that is accessed through a Nether Portal built in the Overworld.

Nether Portal: Structure built by a player to access the Nether. Often found incomplete in the Overworld causing visual clues to materials needed to assemble.

Netherite: Metal element blocks that can be used to craft items. Often used for its powerful qualities in creating weapons and armor.

Night Cycle: Ten minutes of nighttime game play experience. Hostile mobs typically spawn during the night cycle.

NPC: Non-playable character. These are spawned and controlled by the game.

Overworld: The initial world players interact with when starting a new game.

PVP: Player versus player; typically a battle in Survival mode.

Realms: Paid subscription service providing a private server for one owner who can invite players. Permissions can be set for player access when the owner is not online.

Sandbox-Style Game: Provides players the freedom to explore without a linear objective.

Seed: A predetermined set of numbers that serves as a digital geo-marker for players to create a world starting in a specific place on the map.

Servers: A specially designed program for hosting a private world with restricted access. Realms is an example which is hosted by Minecraft. Other servers can also be on a private local area network (LAN) hosted by a private entity.

Skeleton: Mob that does damage with bow and arrow.

Skins: Visual aspects of the players on-screen character that can be changed and modified with in-game options or purchased in the Minecraft Marketplace.

Spawn: The act of a character emerging in the game either at the beginning or following defeat.

Spectator: A selected game option that allows the player to explore the world without consequences of gameplay and can move through structures and landscapes. Provides a "super power" quality that can also compromise private spaces.

Survival Mode: Offers a more specific challenge that requires players to manage their health by navigating threats in the world and finding ways to keep themselves safe by interacting with, avoiding, or confronting mobs. Difficulty can be set to *peaceful, easy, normal,* or *hardcore.*

Teleport: A command that moves the player to another player.

Torch: Item found in inventory or crafted in Survival mode.

Water: Mimics the real-world element. Can be utilized for build elements.

World: The heart of Minecraft gameplay as the platform for Creative or Survival. Can be ongoing or initiated with each "New World" creation.

Zombie: Mob that attacks players, spawning at night.

Further Reading

Minecraft. (n.d.). *Minecraft Wiki.* https://minecraft.wiki/w/Minecraft

Appendix F

Digital Consent Form

Client Name: ____________________ Date of Birth: ____________________

Parent/Guardian Name: ____

Clinician Name & Practice: ____

Date: ____________________

1 **Purpose and Therapeutic Benefits**
This form describes the use of *Minecraft* as a therapeutic tool in your child's therapy. Under clinician guidance, *Minecraft* can be used to help your child:

- Develop emotional awareness through intentional therapeutic play in a controlled environment.
- Identify and practice coping skills while playing the game and offline.
- Express thoughts and feelings that may be difficult to verbalize.
- Work on goals related to problem-solving, flexibility, and emotional regulation.
- Practice navigating social dynamics in a safe, therapeutic context.

2 **Secure Preparation and Anonymous Identity**
To ensure a safe and confidential therapeutic experience, we will use private, invitation-only gameplay. This is NOT a public online game. Access is strictly limited to the clinician and approved clients during scheduled sessions.

Clinician's GamerTag: ________________________________

Client's Approved GamerTag: ____________________________

*(A non-identifying username created with clinician support.)

3 **Potential Risks and Our Safety Protocols**
While we take every precaution, using any online platform involves potential risks. We mitigate these through the following protocols:

No Public Interaction: The gameplay is private to the clinician and client unless group agreements are made, in which case only approved clients can join.
No In-Game Voice Chat: All audio communication will occur through our secure, HIPAA-compliant telehealth video platform (e.g., Zoom, Google Meet).

4 **Privacy, Data, and HIPAA Considerations**
The following demonstrates how your child's privacy and confidentiality is protected, as required by law and the Health Insurance Portability and Accountability Act (HIPAA).

Protected Health Information (PHI): Your child's full name, date of birth, and reasons for therapy are never shared or used within the game.
Data Storage and Retention:

- In-game chat logs and any session recordings are treated as medical records.
- This data is stored on encrypted, password-secured devices or HIPAA-compliant cloud storage.
- All digital records are retained for a period of [ ] years, as required by state law, before being securely destroyed.

Inherent Risk: Despite best efforts, absolute privacy online cannot be guaranteed (e.g., risk of a data breach by the server hosting company).
Business Associate Agreement (BAA): A BAA is a HIPAA-required contract that holds a vendor legally responsible for protecting your health information. It is important to understand that the consumer versions of Minecraft (Bedrock, Java) and their online services (Xbox Live, Nintendo Switch, PlayStation Network) do not provide BAAs to clinicians. While we use a secure, separate video platform for our conversations that does have a BAA, the Minecraft gameplay itself operates on platforms that fall outside of this specific HIPAA safeguard. **Does not apply to Minecraft Education users.*

5 **Group Session Agreements**
For group sessions, a safe and respectful environment is essential. All clients agree to:

Be Respectful: Use kind and supportive language (pick-up vs. put-down statements).

Collaborate, Don't Destroy: No "griefing" or destroying others' creations.

Follow Clinical Guidance: Adhere to the clinician's directions and therapeutic activities.

Disruptive behavior will be addressed therapeutically in the group first. Persistent issues will require collaborative dialogue with the client and caregiver to ensure the best fit of the group and relationship with others.

6 **Protocol for Technology Failure**

Technical issues can occur. The plan to manage them is:

Connection Problems: If you are disconnected, please try to rejoin immediately. If the issue persists, the clinician will contact you via the phone number on file within 5–10 minutes.

Clinician Connection Problems: If problems arise for the host, the clinician will attempt to restart. If it remains unstable, the session will continue via telehealth video to process the emotions surrounding the event, or will be rescheduled.

Missed Time: Every effort will be made to make up for session time lost due to technical failure on the clinician's end.

7 **Parent/Caregiver Responsibilities**

To ensure safety and effectiveness, you agree to:

Appropriate Access: Obtain a suitable device and ensure a stable internet connection.

Purchase the Game: *Minecraft* is a paid game and ensure the correct edition is installed. **Does not apply to sessions with Minecraft Education users.*

Maintain Client Confidentiality: Provide a private, quiet space for your child's session.

Comply with Minecraft's End User License Agreement (EULA) and Terms of Service.

8 **Termination and Ending Therapy**

At the end of the therapeutic work, any digital content related to the client and/or group will be permanently deleted. Exceptions to this are case-dependent and subject to change based on the treatment plan and scheduling.

9 **Social Media and Online Presence Boundary**

Social media engagement and/or playing the game outside of the appointment time is prohibited. The clinician does not monitor and/or link up with the client on any social media platforms and will not be available to play recreationally. The client will only join up with the client during agreed-to, scheduled appointment times.

10 **Consent**
By signing below, I acknowledge that I have read and understood this consent form, have had my questions answered, and agree to the use of *Minecraft* as a component of my child's therapeutic sessions under the terms described above.

____

Signature of Parent/Guardian

____

Printed Name of Parent/Guardian

____

Date

Disclaimer for Readers: This template is intended for mental health professionals who use *Minecraft* in therapy. It should be reviewed by a legal professional familiar with your local healthcare laws before being used clinically. The therapeutic use of Minecraft is not affiliated, associated, or endorsed by Mojang Studios or Microsoft Corporation. Minecraft is a registered trademark of Mojang AB, now owned by Microsoft.

Index

Note: Page numbers in **bold** refer to tables.

For Product Safety Concerns and Information please contact our EU representative GPSR@taylorandfrancis.com
Taylor & Francis Verlag GmbH, Kaufingerstraße 24, 80331 München, Germany

www.ingramcontent.com/pod-product-compliance
Ingram Content Group UK Ltd.
Pitfield, Milton Keynes, MK11 3LW, UK
UKHW022349190926
475702UK00015B/2195
* 9 7 8 1 0 4 1 0 1 4 4 8 5 *